CHOPIN

By the same author

ADAM ZAMOYSKI

Chopin
Prince of the Romantics

Harper
Press

HarperPress
An imprint of HarperCollins*Publishers*
77–85 Fulham Palace Road,
Hammersmith, London W6 8JB

www.harpercollins.com

Published by HarperPress in 2010
Copyright © Adam Zamoyski 2010
2

The author asserts the moral right to
be identified as the author of this work

A catalogue record for this book
is available from the British Library

ISBN 13 978-0-00-734184-9

Set in Minion by Palimpsest Book Production Limited,
Grangemouth, Stirlingshire

Printed and bound in Great Britain by
Clays Ltd, St Ives plc

Mixed Sources
Product group from well-managed
forests and other controlled sources
www.fsc.org Cert no. SW-COC-1806
© 1996 Forest Stewardship Council

FSC is a non-profit international organisation established to promote the
responsible management of the world's forests. Products carrying the FSC label
are independently certified to assure consumers that they come from forests
that are managed to meet the social, economic and ecological needs of
present or future generations.

Find out more about HarperCollins and the environment at
www.harpercollins.co.uk/green

To Emma

CONTENTS

ILLUSTRATIONS

Astolphe de Custine.

Wojciech Grzymała.

Julian Fontana.

Maria Wodzińska.

Chopin, watercolour by Maria Wodzińska, 1836.

George Sand.

Marie d'Agoult.

George Sand's house at Nohant.

Chopin in the early 1840s.

Chopin, drawing by Franz Xaver Winterhalter, 1847.

Ignaz Moscheles.

Pauline Garcia-Viardot.

Auguste Franchomme.

Adam Mickiewicz, sketch by Delacroix.

Stefan Witwicki.

Bohdan Zaleski.

Eugène Delacroix.

Chopin, caricature by Pauline Viardot, 1844.

Marcelina Czartoryska.

Maria Kalergis.

Chopin, photograph taken during the last months of his life.

Jane Stirling.

Preface

Two centuries have passed since Chopin came into this world, yet his legacy is all around us today. The quiet revolution he wrought influenced the development of Western music profoundly, and he is still one of the very few most widely studied and revered composers. For many, he is the object of a cult. Yet most people know little of his life, of the man, his thoughts and his feelings; his public image is a sugary blur of sentimentality and melodrama.

The aim of this book is to cut through the myths and legends, to delve into everyday reality in order to tell the story of his life, and to reveal all that can be discovered of Chopin as a person. I had already attempted this in a previous book, published in 1979, and since this has been out of print for many years, I decided to update it, taking into account all the new material that has come to light and the many excellent studies on specific aspects of Chopin's life that have appeared since then.

I also decided that some of these were worth exploring further. I felt I should devote more space to the composer's state of health, which has been the subject of professional study in recent years. And I wished to place him within the intellectual and spiritual environment of his day, about which I had learnt much in the intervening period. In the process, I found myself reworking the text thoroughly. So, although I held to my original approach and did not fundamentally alter the structure, I believe this to be in many respects a different book, and that is why I have issued it under a new title.

Adam Zamoyski
London, 2009

ONE

A Prodigy Restrained

On 30 October 1849 a large crowd gathered at the church of La Madeleine in Paris, and hundreds of carriages clogged the surrounding streets, causing a jam that stretched as far as the place de la Concorde. The front of the enormous temple-like church was draped with panels of black velvet bearing the initials 'F.C.' embroidered in silver. Entry was by ticket only, and those who had not managed to obtain one thronged the monumental steps.

'At noon, the grim servants of death appeared at the entrance to the temple bearing the coffin of the great artist. At the same time a funeral march familiar to all admirers of Chopin burst from the recesses of the choir. A shiver of death ran through the congregation,' recalled the French poet Théophile Gautier. 'As for me, I fancied I could see the sun grow pale and the gilding of the domes take on an evil greenish tint . . .'[1]

Mozart's Requiem was sung, with the legendary mezzo-soprano Pauline Garcia-Viardot and the famous bass Luigi Lablache supported by the orchestra and choir of the Paris Conservatoire, the finest in Europe. During the offertory, the organist of the Madeleine played two of Chopin's preludes.

After the service, the coffin was borne from the church to the cemetery of Père Lachaise. The mourners were led by Prince Adam Czartoryski, widely regarded as Poland's uncrowned king, and the pall-bearers included the most famous operatic composer of the day, Giacomo Meyerbeer, and the painter Eugène Delacroix. Behind the coffin came dozens of musicians and artists, and thousands of the dead man's friends and admirers, with even the grandest ladies walking on foot, their escutcheoned carriages following in a long cortège. At the cemetery, the coffin was lowered into the grave without a homily, and the mourners dispersed in silence.[2]

With the possible exception of Beethoven, no musician had ever had such a splendid funeral, and few have been so mourned. A year later, a monument was placed over the grave, and this quickly became, and remains to this day, not only a place of pilgrimage but also the recipient of letters and messages. Some merely express admiration and gratitude, but most are personal communications, often passionate and sometimes pathological in nature, professing a decidedly possessive love.

Chopin has been worshipped not only for his music, but for himself, and not only worshipped but desired and appropriated. This most private and diffident of men has been taken over by musicians, musicologists, artists, biographers, film-makers and even politicians who believed they understood him and knew him intimately, moulding his image to their own purposes. Musicians have imposed their own often highly subjective interpretations on his music, musicologists have rewritten it, artists have painted him as they would like to see him, biographers have introduced their own dramatic imagination into his life, film-makers have dripped blood on the keyboard and politicians have attempted to claim him, for France, for Poland, for Slavdom and even for Poland's Jewish community.

Chopin was reticent by nature and extremely guarded when it came to private matters. He was too lazy to keep a diary and too self-deprecating to write his memoirs. He left no wife or son who might fashion his image for posterity. This left the field open to acquaintances who, as is usual in such cases, adapted or invented in order to project the desired image of themselves. The majority of Chopin's private papers were destroyed, in two world wars, a national insurrection and a personal vendetta. Biographers have therefore resorted to speculation and fantasy to fill the gaps, with every generation projecting its own aesthetics and desires on the blank canvas. It is only comparatively recently that historical discipline was brought to bear, and that the composer's origins have been fully established.

They lie with a family of indigent peasants by the name of Chapin who moved at the end of the seventeenth century from the village of Saint-Crépin in the Dauphiné region of France to the more prosperous duchy of Lorraine. By the mid-eighteenth century they were wine-growers and wheelwrights in the village of Marainville-sur-Madon in the Vosges, and their name had changed to Chopin. The Duchy of Lorraine was then ruled by King Stanisław Leszczyński, father-in-law of Louis XV, who had received it in 1737 as a consolation prize for losing his Polish throne, and it became home to many of his Polish supporters and courtiers. It was in Marainville that the composer's father, Nicolas, was born in 1771, to François Chopin, the village administrator (though there was a persistent rumour, allegedly encouraged in later life by Nicolas himself, that he was the natural son of the local châtelain, a courtier of King Stanisław).

In 1780 the château of Marainville was bought by a Polish nobleman, Michał Jan Pac. His estate manager, Adam Weydlich, also a Pole, was married to a middle-class Parisienne who, it seems, taught the young Nicolas Chopin to read and write, and possibly to play the flute. When, after the death of Pac and the sale of the estate in 1787, the Weydlichs returned to Poland, they took the sixteen-year-old Nicolas with them. In Warsaw, he was installed in the household of Weydlich's brother Franciszek, who taught German and Latin at the Cadet School.

He earned his keep by working for a couple of years as accountant at the Warsaw tobacco factory and, after it closed in 1789, acting as tutor to the Weydlich children. He was honest and reliable, and must have acquired a considerable degree of education, as well as well-placed protectors, as he then became tutor to the son of the mayor of Warsaw, Jan Dekert, and in 1792 to the children of the Dziewanowski family on their estate at Szafarnia.

Two years earlier, an opportunity had presented itself to Nicolas to visit his family in Marainville, as someone had to go there in connection with Pac's estate. But he did not avail himself of this, and indeed appears never to have sought to make contact with them again. He was also probably discouraged from going by the possibility of being trapped in revolutionary France and even drafted into the army. This did not shield him from war, which came in 1792, when Russian armies invaded Poland. After a brief campaign, the country lost a large part of its territory to Russia and a smaller one to Prussia, and was occupied by Russian troops. In 1794 a national insurrection broke out in an attempt to liberate the country from Russian control. Nicolas Chopin enlisted in the Warsaw militia, and was wounded in the Russian assault on the city, which effectively put an end to the insurrection.[3]

Later that year or at the beginning of the next, he moved to the country estate of Kiernozia, to act as father-figure as well as tutor to the newly orphaned children of Maciej Łączyński (one of whom, Maria, was to become famous after her marriage to Anastazy Walewski as Napoleon's mistress). Nicolas remained there until 1802, when he moved to a similar job in the household of Count Skarbek on the estate of Żelazowa Wola, where he looked after the Count's four children. In 1806 the thirty-five-year-old Nicolas Chopin married Tekla Justyna Krzyżanowska, the reputedly beautiful and sweet-natured twenty-four-year-old daughter of an impoverished nobleman who had worked for Skarbek as an estate manager.

The following year the Chopins had a daughter, Ludwika, and moved into one of the outbuildings of the manor, a spacious single-storey house with a thatched roof, in which they occupied a couple of rooms. It was in one of these whitewashed rooms with its clay floor that their son was born in 1810. He was christened Fryderyk Franciszek in honour of his godfather, the young Count Fryderyk Skarbek, and Nicolas Chopin's own father, François. The baptismal register of the parish church of Brochów, near Żelazowa Wola, states that the child was born on 22 February, but the Chopin family and the composer himself always gave the date of his birth as 1 March. To complicate matters further, his age was consistently increased by a year whenever he was mentioned in the press or appeared in public as a child, giving rise to the impression, held by some of his friends, that he had been born in 1809. The parish register is not a record of birth, and the date mentioned would have been supplied by Nicolas Chopin or his wife. There is therefore no reason to favour either date, and one can only be thankful that the year, 1810, is certainly accurate.[4]

The Chopins moved to Warsaw only six months after the birth of their son. The city and its surrounding area had been liberated from foreign rule following Napoleon's victory at Jena in 1806, and in 1807 reconstituted as a new state, the Duchy of Warsaw. Politically a satellite of France, the Duchy was modelled on the French pattern, and the French language became more of a necessity than a luxury, which favoured Nicolas Chopin. He obtained a post teaching French at the Warsaw high school, the Lycée (*Liceum*), starting in October 1810, and later another at one of the military training schools.

Warsaw was an unusual metropolis, whose aspect reflected its chequered past. There was a medieval walled city jostling for space on the escarpment overlooking the Vistula with the Royal Castle, by then sadly dilapidated. To the south of this stretched a few elegant eighteenth-century streets and, beyond that, a curiously rural city of palaces and villas, many with extensive grounds, interspersed with humbler dwellings and wooden hovels. One traveller likened it to a drawing room full of furniture, some of it very fine, which had never been properly arranged. Many of the palaces had become public buildings, while others had been divided up into apartments.

The Lycée was housed in a redundant palace built by the Saxon kings of Poland, a grandiose eighteenth-century building with white stucco façades. As there was no accommodation provided for pupils from the country, teachers were encouraged to take apartments in one of the wings of the palace if they were prepared to take in paying boarders. The thrifty Nicolas Chopin seized on this opportunity to increase his income, and moved into the Saxon Palace with his family. He took in six boys, who slept in two rooms and took all their meals with the family.

Nicolas identified himself entirely with his adopted country, and considered himself a Pole. In this he was not being eccentric. Most of his colleagues at the Lycée, from the Rector Samuel Bogumil Linde down, were of foreign origin, and sported names such as Kolberg, Ciampi and Vogel, but had become enthusiastically Polish in outlook. Nicolas Chopin always insisted on speaking Polish, and would not tolerate any other language in his home, even though he spoke it badly and had to resort to French when writing letters.

He was a competent teacher, stern and literal, and was described by one of his pupils as 'a rather ceremoniously grave personage with a certain elegance of manner'.[5] He was not religious, and felt no reverence for the institutions of monarchy and aristocracy, but he was no revolutionary; he believed firmly in acknowledging the ruling power and accepting the limits imposed by the society he lived in. His attitude to art and music was prosaic, although he played the flute a little, until his baby son broke it, and later took up the violin.

The only artistic influence in the household was provided by Justyna, who could play the piano well and sing quite respectably. In contrast to her husband, she was very religious. She was gentle and quiet, but although her role in the family was confined to that of mother and housekeeper, she stood out by her dignified bearing and social graces. Her presence was a considerable comfort to her son, providing as it did a counter-balance to his severe, scrupulous and pedantic father. The eldest daughter, Ludwika, was intelligent and gifted, and also played the piano well from an early age. Izabela, born a couple of years after Fryderyk, was a spirited girl with no intellectual or artistic pretensions, but the youngest, Emilia, was exceptionally gifted, writing poetry by the age of eight.

The little Chopin was of delicate health. Slightly built and chronically underweight, he was prone to all the ailments of childhood. Such staples as smallpox threatened, and it was impossible to avoid contact with the ubiquitous tuberculosis, which would carry away one of his siblings, at least one of his teachers, several of his father's boarders and eventually his father too. He needed a well-ordered childhood and healthy conditions if he was to survive for long, and the Chopin household provided this.

In 1817 the Lycée was moved to a less grandiose but more appropriate site. This was the Kazimierzowski Palace, a much-reconstructed seventeenth-century former royal residence, a large building with a colonnaded portico flanked by two detached wings. The Chopins occupied an apartment in one of the wings, and now took in ten boarders. The palace was pleasantly situated in what had once been a botanical garden, which sloped away towards the Vistula behind the main building, and the Chopin children, along with those of other teachers and the boarders, made this territory their own.

The various stories which have been dredged up in order to illustrate Chopin's extraordinary sensitivity as a baby – that he would burst into tears if someone played the piano badly, or, alternatively, sit for hours under the instrument listening in spellbound rapture – can be disregarded. They are the sort of detail that someone 'remembers' fifty years later, and even if true are largely meaningless, for there can be few babies who will not either bawl their heads off or else listen in fascination if a musical instrument is played in their presence. One cannot ascribe this to artistic sensitivity at the nappy stage, any more than one can believe a story coined after the composer's death to the effect that one night he crawled out of his cot, hoisted himself onto the piano stool and began to improvise Polonaises, to the astonishment of his family, drawn from their beds by the sound of music.

Chopin was introduced to the piano by his mother when he was four, and by the age of six he was noted for his ability to play relatively difficult pieces as well as for his gift for playing around with a few notes or a motif and producing simple melodic variations. In 1816 he started taking piano lessons from an old friend of his father's, the sixty-year-old Adalbert Żywny. Żywny had come to Poland from his native Bohemia and played the violin in a Polish aristocrat's court orchestra before becoming a freelance music teacher in Warsaw. He was a tall man with a huge purple nose and no teeth. He wore a lopsided, old-fashioned and yellowed wig, and a thickly quilted frock-coat of eighteenth-century cut, which, along with his cravat, his waistcoat and even his vast Hungarian boots, was thoroughly impregnated with snuff. He never bathed, confining himself to a rub-down with vodka on hot summer days, and his only attempt at elegance was a collection of fancy waistcoats. These he had had made up from a job lot of breeches he had bought cheaply when King Stanisław Augustus's wardrobe was auctioned off after the last partition of Poland in 1795. It is not clear whether this rather curious link with Poland's glorious past was intentional or not, but Żywny too had become very Polish, not the least of the attributes which endeared him to

Nicolas Chopin. Little Chopin adored him, and he became a regular visitor to the household, usually dining with the family and often spending his evenings with them.[6]

Żywny was an eighteenth-century musician; his gods were Bach, Haydn and Mozart. The only contemporary composers he acknowledged were Hummel and Moscheles, he had no time for Beethoven or Weber, and positively hated the new Italian school of Spontini and Rossini. His pedagogic method was much as one might expect. 'Apart from his commodious half-pound snuff-box, the lid of which was decorated with a portrait of Mozart or possibly Haydn, and his large red chequered kerchief,' wrote one of his pupils, 'Żywny always had about him a gigantic square pencil which he used for correcting printers' errors in the scores, or else for rapping his less diligent pupils over the head or knuckles.'[7] He was in many ways an unlikely person to initiate one of the nineteenth century's most re-volutionary composers; yet he proved an ideal teacher, because of his limitations rather than in spite of them.

By the time Żywny had come to teach Chopin, the boy had already developed a familiarity with the keyboard which he himself probably lacked. 'The mechanism of playing took you but little time, and it was your mind rather than your fingers that strained,' Nicolas Chopin later wrote to his son, adding that 'where others have spent days struggling at the keyboard, you hardly ever spent a whole hour at it'.[8] Faced with this prodigy, Żywny wisely refrained from interfering. Not being a pianist himself, the only thing he could have taught Chopin was the accepted method of fingering and the traditional hand movements. In view of the boy's instinctive dexterity, he did not bother with these technicalities. Instead, he concentrated on acquainting his pupil with great music, by guiding him through the keyboard works of Bach, Haydn and Mozart, as well as a little Hummel, explaining the theory behind them as he went.

The result of this unorthodox musical education was that

Chopin was allowed to develop his own method of playing, hitting the notes he wanted with the fingers he thought appropriate, not with those specified by textbooks. At the same time he developed a love for and an understanding of the great classical composers which he was never to lose, and which was to set him apart from most of his contemporaries.

This musical education was complemented by the music Chopin heard in homes and drawing rooms around Warsaw. Some of this was taken from the popular Italian operas of the day, but much of it was national in character. Polish piano music was dominated by the Polonaise, a musical form built on the rhythm of a slow, minuet-like court dance dating back to the sixteenth century. This rhythm had been familiar to many composers, including Bach, Telemann and Mozart, but they had merely used it as a tempo for melodies of their own. Towards the end of the eighteenth century Polish composers had begun to write Polonaises of a more authentic character. The trend was taken up by Prince Michał Kleofas Ogiński, a distinguished amateur composer, as well as the pianist Marya Szymanowska, and by the beginning of the nineteenth century the Polonaise had started a new life as a short piece for the piano.

Unsurprisingly, Chopin's own first steps in composition took this form. By the age of seven he was already composing short pieces which Żywny would help him write out, as he had not yet mastered this skill. Few of these survive. Those that do are unremarkable, and are only impressive if the boy's age is taken into account. It was in 1817 that Chopin's first printed work appeared, privately published by Canon Cybulski of St Mary's church, a friend of the Chopin family. It was entitled 'Polonaise in G minor, dedicated to Her Excellency Countess Victoria Skarbek, composed by Frederick Chopin, a musician aged 8'. It is probable that his godfather, Count Fryderyk Skarbek, who had just returned from studies abroad and taken up a teaching post at Warsaw University, had helped to pay for this, which would account for the dedication to his sister. His godfather was also responsible for the article on Chopin which appeared in January 1818 in the *Warsaw Recorder* (*Pamiętnik Warszawski*) and hailed the young composer as 'a true musical genius'. 'Not only can he play with great facility and perfect taste the most difficult compositions for the piano,' Skarbek wrote, 'he is also the composer of several dances and variations which do not cease to amaze the connoisseurs.'[9]

The first known reference to Chopin's appearance outside the family circle is to be found in the diary of a young lady who went to a soirée at Countess Grabowska's, where 'young Chopin played the piano, a child in his eighth year whom the connoisseurs declare to be Mozart's successor'.[10] Countess Grabowska, a friend of the Skarbeks, was the wife of one of the governors of Warsaw University, who was later to become Director of the Government Commission on Education. He belonged to a conservative patriotic milieu which had adopted a pragmatic approach to the realities of Poland's position.

After Napoleon's disastrous Russian campaign of 1812, the whole of Poland had been overrun by Russian troops, and Tsar Alexander was determined to hold on to as much of it as possible. At the Congress of Vienna in 1815 he managed to force through his solution to the Polish problem and created a small Kingdom of Poland whose constitutional king was the Tsar of Russia. It was a precarious compromise, and while many patriots regarded it as little better than captivity, a group of aristocrats worked at promoting the national cause within the limited autonomy it allowed.

The prime salon of this circle was that of the Blue Palace, the Warsaw residence of Count Stanisław Zamoyski. It was also the Warsaw home of his brother-in-law Prince Adam Czartoryski, whose close friendship with Tsar Alexander, distinguished diplomatic career and position as head of what was arguably the richest and most influential family in the Kingdom, made him a key figure in Polish society and politics. The Blue Palace was frequented by the most venerable figures of the past as well as the youngest members of the Polish aristocracy. Countess Zamoyska and her sister, Princess Marya of Württemberg, organised entertainments and *thés dansants* for children between the ages of eight and twelve, designed to instil good manners and patriotic values, which Chopin probably attended.[11]

The Countess was also the founder of the Warsaw Benevolent Society, and it was not long before she recognised Chopin's fund-raising potential. Julian Niemcewicz, the poet and Nestor of Polish literature, a devotee of the Blue Palace, describes a meeting of the Society in one of his one-act plays:

> *The Countess: You see how little money we have; all our efforts come to nothing. We are begging high and low, but everyone is deaf to us, or rather, to the voice of the poor. There is nothing for it but to carry on with our usual methods, but with certain modifications. I flatter myself that Monsieur Łubieński and I have perfected our techniques. There is to be a concert next Tuesday in which little Chopin is to play; if we were to print on the bills that Chopin is only three years old, everyone would come running to see the prodigy. Just think how many people would come and how much money we would collect!*

> *All: Bravo! Bravo! A wonderful idea, excellent! Let us print on the bills that Chopin is only three years old!*

> *Princess Sapieha: I think it would make even more of a sensation if we wrote on the bills that little Chopin will be carried in by his nanny.*

> *All: Bravo! Bravo! What a capital idea, princess!*[12]

What was probably the first of these concerts took place on 24 February 1818. Whatever the bills may finally have said, the press notice actually gave Chopin an extra year, stating that he was nine. The concert took place in the ballroom of a public building often used for such events, the former Radziwiłł Palace, and Chopin played a concerto by the Czech composer Adalbert Gyrowetz. It was his first appearance before such a large audience, and almost certainly the first time he had performed a work of this length.

After this event Chopin's fame spread throughout the capital, and it was not long before a carriage would draw up before the Chopin apartment to carry the eight-year-old boy off to the Belvedere Palace, the residence of Tsar Alexander's brother Grand Duke Constantine, commander-in-chief of the Polish army. Constantine was a martinet who spent his days drilling his soldiers mercilessly, often forcing them to perform feats that could only end in their death or that of their horses. He epitomised everything that was grotesque and brutal about Russian rule in Poland, and he was universally reviled.

Nicolas Chopin was not one to allow sentiment to get in the way of his son's prospects. It was an honour for the boy to be asked to play at the Belvedere, and a triumph when it turned out that he could soothe the Grand Duke's notorious fits of temper with his playing. Chopin presented him with a military march of his own composition, and it was said the Grand Duke was so delighted that he had it scored for full military band and played at parades. What was more remarkable was that Chopin was not fetched merely to entertain the Grand Duke and his wife, but to play with his beloved natural son and Alexandrine de Moriolles, the daughter of his tutor.[13]

Chopin's was an unusual upbringing; from his sheltered home with its middle-class atmosphere, he was propelled into some of the most elegant drawing rooms in Europe, where he performed before the greatest personages in the country, was spoilt by their wives, and played on an equal footing with their children. He quickly acquired polished manners as well as an ability to feel at ease in the most exalted company and mix with any kind of person, and while he was sociable and a little precocious, he was not, by all accounts, conceited. There is a plausible anecdote relating to one of his first public appearances; when he returned home, his mother asked him what the audience had liked best, to which he is alleged to have replied: 'My new English collar.' Whether this is true or not, it is in character, as he would remain remarkably modest about his music throughout his life. This was largely the consequence of his father's determination not to let his talent go to his head, and insistence on treating his son's gift as a pleasant amenity rather than the central feature of his life. This redounds to Nicolas Chopin's credit, considering how ruthlessly most child prodigies were exploited by their parents.

Nicolas Chopin was a product of the eighteenth century, and to him the profession of musician was hardly more respectable than that of actor. Having risen in the world himself, he was determined that his son should continue the ascent. Even when obliged to acknowledge his son's exceptional gift, he would not allow him to exploit it in what he considered a socially demeaning way.

Chopin was shown off whenever this might improve his prospects. In 1818 the mother of Tsar Alexander and Grand Duke Constantine, the Empress Maria Feodorovna, visited Warsaw and indulged in the usual round of visiting institutions and schools. When she graced his class at the Lycée, the eight-year-old Chopin presented her with two Polonaises. At the end of 1819, when the famous singer Angelica Catalani came to give some concerts in Warsaw, the boy was again exhibited; she was so impressed that she presented him with an inscribed gold watch. He was also a regular performer at the Benevolent Society's concerts, and often played at soirées in aristocratic houses. Charity events were permissible, as he performed alongside aristocratic amateur musicians or children reciting poetry, but there was no question of the boy playing for money or taking part in commercial concerts, for that would have branded him as a professional musician.

How Chopin saw himself by the time he had reached the age of eight is impossible to tell, but one thing is certain: that he already knew music to be his most personal form of expression. Every year on his name day in December, Nicolas Chopin was presented with little hand-painted greetings from his son. The verse offering for 1818 opens with the words: 'Dearly beloved father; it would be easier for me to express my feelings in musical phrases . . .'[14]

He had by now learned to write down music, as can be seen from the beautifully written-out Polonaise he dedicated and presented to Żywny on the latter's birthday in 1821, one of the few surviving compositions of this period. The majority of the pieces he wrote at this time remained in manuscript form among his own papers, with which they were later destroyed by Russian troops, or were written into albums, most of which suffered similar fates. Judging from the one or two pieces which have survived, they were clever but hardly distinguished.

At about the same time it became clear that Żywny's task was over, and that there was no more he could do for Chopin. He remained a close friend of the family and often brought his violin to play duets with his pupil, but stopped giving him lessons.

While Żywny was not replaced by another teacher, and Chopin essentially worked at the piano on his own, he was not left entirely without guidance. The piano and organ teacher at the Conservatoire, the Bohemian-born Wilhelm Vaclav Würfel, who had worked in Vienna where he won the admiration of Beethoven, was a friend of the Chopin household, and he guided the boy on a friendly basis.

Another who contributed to Chopin's musical education was Józef Elsner, a Silesian who had established himself in Warsaw some thirty years before. He was a prolific composer of operas, masses, oratorios, symphonies and chamber music, whose recently revived works reveal him as an interesting and original musician. He was also an excellent teacher, and had been appointed head of the newly founded Warsaw Conservatoire.

He was interested in drawing Chopin into this institution, so he gave him a few lessons in musical theory and presented him with a book on the rules of harmony. But for the time being Nicolas Chopin's views on the boy's future prevailed, and he would have no formal musical instruction over the next four years.

TWO

School Days

The review of a charity concert in which Chopin had taken part in February 1823 concluded with the following observation:

> *The latest number of the Leipzig musical gazette reports, in an article from Vienna, that an equally young amateur by the name of List [sic] astonished everyone there by the precision, the self-assurance, and the strength of tone with which he executed a concerto by Hummel. After this musical evening, we shall certainly not envy Vienna their Mr List, as our capital possesses one equal to him, and perhaps even superior, in the shape of young Mr Chopin . . .*[1]

Chopin himself would not have envied the Viennese prodigy. For while Franz Liszt, one year his junior, was steered into the gruelling career of performing musician, Chopin enjoyed a normal childhood. Later that year he donned the semi-military uniform of blue frock-coat with a single row of buttons and a high collar with a white stripe on it, and joined the fourth form of the Warsaw Lycée like any other schoolboy.

While he was by no means robust, he was neither sickly nor timid, and was among the most popular members of his class. Unaffected and unselfconscious as he was, 'little Frycek' had no difficulty in making friends. He won the avuncular and slightly protective friendship of older boys, such as Jan Białobłocki and Tytus Woyciechowski, respectively five and two years his senior.

But he was also at the heart of a gang of the livelier members of his own class, such as Dominik Dziewanowski, Julian Fontana and Jan Matuszyński.

Chopin had an irreverent wit and a keen eye for the ridiculous. He drew incisive caricatures and satirised Poles speaking French or foreigners speaking Polish. He fooled about on the piano, making musical jokes or providing an accompaniment to stories. But it was his gift for mimicry that really astonished people. He could transform not only his expression, but his very appearance, and was barely recognisable when imitating one of the Lycée masters or some public figure. Many years later, the celebrated French actor Pierre Bocage was to say that Chopin had wasted his talents by becoming a musician.

But while he neglected no opportunity for fun, Chopin also worked hard, and at the end of the academic year in July 1824 he collected the fourth-form prize jointly with Jan Matuszyński. The real prize, however, was an invitation to go and stay in the country with his classmate Dominik Dziewanowski.

Apart from the occasional short visit the Chopin family had made to the Skarbeks at Żelazowa Wola, this was Chopin's first real taste of the country. The Dziewanowski estate, Szafarnia, lay not far from Żelazowa Wola, on the flat Mazovian plain, west and slightly north of Warsaw, the only part of the Polish countryside with which Chopin was ever to become familiar. The estates in that area were not rich, and the country houses reflected this. The house at Szafarnia has not survived, but it probably conformed to the general pattern of timber or rendered brick manor houses: long and low, classical in style, with a colonnaded portico. These houses were often elegant, occasionally even grandiose in their conception, but the execution was sometimes rustic. The same went for life inside them, with the accent on comfort: there would be a piano in a fine drawing room, but there might be geese wandering about the back porch.

Chopin's holiday in Szafarnia had undoubtedly been dictated, at least in part, by concern for his health, which was far from good; it is possible that he had contracted tuberculosis, which was widespread. He was armed with pills and put on a strict diet: six or seven cups of acorn coffee per day, various tisanes, plenty of food, a little sweet wine, very ripe fruit, but, much to his chagrin, no bread.

This did not mar his enjoyment, and his letters home are full of the excitement caused by the novelty of his experiences. The books he had brought from Warsaw were hardly opened, and although he played the piano a great deal, he wrote little during his stay. Most of his time was spent out of doors, running about with his friend Dominik, going for drives through the surrounding countryside, visiting their friend Jan Białobłocki, whose parents' estate lay not far away, and even riding. 'Don't ask whether I ride well or not,' he wrote to a friend in Warsaw, 'but I do ride; that is to say the horse goes slowly where it wants, and I sit on it in terror, like an ape on the back of a bear; I haven't fallen off yet, because the horse hasn't bothered to throw me.'[2] This was hardly surprising, since it was being led about on a rein by Dominik's aunt Miss Ludwika Dziewanowska.

Chopin wrote most of his letters home in the form and under the heading of the *Szafarnia Courier*, a pastiche on the *Warsaw Courier*, using the same layout of Home News, Foreign News and Society News. The customary censor's stamp was in this case applied by Miss Ludwika. The *Szafarnia Courier* is full of schoolboy wit, with detailed news of how many flies settled on his nose, arch descriptions of battles between farmyard animals, Homeric accounts of quarrels between servants and notes on the misdemeanours of the domestic cat. There is also a great deal on the comings and goings of the Jewish traders who were a ubiquitous part of country life, and whom Chopin treats with predictable mockery. But the *Szafarnia Courier* also gives some idea of his wry, hyperbolic sense of humour and of his tendency to ridicule himself, the Pichon of the entries:

On 26th Inst. Monsieur Pichon visited the village of Golub. Amongst other sights and wonders of this exotic place, he saw a pig (imported) which for some time totally absorbed the atten-tion of this distinguished voyageur.[3]

Monsieur Pichon is suffering great discomfort on account of the mosquitoes, of which he has encountered fabulous quantities at Szafarnia. They bite him all over, except, mercifully, on the nose, which would otherwise become even bigger than it is.[4]

On 1st Inst. Monsieur Pichon was just playing 'the Jew' [a newly composed Mazurka on a Jewish dance theme], *when Monsieur Dziewanowski, who had business with one of his Jewish tenants, asked the latter to pronounce judgement on the young Jewish virtuoso's playing. Moses came up to the window, inserted his exalted aquiline nose into the room and listened, after which he declared that if Mons. Pichon were to go and play at a Jewish wedding, he would earn at least ten thalers. Such a declaration encouraged Mons. Pichon to study this kind of music with diligence, and who knows whether one day he may not give himself over entirely to this branch of the arts.*[5]

The fourteen-year-old boy found everything about life in the country new and interesting, but what fascinated him more than anything else were the unfamiliar sounds. The only popular music he had heard before was Warsaw street musicians' render-ings of folk songs and dances. As he listened to peasant girls singing their songs of love or sorrow, to the old women chanting in the fields, and to the drinking songs issuing from village taverns, a whole new world of music opened up before him. When he returned to Warsaw in September, it was with his head full of these new harmonies.

He had by now achieved such mastery of the keyboard that the Polonaises he turned out were far superior in technical terms to their Ogiński model. With the A flat major Polonaise, written in 1821 and dedicated to Żywny, he had moved on to writing in the so-called 'brilliant' style; it is a sparkling bravura piece designed to show off the virtuosity of the performer rather than to plumb the depths of musical expression. At the same time, he continued to seek the key to a deeper understanding of the language of music, following his own instinct and taking advantage of every opportunity to expand his knowledge.

He was profoundly affected by the new Italian music, represented most notably by the operas of Spontini and Rossini, now fashionable in Warsaw. It was being promoted by the conductor and composer Karol Kurpiński, himself the author of several operas in a similar style. Chopin was struck by the melodic brilliance and the 'singing' quality produced by the Italian composers, and strove to bring some of these into his own playing.

In his fourteenth year he began writing waltzes and Mazurkas (the Gallicised name of the *mazur*, the principal dance of the peasants of Mazovia) as well as Polonaises, often for more than one instrument. Lack of evidence precludes any serious analysis of his output, and the main source of information on the compositions of this period is the album of Countess Izabela Grabowska, which was fortunately described by a musicologist before it was lost in the war. The Countess was a cousin of Fryderyk Skarbek and an enthusiastic violinist, and as she lived not far from the Chopin apartment, the young composer spent a good deal of time with her.

Most of the music in the album was written, possibly in collaboration with the Countess, around 1824. The book contained a large number of compositions for the piano, and quite a few for piano and violin. The musicologist who examined it thought many of these unremarkable and imitative of Hummel, and noted a lack of experience and a certain untidiness in the way the harmonies were developed. But he was also astonished by the number of passages which showed originality and seemed to announce Chopin's mature work.[6]

Chopin expanded his education and experience by taking part in a variety of musical events, most of them of an amateur nature. Documentary evidence is scarce, but we do know that he was closely involved in a series of musical performances put on by a friend of Nicolas Chopin, Józef Jawurek, the director of music of the Warsaw Evangelical church, which had a fine neo-classical rotunda with good acoustics. In 1824 and 1825 Chopin took part, along with his sister Ludwika and Jan Białobłocki, in performances of Haydn's *Creation* and works by Elsner, and it is highly likely that he was involved in other similar events.[7]

In April 1825 the capital prepared for an official visit from Tsar Alexander, and it was Chopin who was singled out by the Warsaw instrument-maker Brunner and the inventor Professor Hoffmann to show off their latest invention, the eolomelodicon, at a public concert. It was a sort of miniature organ, and Chopin played part of a Moscheles piano concerto and an improvisation of his own on it at a grand instrumental and vocal concert at the Conservatoire on 27 May. As the makers had hoped, both the instrument and the boy's playing caused such a stir that the Tsar came to hear of it, and a special recital was organised for him. This command performance took place in the Evangelical church, with Chopin dressed in his Lycée full-dress uniform of blue tailcoat, breeches and stockings, pumps with silver buckles and white gloves. The Tsar was so taken with his playing that he presented him and the makers of the instrument with diamond rings.[8]

This recognition coincided with the first commercial publication, on 2 June 1825, of one of Chopin's works, the Rondo in C minor, op.1. The Benevolent Society managed to persuade all the artists who had taken part in the May concert to repeat their performance for charity on 10 June, and on this occasion Chopin played the newly published Rondo on the strange instrument, and then launched into a long improvisation, which earned him his first mention in the press outside Poland. The *Allgemeine Musikalische Zeitung* of Leipzig reported that 'young Chopin distinguished himself in his improvisation by a wealth of musical ideas, and under his hands this instrument, of which he is a great master, made a deep impression'.[9]

International acclaim was one thing, but the laws of the Chopin family were rigid, and as the boy only had a month left before his end-of-year exams, he was made to apply himself to his work. 'I have to sit and sit, sit, still sit, and perhaps sit up all night,' he wrote to his friend Białobłocki, who had now settled in the country, adding in a subsequent letter that he would at best scrape through the exams.[10] In the event, he once again jointly topped his class, this time with his friend Julian Fontana. The next day he rushed out to buy himself a new pair of corduroy breeches and then climbed into a carriage with Ludwika Dziewanowska, who had come to take him and Dominik to Szafarnia.

The summer of 1825 was so fine that Chopin hardly played any music. He spent his days out of doors with his friend, walking, riding, shooting, and occasionally going off on longer excursions with the whole house party. They visited various neighbouring estates, dropped in on Jan Białobłocki, who was ill with tuberculosis, and on one outing got as far as the city of Toruń. Chopin spent the day there admiring the Gothic churches, which impressed him by their age, sampling the celebrated local gingerbread, and visiting the house in which Copernicus was born. He was appalled by the condition of the house, and incensed that the room in which the great astronomer was born was now inhabited by 'some German who stuffs himself with potatoes and then probably passes foul winds'.[11]

The climax of the summer was the harvest festival, which Chopin described at length in a letter to his parents. 'We were sitting at dinner, just finishing the last course,' he wrote. 'We suddenly heard in the distance a chorus of falsetto voices; old peasant women whining through their noses and girls squealing mercilessly half a tone higher, to the accompaniment of a single violin, and that only a three-string one, whose alto voice could be heard repeating each phrase after it had been sung through.'[12] The two boys left the dinner table and went out to watch the column of peasants approaching, led by four girls carrying the traditional wreaths and bunches of harvested crops. When they reached the manor house, the harvesters sang a long piece in which there was a verse addressed to each of the people staying there. When Chopin's turn came, they teased him for his weedy looks and his interest in one of the peasant girls.

The girls carried the wreaths into the house, where they were ambushed by a couple of stable boys who drenched them with buckets of water. Barrels of vodka were rolled out, candles were brought onto the porch, and the violinist struck up a hearty *mazur*. Chopin opened the dancing with a young cousin of the Dziewanowskis, and carried on with other girls. He then took over from one of the peasants who was playing a double-bass, which was down to one string, and accompanied the flagging violinist. The warm, starry night was well advanced before Chopin and Dominik were called to bed and the peasants moved on to the village to continue their carousing. The whole evening made a vivid impression on Chopin, and left him a little wistful. His reminiscence of the jollity was tinged with a note of melancholy, and he had a vague foreboding that he would not be spending many more such carefree holidays in the Polish countryside.

He returned to Warsaw in September to embark on his final year at the Lycée. His father had at last given him a room of his own so he could apply himself to his studies; it was dwarfed by his piano, and rapidly filled up with sheet music, piled on shelves, chairs and cupboards. The composers most in evidence, apart from Bach, Mozart and Hummel, were Friedrich Wilhelm Kalkbrenner, a renowned pianist who composed mainly for that instrument, and Ferdinand Ries, a pupil of Beethoven who also wrote principally for it.

Music-making took up every available moment. Chopin took over from the organist of the Convent of the Visitation and played every Sunday at the Lycée and University Mass. With his sister Ludwika and other friends he sang in the choir of the Evangelical church. He was also often to be heard playing in drawing rooms around Warsaw. A contemporary diary gives the first detailed account of his playing, at a soirée given by Teresa Kicka. It describes how, after playing several works, he launched into an improvisation which he drew out for a very long time. This form of *ad libitum* playing revealed Chopin at his most poetic and inventive, and fascinated those fortunate enough to hear him. But the exercise visibly drained him as he played, and he began to look so pale and exhausted that the poet Niemcewicz eventually went up to him and pulled his hands away from the keyboard.[13]

Chopin was much too energetic for his constitution. During the Christmas season, for instance, he was often at the opera, at a concert or at a party, with the result that he was rarely in bed before two o'clock in the morning. He was incapable of taking things easy, and always had to join in whatever was going on. In a witty versified account, he described one occasion when he spent half of a party playing dances on the piano for the other guests, and then started dancing himself, not staid Polonaises or Quadrilles, but energetic *mazurs* and other country dances, during one of which he slipped and crashed to the floor, twisting his ankle.[14] At the beginning of 1826 he fell ill. The symptoms were an inflammation of the throat and tonsils, and he retired to bed with a nightcap on his head and leeches at his throat.

His studies do not seem to have suffered from the illness, the active life he was leading or indeed from the now impressive volume of music he was writing. At the end of his final year at the Lycée, in July 1826, he once more managed to get through his exams, this time winning an honourable mention, along with Tytus Woyciechowski and Jan Matuszyński. This earned him a treat on the day after the exams: a trip to the opera to see the new production of Rossini's *La Gazza Ladra*. But there was to be no month in the country that summer.

His younger sister Emilia was suffering from tuberculosis, and the disease had reached a critical stage. Her parents had decided to try the last resort of a spa cure, and their choice had fallen on Bad Reinerz (Duszniki Zdrój) in Silesia. Chopin was to be taken along as well, on the principle that it could only do him good too, and at the end of July Justyna set off with the two of them.

Life at Bad Reinerz was governed by a strict routine. The Chopins had to be at the spring by six in the morning for the first glass of mineral water. This was later complemented by draughts of whey, which were held to be good for the chest, and more glasses of mineral water at intervals during the day. A wheezing orchestra played while the clientele queued up for their glasses to be filled or walked up and down sipping the water. For Chopin, the only attraction of the place was the scenery: he had never seen anything more exciting than the flat Mazovian plain, and he was predictably impressed by the mountains in which the town nestled. He went for walks and enthused about the breathtaking views, but was depressed by the fact that he could not translate his sensations into his own medium. 'There is something I lack here; something which all the beauties of Reinerz cannot make up for,' he wrote to Elsner in Warsaw. 'Imagine – there is not a single decent piano in the whole place.'[15]

Nevertheless, when a couple of children were suddenly orphaned by the death of their father who had come to take the waters, Chopin offered his services to help them. A piano was found, and he gave a recital in the *Kurhaus* for their benefit.[16] It was so warmly received by the visitors to the spa that he was persuaded to give another. Humble as it was, this acclaim from an audience who had no idea of who he was provided another small measure of encouragement to the boy. It was also a weapon to be used in the battle against his father's wish that he should enter the University rather than the Conservatoire. Both Żywny and Elsner must have been persuasive allies, and by the time Chopin returned to Warsaw, a decision had been reached on his future. It was a compromise: he was to enter the Conservatoire, and at the same time to attend lectures on certain subjects at the University.

THREE

Musical Genius

'I go to bed at nine; all tea parties, soirées and balls have gone by the board,' a despondent Chopin wrote to Jan Białobłocki as he began his studies at the Conservatoire in the autumn of 1826. He was beset by a succession of minor ailments, such as toothache, neuralgia and digestive problems. 'I drink emetic water on Dr Malcz's orders and stuff myself with oat gruel like a horse.'[1] It was hardly a propitious start to his hard-won musical studies.

The Warsaw Conservatoire, founded in 1821, offered entrants a number of courses to choose from. The one selected by Chopin consisted of three years of musical theory and counterpoint, the last of which was to be devoted to practical work such as writing masses and oratorios to Polish and Latin texts, vocal compositions of various types, works for orchestra, and chamber music. But he seems to have created his own curriculum from the start. When he joined the Conservatoire in September 1826, he took six lessons a week in counterpoint from Elsner and spent the rest of the time working on his own. Elsner was an enlightened teacher, who saw his role as that of adviser. 'When teaching composition, one should never provide recipes, particularly with pupils of obvious ability,' he explained; 'if they wish to rise above themselves, they must find their own, so that they may have the means of discovering that which has not been discovered yet.'[2] But Chopin found even this relaxed discipline taxing.

In accordance with the compromise reached with his father, he was also attending lectures at the University. Although the original idea had been that he should take a course in general subjects, he soon narrowed this down. The only course he seems to have followed seriously was that on Polish Literature given by the poet Kazimierz Brodziński, whose lectures covered a range of subjects, from aesthetics to folklore, which he was busily recording.[3]

Chopin had been born into a society that was in the process of reinventing itself: the old Poland embodied in the Commonwealth had failed and been dismembered at the end of the eighteenth century, and patriots bent on the re-establishment of a Polish state were aware that they must create a new synthesis of nationhood on which to build it. This involved, amongst other things, cultural redefinition based on a reassessment of the past and the integration of the mass of common people into the national project. Wittingly or not, Chopin was, through his music, doing just that, by distilling the essence of the old chivalric ideals on the one hand and reaching into the soul of popular culture on the other to create a new national idiom immediately recognisable to all. In this, he virtually epitomised the *zeitgeist* of his generation. Yet in certain fundamental ways he stood apart from his peers.

Given the accent placed in the Chopin household on education, and particularly on literature – his sisters Ludwika and Emilia had published poems and even a jointly written novel for children – Chopin could hardly fail to be aware that his generation was making literary history. Yet he failed to show any deep understanding of contemporary Polish writers. He did set to music some of the poems of the leading Romantic Adam Mickiewicz, as well as works by his friend the much lesser poet Stefan Witwicki, but he was far too down-to-earth in his approach to life to catch the spirit of exaltation that nourished the Romantic movement. He saw himself as a craftsman, focused exclusively on achieving greater skill and deeper knowledge in his chosen craft of music.

And even in this chosen craft, Chopin remained remarkably aloof from contemporary trends. His reverence for Bach continued undiminished – more than a decade later, he could still play all the Preludes and Fugues from memory, explaining: 'That is something one never forgets!'[4] As he learnt more about the theory of music, he developed a greater respect for Haydn, whom he valued for his 'experience', and for Mozart, who became his God. The only fashionable music Chopin was enthusiastic about was that of the Italian school. Elsner, who disliked it, steered him towards the music of Hummel, Ignaz Moscheles and the Irishman John Field – hardly exponents of the Romantic movement.[5]

Chopin's attitude to the world was far removed from that of the typical Romantic. As he entered his eighteenth year he had his first close experience of death, when his fourteen-year-old sister Emilia died of consumption before his eyes. He was profoundly shaken. Where most of his peers would have poured out their grief and indulged their emotions, he did not wallow in his pain – he locked it away in a compartment of his mind where he could revisit it privately.

Soon after Emilia's death the family moved house, to an apartment in one of the wings of the Krasiński Palace, just across the road from the Lycée. Nicolas Chopin had acquired a third job, teaching at the advanced military school of artillery and engineering, presided over by the revered General Józef Sowiński, who had lost a leg fighting for Napoleon at the battle of Borodino in 1812, and who became a friend of the family. Nicolas had saved enough to be able to do without boarders, which was fortunate as the other two Chopin girls were growing into young ladies, and the presence of young men in the home might have presented a hazard. The new apartment contained a drawing room with a fine view over the most handsome street in Warsaw, and, being so close to his previous home, the move did not affect Chopin's way of life. On the other hand, it was quieter, and the family now enjoyed greater privacy. Chopin had his own 'refuge', a small room at the top of a rickety staircase which accommodated his piano.

This was just as well; that year of 1827 was also something of a landmark in Chopin's musical development, for it was now that he made his first attempts at writing for orchestra. The most interesting of these are the set of Variations for Piano and Orchestra on the theme of the *La ci darem la mano* duet from Mozart's *Don Giovanni*, which, as the *Gazette Musicale de Paris* asserted more than seven years later, 'announce the superiority of Chopin's nature with as much precision as felicity'.[6]

Chopin's ability to write for the orchestra has often been questioned, and unfavourably compared with Beethoven's magnificent interweaving of piano and orchestra. But to do this is to miss the point. Chopin used the orchestra essentially as an accompaniment to the piano, which it was meant to support rather than overshadow or outshine, and it is the piano that he used to develop his musical ideas.

He was growing increasingly sure of himself and the direction in which he was moving, and he was further encouraged by Hummel, who arrived in Warsaw to give a couple of concerts in April 1828, and who appears to have been impressed by Chopin. This first mark of recognition from an eminent musical personage was probably what prompted him to send copies of the Variations and his first Piano Sonata to publishers in Leipzig and Vienna.[7]

Chopin was now working on a new Rondo for two pianos, and this absorbed all his attention that summer, spent in a fine country house at Sanniki with his friends the Pruszak family. He was back in Warsaw at the end of August, just in time to see Rossini's *Barber of Seville* and his latest opera, *Otello*, but the production was so bad that he longed to strangle the whole cast.

His joy was all the greater when, a few days later, the chance of visiting a foreign capital presented itself.

A colleague of Nicolas Chopin, Professor Feliks Jarocki, had been invited to take part in a congress of naturalists and physicians organised in Berlin by Alexander von Humboldt. Since all his expenses were being paid, he offered to take young Chopin with him. The boy was overjoyed at the prospect of hearing renowned orchestras and choirs, and the chance to meet composers such as Gasparo Spontini who made up the city's musical establishment. He had one acquaintance in Berlin who he felt sure would help him gain admittance to this charmed world: Prince Antoni Radziwiłł, a Polish aristocrat married to one of the Prussian royal princesses and the King's Lieutenant in what was then the Duchy of Posen, the part of Poland ruled by Prussia. He was a distinguished amateur musician, and had met Chopin on one of his visits to Warsaw.

Berlin turned out to be something of a disappointment. After five days in a mail coach, the two travellers arrived in mid-September. Chopin's first impressions were unfavourable: he found the streets formal and empty, and thought the women ugly. He had to dine at the hotel with Jarocki and the other visiting scientists, whom he found uninteresting and slightly ridiculous. Prince Radziwiłł was absent, and on the one occasion when Chopin did find himself in the same room with Spontini, Zelter and Mendelssohn he was too shy to introduce himself. He visited the local piano-makers, but there were no instruments in stock for him to try. He saw operas by Spontini, Onslow, Cimarosa and Weber, but was disappointed by the productions and the standard of the singing. The only thing that 'came close to the ideal I have of great music' was Handel's *Ode on St Cecilia's Day*, which he heard at the Singakademie.[8] It was the first time he had been struck by Handel's work, and his respect for that composer was to grow steadily. Years later, when Mendelssohn showed him a new edition of Handel's work, Chopin would experience 'a truly child-like joy'.[9]

The congress ended with a banquet during which the venerable professors dropped their inhibitions. They stuffed themselves in a way Chopin found hard to believe, and drank a good deal as well, with much clinking of glasses. When Zelter and his choir intoned a ceremonial cantata they all joined in, waving their arms and bawling their heads off. Chopin was quite happy to climb into a coach bound for Warsaw the next day. But, disappointing as it had been, the Berlin trip only whetted his appetite for foreign travel, and as he began his final year at the Conservatoire he dreamt of going further afield.

Chopin was now almost nineteen years old. He had grown into an interesting-looking young man, physically somewhat puny, but with a refined countenance and manner. This, as well as his sociability and his musical gift, meant that he was much sought after. He hated missing out on any gathering, and the consequent round of tea parties, dinners, soirées and balls exhausted him. 'You know how awful it is when all you want to do is go to bed, and suddenly everyone wants you to start improvising,' he complained, somewhat disingenuously, to a friend; he always complied, and, having sat down at the piano, would improvise for hours.[10]

This was the year devoted to practical exercises, but Elsner did not demand any of the regulation masses or oratorios from Chopin. The best-known compositions from this period are the Rondo on Cracovian Themes (op.14), also known as the *Krakowiak*, and the Fantasia on Polish Airs (op.13), both for piano and orchestra. Although some years later a Parisian critic was to hail the Fantasia as a landmark in musical history, it is hard to see it as one now.[11] These pieces are notable for a number of reasons, not the least of which is the intricacy and beauty of the piano parts. But they belong in the tradition of the brilliant style, in which surface decoration is more important than underlying structure. A greater degree of daring and originality obtains here than in any of Chopin's previous or indeed later writing for orchestra, and there are passages in which the latter assumes an active role and ceases to be merely an accompaniment for the piano. But perhaps the most interesting aspect of these and other works from the same period is the way in which Chopin handles the folk element in them.

Following his exposure to authentic folk music in 1824, Chopin had started collecting country tunes and using them in pieces for the piano. This was accepted practice, and many musicians either transcribed folk songs for various instruments or wrote variations on them. But Chopin was less interested in the tunes themselves than in the structure and essential character of this kind of music. The difference between what most musicians did with folk music and what he was attempting could be likened to the difference between using ready-made phrases of a foreign language, and learning the language and constructing one's own phrases. By 1828 he had mastered the folk idiom so far that he could write original Mazurkas, often using elements of melodies he had heard in the country, but more often creating his own. This process eventually led him to create what was in effect an entirely new mode of musical expression through the melodic language of a people. An analogous treatment of the Polonaise form evolved with time into a pure expression of the historic, courtly ethos which had inspired the dance. He was no longer writing a country dance or a court dance; he was writing poems in the musical language of Mazovia, or alternatively in that of the vanished world of the Polish noble past.

At the same time, Chopin did apply himself to a work in the grand style – a concerto for piano and orchestra. This was probably meant to fall within the category of his practical work for Elsner, but it may also have been prompted by the need to have a substantial composition to show off – pianists were expected to demonstrate their virtuosity through their own works, not by interpreting others'. This was all the more important as Chopin was now planning a tour abroad. In April 1829, Nicolas Chopin petitioned the Minister of Education for the requisite funds. The move was not without precedent, as an older Conservatoire colleague of Chopin's, the pianist Tomasz Nidecki, had been given a foreign travel grant a couple of years before. Nicolas reminded the Minister that his son had 'had the honour of being heard by the late Tsar', and that His Imperial Highness the Grand Duke 'had often been most graciously pleased to allow him to give evidence of his growing talent in His Most Serene presence'.[12]

The Minister, Count Grabowski, endorsed the petition and recommended a handsome grant for three years, during which the young man was to visit Germany, France and Italy, but his superior, the Minister of the Interior, turned it down, with the observation, scrawled in the margin, that 'Public funds cannot be frittered away on this kind of artist'.[13]

The disappointment caused by the failure of this petition was soon forgotten in the excitement created by the arrival, a few weeks later, of the legendary violinist Niccolò Paganini. Chopin went to most of the ten concerts he gave in Warsaw, and was bowled over by the virtuosity of his playing. Paganini was the first musician to elevate his instrument from its traditional role within the orchestra or quartet, and Chopin can hardly have failed to draw parallels with what he was doing himself regarding the piano.

Returning home after one of the concerts, Chopin composed a set of variations entitled *Souvenir de Paganini*. More important, he now set to work on a new idea of his own – of producing exercises that would help him draw a wider range of sound and greater expression from his chosen instrument. The first of these studies, or Études (nos. 8, 9, 10, and 11 of op.10), were written over the next six months, and with time they were to revolutionise his use of the piano.

Paganini's visit was followed by a series of concerts by the violinist Karol Lipiński, who had at one stage been regarded as one of Paganini's principal rivals, but in Chopin's view his concerts only underlined the superiority of the Italian's genius. The same was true of the concerts given soon afterwards by the Hungarian pianist Stephen Heller; his playing was marked by a superior musical intelligence, but lacked the special qualities Chopin was beginning to look for.

A more portentous event for Chopin was a concert organised by Carlo Soliva, the singing instructor at the Conservatoire, to show off his pupils. One of these, Konstancja Gładkowska, struck the young man not only by her fine voice, but also by her appearance. She was dark-haired and pretty, with a face that exuded melancholy rather than vivaciousness. Of her character, not much is known. Chopin was immediately smitten, but he was too shy to let this show, and made no attempt to attract her attention over the next few months.

He was now faced by an important hurdle, in the shape of his final exams at the Conservatoire; Nicolas Chopin would certainly take note of the results and plan his son's future accordingly. It is not known what form the exams took, but they were partly based on his work over the past three years. As he considered this, Elsner noted in his diary that Chopin had 'opened a new era in piano music through his astonishing playing as well as through his compositions'.[14] In the official verdict on the exams in the Conservatoire register, he was more categorical: 'Chopin, Fryderyk; third year student. Outstanding abilities; musical genius.'[15]

This would have been the logical moment for Chopin to set off on a foreign tour, but there seemed to be no way of financing it. The best he could do for the time being was to join a party of friends from the University who were going on a jaunt to

Vienna. They left Warsaw immediately after the exams, on 21 July. On the way they visited the historic city of Kraków, and from there went on a couple of excursions, one down the Wieliczka salt mines, another through the scenic valley of Ojców. The cart they were travelling in got lost and then stuck in a stream, leaving them to wander for hours in the pouring rain before they found shelter and some straw for the night. That Chopin did not catch cold suggests that his health had improved considerably.

The little party reached Vienna on the last day of July 1829, and Chopin took an immediate liking to the city. He saw several operas, by Boieldieu, Meyerbeer and Méhul, went to a number of concerts, and found perfection everywhere. He had mastered the reticence which had held him back in Berlin, and immediately took steps to get acquainted with the musical establishment. He called on Haslinger, the publisher to whom he had sent the scores of the *La ci darem la mano* Variations and the C minor Sonata; on his old friend and teacher Wilhelm Würfel, who had moved back to Vienna; and on a venerable Polish music-lover, Count Husarzewski. They in turn introduced him to others, including the venerable Ignaz Schuppanzigh, violinist and leader of the quartet which had performed all Beethoven's chamber music for him; the two foremost piano-makers, Stein and Graf; and, most important, the director of the Kärntnerthor Theatre, Count Gallenberg.

'I don't know what it is, but all these Germans are amazed by me, and I am amazed at them being so amazed by me,' Chopin wrote to his parents a few days after his arrival.[16] Haslinger, who had probably put aside the score of the Variations by an unknown Pole without looking at it, changed his attitude radically when the young man sat down at the piano in his shop and played them through. He promised to publish them if Chopin agreed to play them in public, and the project was taken up with enthusiasm by others. Würfel believed that the Viennese public was 'hungry for new music', Husarzewski predicted a resounding success, and Count Gallenberg offered his theatre free if Chopin wished to give a concert. Chopin himself was irresolute, and feared that Elsner and his family might not approve, but let himself be persuaded.[17]

The Kärntnerthor Theatre was booked for 11 August and, at Chopin's request, a Graf piano provided. An orchestra was assembled, and a search made for others who might fill out the programme – all concerts at the time took the form of a succession of different artists performing in a variety of musical forms. There were problems at the rehearsal that afternoon, as the two pieces Chopin intended to play with the orchestra (the *La ci darem la mano* Variations and the *Krakowiak* Rondo) were written out in his usual careless way, and the disgruntled orchestra began to mutiny. They refused to play the *Krakowiak*, and it was only thanks to the diplomatic efforts of Tomasz Nidecki, whose travels had brought him to Vienna, that the concert took place at all. Nidecki made a clean copy of the scores of the Variations, which the orchestra eventually agreed to play. 'At seven o'clock in the evening I made my appearance on the Imperial and Royal stage!' Chopin wrote to his parents the following day.[18]

The concert opened with the orchestra playing the overture from Beethoven's *Creatures of Prometheus*, after which Chopin appeared on stage to play his Variations. He was not nervous of the Viennese audience, but was a little put out to find a highly rouged gentleman sitting down next to him, boasting that he had turned pages for Hummel and Moscheles. The skirmish with the orchestra that afternoon had ruffled him, and he launched into the piece with 'exasperation', half expecting them to set a trap for him. But they played perfectly, while the delighted audience applauded after each variation and called him back for a second bow at the end. After an interlude of *lieder* sung by a lady from Saxony, Chopin reappeared on the stage to play a 'free fantasy' without orchestra. He started off by improvising on a theme from Boieldieu's *La Dame Blanche*, which was playing to full houses in Vienna at the time, but was subsequently asked by the director of the theatre to play 'something Polish', whereupon he launched into an improvisation on a peasants' wedding song, which, in his own words, 'electrified' the audience. When he had finished, the orchestra itself broke into applause, and he was called back for a second bow. Count Dietrichstein, the Emperor's director of music, came onto the stage and publicly congratulated Chopin, urging him to prolong his stay in Vienna.[19]

Chopin could hardly believe his triumph. He had grown used to popularity in Warsaw, but a reception like this from an audience which was used to hearing the greatest masters was something else. His friends had dispersed themselves strategically among the audience and reported its reactions to him, the worst of which came from an old lady who enjoyed the music, but sighed: 'What a pity the young man hasn't got a better tournure!'[20] But what really went to his head was the sincere admiration of renowned older musicians like the composer Conradin Kreutzer, the virtuoso violinist Josef Mayseder and Gyrowetz, whose concerto Chopin had played at his first public concert eleven years before. It is true that when asked how he had managed to grow into such a fine musician in Warsaw, he answered that 'With Messrs Żywny and Elsner even a half-wit would learn,' but this was probably said more out of bravado than conviction.[21]

The only criticism to be heard, not for the first or the last time in Chopin's life, was that his playing lacked vigour and volume, or was, as he himself put it, 'too delicate for those accustomed to the piano-bashing of the local artists'. This did not concern him unduly, but he felt obliged to warn his parents not to worry about it either, writing: 'I expect that criticism to be made in the papers, particularly as the editor's daughter enjoys nothing like a good thump at her piano.'[22] While having dinner at the hotel after the concert, Chopin overheard unfavourable reactions from a man who had just come back from the Kärntnerthor, but as he remarked philosophically, 'the man who will please everyone has not been born yet'.[23] It was not the first time he noticed that he pleased the more refined.

Prince Lichnowsky, Beethoven's friend and patron, could not find words enough to praise Chopin, a reaction shared by others with resounding names such as Schwarzenberg and musical reputations like that of Czerny, a pupil of Beethoven and teacher of Liszt, whom Chopin found 'warmer than any of his compositions'.[24] They suggested he give a second concert, and he accepted without protest, excusing himself to his parents for his presumption with the observation that people in Warsaw would not believe that the first had been a success unless it was repeated.

Exactly a week later, on 18 August, Chopin again appeared at the Kärntnerthor. By this time Nidecki had helped him to rewrite the parts of the *Krakowiak* Rondo, so he was able to perform that. 'Everyone from Kapellmeister Lachner right down to the piano tuner was astonished by the beauty of the piece,' Chopin wrote home with pride.[25] Again he was called back for a second bow, and even a third, after which the audience called for an encore, a rare occurrence in those days. Rarer still, the orchestra was prepared to join in, so he was able to play the *La ci darem la mano* Variations as an encore. If the success of the first concert had seemed a little unreal, there was no mistaking the reaction of the audience now. Chopin had got what he had been longing for: an appraisal at the hands of an unbiased and discerning public. As he quipped after the event, he would give up music and become a house-painter if he heard any unfavourable criticism after this.[26]

Chopin was still, at the age of nineteen, naïve and inexperienced, and this first brush with the commercial side of musical life did not fail to disillusion him. The tetchiness of the orchestra, underscored by petty jealousy, Haslinger's calculations regarding the printing of the Variations, and the gracious way in which Count Gallenberg lent his theatre while taking money for tickets without volunteering to pay a fee had opened his eyes, and he felt 'cleverer and more experienced by four years'.[27] But such considerations counted for little when set against his reception and the reviews which began to appear as he was preparing to leave the Austrian capital.

'Chopin surprised people, because they discovered in him not only a fine, but a very eminent talent,' one of them explained, going on to say that 'on account of the originality of his playing and compositions, one might almost attribute to him already some genius, at least as far as unconventional forms and pronounced individuality are concerned'. It went on to identify 'a certain modesty which seems to indicate that to shine is not the aim of this young man', and summed up accurately Chopin's attitude when playing before an audience: 'He emphasised but little, like one conversing in the company of clever people, not with the rhetorical aplomb which is considered by virtuosos as indispensable.' The reviewer hailed him as a 'true artist', pointing out that his improvisation had delighted a public 'in whose eyes few improvisers, with the exception of Beethoven and Hummel, have as yet found favour'.[28] Another called him a 'master of the first rank', declaring that his compositions bore 'the stamp of great genius' and comparing his appearance in the musical world to that of 'the most brilliant meteors'.[29] The reviewer who must have pleased Chopin more than all the others wrote:

> He is a young man who goes his own way, and knows how to please in this way, although his style of playing and writing differs greatly from that of other virtuosos, and indeed chiefly in this; that the desire to make good music predominates noticeably in his case over the desire to please.[30]

It was in high spirits that Chopin and his friends left Vienna for Prague, the next city on their itinerary. They spent three days there, sightseeing and calling on some of the local musicians, after which they travelled on towards Dresden, pausing at Toeplitz, whence they went on an excursion to Wallenstein's castle at Dux. While in Toeplitz, Chopin stumbled on a Warsaw acquaintance who was a distant relative of the lord of the place, Prince Clary, and who took him along to meet the Prince that evening. Chopin's pleasure at being in such company is evident:

> *We went in; the company was small but select – some Austrian Prince, a general whose name I forget, an English sea-captain, several young dandies, apparently Austrian Princes too, and a Saxon general called Leiser, covered in medals, with a scar on his face. After tea, before which I talked a good deal with Prince Clary himself, his mother asked me whether I would 'deign' to sit down at the piano (good piano – Graf's). I did 'deign', but asked the company to 'deign' to give me a theme to improvise on. Thereupon the table at which the fair sex were knitting, embroidering and crocheting came to life with cries of* 'Un thème!' *Three Princesses consulted together and finally sought the advice of Mr Fritsche (young Clary's tutor I think), and he, with general assent, gave me a theme from Rossini's Moses . . .*[31]

The Clarys invited Chopin to spend another day in Toeplitz, but he wanted to press on to Dresden, where he arrived with his friends on 25 August. He visited the celebrated art gallery, went to the theatre to see Goethe's *Faust*, called on some of the city's musicians, and then left for Warsaw, feeling like a homecoming hero.

FOUR

Adolescent Passions

Chopin had an unpleasant surprise when he reached Warsaw on 12 September. The *Warsaw Courier* had somehow managed to misconstrue the reviews of his concerts and had published what amounted to an unfavourable account of his Viennese triumph. He was able to show his friends the original versions, but it was too late to scotch the general impression of failure which had attached itself to his trip.[1]

This only made Warsaw seem more provincial, and he could not even take solace in the sympathy of his friends. Białobłocki had died, Tytus Woyciechowski had retired to the country to look after his estate, others had gone abroad or, like Matuszyński and Fontana, were working hard at their university studies. Chopin had nothing to do, as he had finished his education and was waiting for the opportunity to begin his travels. As before, the main obstacle was lack of money. While he had been in Vienna, the rest of his family had paid a visit to Prince Antoni Radziwiłł at his summer residence of Antonin, and the consequence of this was an invitation for Chopin to spend the season in Berlin with the Prince. But he was not keen on the idea. Berlin had seemed provincial to him, and he longed for Vienna, Italy and Paris. He must have also considered the possibility of visiting England, for he was now, along with Julian Fontana, taking English lessons – from an Irishman called Macartney, who was usually drunk and trying to borrow cash from the two boys.[2]

Chopin struggled on with his F minor Concerto (op.21, usually referred to as no.2, although it was the first he wrote) and with the first set of Études. He went to every performance at the opera and to every concert, however uninspiring, and spent much time at Brzezina's music shop. Like all similar establishments, this was a cross between a shop and a drawing room, with something of the atmosphere of a coffee house thrown in. People interested in music would drop in, see what had arrived from abroad, browse, play pieces through on the piano, and discuss musical topics. Chopin and other musicians used to meet on given days at the rooms of Joseph Kessler, formerly pianist to Count Potocki at Łańcut and now a music teacher in Warsaw. What they played depended on who turned up with what instruments. This way they managed to play through many chamber works that autumn, including pieces by Spohr and Hummel, and a Trio by Beethoven. 'I have not heard anything quite so great for a long time – in this piece Beethoven makes fools of us all,' Chopin wrote afterwards to Tytus Woyciechowski.[3]

Now that Chopin had time on his hands, he entered into the life of the city to a greater extent, and frequented the coffee houses and other haunts of the young intelligentsia, who were in a state of political ferment. The death of Tsar Alexander I in 1825 and the accession of his brother Nicholas I to the throne had altered the political climate in Poland. While all but the most radical had been prepared to accept the Russian hegemony under Alexander, this was becoming extremely difficult under the increasingly autocratic rule of his successor. Chopin's generation grew restive as it watched the constitution violated, books censored and manifestations of national feeling suppressed, and by the end of 1829 there was a palpable spirit of rebellion. Coffee houses such as Brzezińska's, which Chopin frequented for coffee in the daytime and punch in the evenings, were the scene of fervent discussions and conspiratorial activity.

But while he was with his generation in spirit, Chopin was not interested in politics, and his closest companions were not revolutionaries but poets. Some, like Stefan Witwicki and Bohdan Zaleski, were also caught up in the nationalist movement, although the one he liked best, Dominik Magnuszewski, was an erratic dilettante poet and amateur musician with a melancholy bent and a sense of alienation from his contemporaries. But from Chopin's letters to Tytus it is clear that he never developed real intimacy with any of them. 'You cannot imagine how much I lack something in Warsaw now,' he wrote. 'I haven't got anyone I can say two words to, anyone I can confide in.'[4] He had a great deal he wished to confide, as he was still nurturing a secret love for Konstancja Gładkowska.

Throughout his childhood and teens Chopin had found the process of musical composition relatively effortless, and he had always been relaxed in his relations with others. Now, at the age of nineteen, he was finding it difficult to fulfil himself either artistically or emotionally, and the resulting sense of frustration pervades his letters. This makes it more difficult to assess his real feelings towards Konstancja, as they are inextricably bound up with that frustration whenever he touches on them. She certainly had no idea of what was going through the composer's mind, and carried on flirting with a couple of officers less bashful than Chopin. The presence on the scene of these strapping young bloods only served to underline his sense of his own physical shortcomings. His reaction was to withdraw into himself and wallow in self-pity.

In October, Chopin's sombre thoughts were dispelled by a pleasant distraction. He had been asked down to the country by his godmother, Mrs Wiesiołowska, *née* Skarbek, whose estate lay close to Prince Radziwiłł's Antonin, and although he was originally unenthusiastic about the idea, he did go on to stay at Antonin afterwards. He had a delightful sojourn in this 'paradise' with its two 'Eves', the young princesses, who managed to chase all thoughts of Konstancja from his head. The Prince was charming to him and showed him his own music, amongst which was an accompaniment to Goethe's *Faust* which Chopin found surprisingly good.[5] As well as talking music they made music, for the Prince was a good cellist. Chopin wrote a Polonaise for piano and cello specially for him and his daughter to play. 'It is nothing but glitter, for the drawing room, for the ladies,' he explained to Tytus. 'I wanted Princess Wanda to learn to play it; I'm vaguely supposed to be giving her some lessons while I'm here. She's young (seventeen), pretty, and it's a real joy placing her little fingers on the keys.' He always warmed to anything delicate, pretty and refined. 'I could have stayed there until I was thrown out,' he later wrote, but he soon returned to Warsaw, having promised to join the Radziwiłłs in Berlin in May 1830, which he hoped would give him time for another visit to Vienna first. Nothing was to come of these plans.[6]

Try as he might, he still could not get his F minor Concerto finished. He was in the ridiculous situation of being in demand and not being able to come up with the required works. On 6 December, his father's name day, he arranged a concert in the Chopin apartment, with the participation of Żywny and Elsner, and on 19 December he took part in a public concert at the Merchants' Club, at which he improvised so brilliantly that he was hailed in the papers as never before. The Polish press, which had largely ignored his existence until now, seems at last to have realised the importance of this national poet of the keyboard. 'Mr Chopin's works unquestionably bear the stamp of genius,' concluded the *Warsaw Courier*; 'among them is said to be a concerto in F minor, and it is hoped that he will not delay any longer in confirming our conviction that Poland too can produce great talent.'[7]

But the F minor Concerto was still unfinished, and it was not until 3 March 1830 that he was able to perform it. On that day he made up a small orchestra in the Chopin drawing room, and played the concerto, with Kurpiński conducting. The newspapers reviewed the concert as though it had been a public event, for there had been a select audience present. The *Warsaw Courier* described Chopin as the 'Paganini of the piano',[8] while the *Universal Daily* carried a very long review, stating, amongst other things, that:

> *The creative spirit of the young composer has taken the path of genius . . . I felt that in the originality of his thought I could glimpse the profundity of Beethoven, and in the execution the art and pleasing qualities of Hummel . . . All the listeners were moved by these works, and those more closely associated with the artist were deeply affected. His old piano teacher was nearly in tears. Elsner could not conceal his joy as he moved about, hearing only praise of his pupil and his compositions. Kurpiński conducted the orchestra himself for the young artist. This is a real talent, a true talent. Mr Chopin must not hide it and must let himself be heard publicly; but he must also be prepared to hear voices of envy, which usually spare only mediocrity.*[9]

Egged on from all sides, Chopin agreed to perform, and on 12 March the *Warsaw Courier* informed the public that he would be giving a concert in the National Theatre. Two days later the same paper announced that all the tickets had been sold, although there were still three days to go before the event.

On the morning of 17 March Chopin rehearsed the concerto with full orchestra, under Kurpiński, and on the same evening played it through before his largest audience to date: eight hundred people. He also played his Fantasia on Polish Airs, sandwiched between overtures by Elsner and Kurpiński and some songs by Paër. In his meticulous diary, Kurpiński noted that, although the theatre had been packed with an enthusiastic audience, the piano used had been too soft-toned, and much of the effect had been lost.[10] Chopin himself was not at

47

all pleased with the performance. He realised that some people could not hear properly, and felt that the music had not got through to the audience, whose enthusiastic applause, he felt, was simply 'to show that they hadn't been bored'.[11]

He could not have been more wrong, for although playing on his own quiet piano had clearly been a mistake, the reception was rapturous. The Warsaw newspapers were dominated by reviews of the performance, which in some cases took up a third of the whole issue. The critics could not make their minds up whether it was his playing or his compositions which were the more remarkable, and comparisons with Mozart and Hummel were bandied liberally. Hardly had the sound of his playing died away than a persistent chant for a second appearance began. This was arranged for 22 March, and a Russian general obligingly lent Chopin a strong Viennese instrument for the occasion. The concert opened with a symphony by Józef Nowakowski, an older Conservatoire colleague, after which Chopin played his concerto, the *Krakowiak* Rondo and an improvisation on a peasant song, again interspersed with other pieces. This time the music got through to everyone, and there was wild enthusiasm in the theatre. People shouted for a third concert, while a French pianist on his way to Moscow, who had dropped in out of boredom, rushed out to buy a bottle of champagne and insisted on toasting the unknown young Pole.

Chopin's playing had by all accounts been at its best. As one review put it: 'It was as though his manner of playing was saying: "It is not me – it is music!"'[12] Another explained that 'Chopin does not play like others; with him we have the impression that every note passes through the eyes to the soul, and that the soul pours it into the fingers . . .'[13] Yet another, by a music-lover called Albert Grzymała, compared his playing to 'a beautiful declamation, which seems to be the natural medium of his compositions'.[14] Perhaps the most interesting reflection, summing up as it did the whole of Chopin's career as a performing artist as well as his attitude to life as a musician, was made by a society lady, whose diary entry for the evening of the concert was printed in the *Polish Courier*, and after heaping praise on him, noted:

> *Chopin's playing is like, if I may express myself in such manner, the social* ton *of an important and substantial person who lacks any pretentiousness, because he knows he has a natural right to everything; it is like a young innocent beauty, whose mind has not been tainted by the idea that she could increase her charms through dress. You could be accused of the same innocence, you interesting artist! The stage requires brilliance, excellence, and even something of the terrible, for while the really beautiful and gentle tones are understood by the few, they make only a weak effect on others, and none at all on the many. But even this reproach is a compliment to you . . .*[15]

The reproach was certainly justified, for now that he had been reviewed and praised more than Paganini and Hummel during their visits, now that the whole of Warsaw had finally understood his playing and his compositions, Chopin did not give the third concert everyone was clamouring for, even though the money involved would have meant freedom to travel wherever he liked. He explained his reluctance to Tytus by saying that he had nearly finished his second piano concerto (the one in E minor, usually called no. 1), and that, wishing to have something new for his next appearance, he would wait until this was ready, which he hoped would be after Easter.

The real reasons for his refusal lay elsewhere. He found the preparations for the concerts exhausting and stressful, as he had to select musicians and decide whose music would be chosen for the programme, which in a small place like Warsaw was a delicate operation. Friends and acquaintances took offence when he failed to reserve boxes for them or personally invite them to the event. 'You wouldn't believe what torture the three days before the concert are,' he wrote to Tytus after the first one; but he was soon to discover that the period afterwards could be equally bruising.[16]

He was horrified by what he considered to be the exaggerated praise and sycophancy that accompanied his appearances: he received verse offerings from hacks; his old friend Alexandrine de Moriolles sent him a crown of laurels; Antoni Orłowski, a colleague from the Conservatoire, was busy writing Waltzes and Mazurkas to themes from Chopin's concerto; and the music publisher Brzezina wanted to print a lithograph portrait of him. At the same time the newspapers carried a number of articles discussing the nature of Chopin's genius and its position in the world of music. One long and somewhat illogical article ended up by thanking Heaven and Elsner that the young composer had not been allowed to fall into the hands of 'some Rossinist', an ill-concealed jibe at Kurpiński.[17]

This provoked an open war between those who were for Elsner and German music, and those who supported Kurpiński and Italian music. Chopin was appalled to find himself at the centre of the fracas, and did everything he could to extricate himself. He begged Antoni Orłowski not to print his compositions, and refused to allow Brzezina to publish a portrait. 'I don't want to read or listen to what anyone writes or says any more,' he wrote petulantly to Tytus, for whose presence he longed more than ever.[18]

The quarrel had nothing whatever to do with Chopin himself, and he need not have felt in any way implicated in its unpleasantness. Yet the hitherto highly sociable and uninhibited composer was beginning to develop alarmingly sensitive spots. He had always been self-conscious enough to see the ridiculous in his own behaviour, and had in the past drawn great pleasure from describing it in letters to friends. It may be that this emanated from a deeper fear of being ridiculed by others;

both his extreme modesty about his work and the arch tone in which he often referred to himself would suggest an underlying pride hiding behind bashfulness. As he reached the end of his teens and began to take himself a little more seriously – seriously enough to nurture a great passion – he shrank from anything that might expose him to criticism or judgement. His first major appearances as a professional musician had made him a public figure, which embarrassed him, and had provoked a squabble which disgusted and alarmed him. The episode only strengthened his conviction that any sort of public activity was bound, in one way or another, to expose him to unseemliness and possibly ridicule.

This was accompanied by an analogous development in his relations with other people. He still found it easy to make friends, and was outwardly sociable, but he grew more and more suspicious and wary of allowing them to approach too close. That is why the absent Tytus was not replaced by any other as Chopin's confidant, and why their intimacy grew instead of waning. It also explains a great deal about Chopin's behaviour with regard to Konstancja Gładkowska.

Warsaw was not a large city, and it would have been impossible for him not to have seen her quite often, either socially or at musical evenings. After his triumphal concerts she must have been more than ever aware of his existence. And yet it would appear that he continued to pine from afar, without attempting to let her know his feelings. Romantic adolescents are often more interested in nurturing emotions than in achieving intimacy with their object, but in Chopin's case the fear of putting himself in an embarrassing position is probably what paralysed any move towards intimacy. It was less risky to keep pining and at the same time to channel his frustration and self-pity towards Tytus, who remained the only real presence in Chopin's heart. 'Nobody apart from you shall have a portrait of me,' he wrote to Tytus after the fuss over Brzezina's attempt to print his portrait; '– one other person could, but never before you, for you are dearer to me.'[19]

This intimacy went beyond the purely emotional. Tytus was a good pianist and wrote a little, and Chopin trusted his taste. Once he even wrote that Tytus had taught him how to 'feel' music.[20] Chopin was always sending him his 'rubbish' or 'laboured bits of dreariness', as he liked to refer to his works, particularly during the spring of 1830. 'When I write something new, I'd like to know how you would like it,' he wrote, 'and I feel that my new concerto in E minor will hold no value for me until you have heard it.'[21]

Chopin's infatuation with Konstancja, and the attendant sense of frustration, were no doubt responsible for this uncharacteristic uncertainty, and for the sudden need to give his music meaning. For the first and last time in his life he was overtaken by the Romantic urge to programme his music both sentimentally and thematically. 'I say to my piano what I would like to be saying to you,' he wrote to Tytus – and what he would like to be saying to Konstancja, he might have added.[22] The Adagio of the new concerto he was writing, which was secretly dedicated to her, is the only piece of his whose meaning Chopin ever tried to explain. 'It is not supposed to be strong, but romantic, calm, melancholy; it should give the impression of gazing at a spot which brings back a thousand cherished memories,' he wrote. 'It should be like dreaming in beautiful springtime – by moonlight.'[23] Other pieces written during the same period are also tinged with sentimentality, like the Nocturnes, op.9, the E flat major Étude of op.10, and some of the songs he wrote to Witwicki's poems, like 'The Wish' or 'Where Does She Love?' (op.74). Even Elsner noticed that some of the music from this period was inspired by 'beautiful eyes'.[24]

During the remainder of March and April Chopin let himself go to pieces. He had intended to finish his second concerto within a few weeks and perform it publicly at the end of April or the beginning of May, as he needed to pursue his career and earn more money, however much it cost him in ruffled sensibilities. He was still vaguely aiming to set out for Berlin in May, and thence go wherever seemed appropriate. But May came and went, and Chopin had neither finished his new concerto nor arranged another performance. While he was heaving sighs in Warsaw, Tsar Nicholas arrived for the state opening of the Polish parliament, and, as usual on such occasions, various artists converged on the city from abroad. These included the King of Prussia's pianist Sigismund Woerlitzer; Miss Belleville, a fine pianist and pupil of Czerny, who had recently played Chopin's *La ci darem la mano* Variations at a concert in Vienna; and the singer Henriette Sontag, a beautiful woman with a magnificent voice for whom Weber had composed the title role of *Euryanthe* six years before. She had retired from the operatic stage after her marriage to Count Rossi and now only sang in concerts.

She gave eleven in Warsaw, most of which Chopin attended. He went into ecstasies over her voice, the elegance and control of which he related to his own touch on the piano, but felt she lacked depth of expression. 'She seems to breathe into the stalls with the scent of the freshest flowers, and she caresses, soothes deliciously, but rarely moves to tears,' he wrote to Tytus.[25] Prince Radziwiłł, who had also arrived in Warsaw, introduced them. They immediately took a liking to each other, and since Henriette was besieged all day long by admiring dignitaries and aristocrats, she asked him to come and call on her in the mornings at her hotel. At this time of day he would find her in her *déshabille*, and he soon became infatuated with her. 'You cannot imagine how much pleasure I have had from a closer acquaintance – in her room, on the sofa – with this "envoy of heaven" as some of the local hotheads call her,' he wrote to his friend, all thoughts of Konstancja temporarily banished from his head.[26]

Chopin had intended to give a concert himself during the Tsar's visit, but for reasons which remain unclear no such event took place. While Miss Sontag sang to the various imperial majesties and Woerlitzer and Belleville played to them, people in Warsaw wondered why Chopin did not. It may be that his contacts with some of those identified by the authorities as subversive elements had something to do with it.

With the end of June, the parliament dissolved and people began to leave the city. At the beginning of July the Haslinger edition of the *La ci darem la mano* Variations arrived in the Warsaw shops, and Chopin agreed to play them at a concert given on 8 July by a singer who had taken part in his earlier appearances. The audience was small, the public wearied by all the activity of the previous weeks, and although the reviews were favourable, the event failed to make any great impact.

Chopin was wondering what to do next. Romuald Hube, one of his companions on the previous year's trip to Vienna, with whom he had been intending to travel to Paris that summer, and then on to Italy, had departed, leaving him stranded in Warsaw. Since Tytus had not come to Warsaw as he had intended, and as Chopin had nothing better to do, he went to stay with him in the country, apparently intending to spend some time there. But after he had been there only two weeks, he read in the papers that Soliva had organised a concert in which Konstancja was to make her stage debut, and he rushed back to Warsaw, much to the annoyance of Tytus.

The event may have been emotionally rewarding for Chopin, but when it was over he was once more at a loose end, harking back to his stay with Tytus. 'Your fields have left me with a dull longing,' he wrote; 'that birch tree before your windows will not leave my thoughts.' In an attempt to dispel these he went to join the rest of his family who were staying with the Skarbeks at Żelazowa Wola.[27] He spent a couple of weeks there, adding the finishing touches to his E minor Concerto. On the warm summer nights the piano would be wheeled out onto the terrace, and Chopin would play to the house party and to the local children who would creep into the park to listen.[28]

In the middle of August Chopin returned to Warsaw, and although he was restless and bored, he took no action to bring forward his departure. 'Nothing draws me abroad,' he wrote to Tytus. 'Believe me that when I leave next week it will only be out of deference to my calling and common sense (which must be very small, since it cannot banish everything else from my mind).'[29] But while plans for a departure 'next week for certain' were announced in one letter, this was followed by another a couple of weeks later in which he informed his friend that 'I'm still here; I don't have enough will to decide on the day . . .'[30] The delays may have had something to do with the alarming situation in Europe: in July a revolution in Paris had swept the Bourbons from the throne and replaced them with a constitutional monarchy under Louis Philippe, another revolution had broken out in Belgium against Dutch rule, and there were rumblings of discontent in various other parts of the Continent. But they probably had as much to do with Chopin's own state of mind.

By the end of the summer he had reached new heights of emotional turmoil, ostensibly on account of Konstancja. Having met her well over a year before and immediately recognised her as his 'ideal' (the very word is redolent of schoolboy ritual), he had still not declared himself to her. 'I could go on hiding my pathetic and ungainly passions for another couple of years,' he wrote to Tytus, at the same time stressing their depth and force.[31] Strong his feelings may have been, but they were certainly not exclusive. The brief infatuations with the Radziwiłł girls and Henriette Sontag are only some of the manifestations of an acute susceptibility to women. From his letters we know that at one soirée in August he saw a girl (who of course reminded him of Konstancja) whom he could not take his eyes off, and who had set his heart on fire by the end of the evening. Another day, in church, he caught the eye of 'a certain person', as a result of which he staggered out in a state of sensuous inebriation and nearly got himself run over by a passing carriage.

These and similar stories are recounted to Tytus in tones of mawkish self-pity, alongside assurances that he, Tytus, is in fact the most important person in Chopin's life. While reaffirming his constant and undying love for the girl, he would write to his friend that he thought constantly of him: 'I do not forget you, I am with you, and it shall be so till death.'[32] It was Tytus who would have a portrait of Chopin before Konstancja, and it was Tytus who was the recipient of what would have been love letters to Konstancja, had Chopin dared write to her. These letters, sometimes friendly, sometimes petulant, sometimes verging on the passionate, are freely strewn with declarations of love and affinity, and contain passages of extraordinary sensuality.

This has prompted some to conclude that the two young men were or had been lovers. On the face of it, the equivocal references to passions, secrets and torment combine with the extremely specific terms of endearment to make this appear plausible. Chopin signs off one letter to Tytus with the following jumble of childishness and coy eroticism:

> *I must go now and wash. So don't embrace me now, as I haven't washed myself yet. – You? If I anointed myself with fragrant oils from the East, – you wouldn't embrace me, not unless I forced you to by magnetic means. But there are forces in Nature, and tonight you will dream that you are embracing me. – I have to pay you back for the nightmare you caused me last night!*[33]

Taken out of context, this may appear a little risqué, as might the endless kisses sent and demanded by Chopin. But these expressions were, and to some extent still are, common currency in Polish, and carry no greater implication than the 'love' people regularly sign off with today. And the traces of infantile eroticism in the letters are of little significance in themselves. The spirit of the times, pervaded by the Romantic movement in art and literature, favoured extreme expression of feeling and glorified transcendent friendship, and it is probably this that lies at the heart of these letters, written as they were at a period in Chopin's life when he came nearest to living out the Romantic ideal.

While the possibility cannot be ruled out entirely, it is highly unlikely that the two were ever lovers. Had the slightly sentimental relationship between the older, stronger boy and his gentler, more emotional classmate really developed into a sexual rapport, it would almost certainly, knowing Chopin's malleable and undecided nature, have become an exclusive and longlasting passion. In such a case there would have been no reason for Chopin to sit about being bored in Warsaw while the bucolic seclusion of Tytus's estate beckoned.

Tytus's role in Chopin's life was nevertheless an important one. 'I swear that only you have power over me, you and . . . no one else!' Chopin wrote, somewhat dramatically, to his friend, and he was hardly exaggerating.[34] His upbringing had marked his character. The strong paternal authority to which he had been subjected had rendered him almost incapable of making a decision on his own. His loving mother and admiring sisters had led him to demand and expect boundless affection from people. The sheltered and regular life of the Chopin household only served to make the outside world and its cares seem more problematic and frightening. While his early exposure to a wide acquaintance had developed in him a gift for easy sociability, this was, apparently, accompanied by a certain fear of giving himself. All this made Chopin dependent, now that he was beginning to live outside his family, on the support of friends. Since he was finding it increasingly difficult to get close to people, he clung more and more to his old friend Tytus. He kept trying to abdicate responsibility, begging Tytus for advice and direction, but Tytus apparently evaded the responsibilities of a mentor and pressed Chopin to take a hold on himself. At the same time he became the recipient of some of Chopin's repressed or frustrated feelings, which is why some of the letters he received from the young composer read like love letters.

In Warsaw, Chopin's only close friends were Jan Matuszyński, who was pursuing medical studies, and Julian Fontana, who had now, after finishing his studies at the Conservatoire, taken up law at the University. Along with Witwicki, they formed a small group which often met at the house of their friend the poet Dominik Magnuszewski. The latter lived with his grandfather, a former judge who seemed to embody the spirit of pre-partition Poland, still dressing in the traditional costume of the Polish nobility. Chopin and his friends loved to listen to him talking about that past which now seemed so distant. The atmosphere of the old Poland had been superseded by the more modern and secular spirit of the 1820s, and Chopin was strongly drawn to what was heroic and elegant about it – it was this he was attempting to capture in the rhythmic and melodic gestures of the more sophisticated Polonaises he was beginning to write.

The atmosphere at Magnuszewski's house was congenial, and here he could let himself go with abandon. 'Everyone always wanted him to improvise,' Magnuszewski's sister recorded. 'He never tried to wriggle out of this, but first he would ask my sister Klara, who had a beautiful voice, to sing something, and it was only afterwards that he would start. We would sit in silence for hours, listening to that music which fired our young souls, and afterwards we would usually start dancing. At that point the dreamy improviser would turn into a lusty player and start thundering out Mazurkas, Waltzes and Polkas until, tired of playing and eager to join in the dancing himself, he would cede the keyboard to a humbler replacement, Fontana, who played fluently and beautifully.'35

By mid-September, Chopin was trying out various movements of his new E minor Concerto in quartet or other forms, and on the twenty-second he arranged a full performance of the work in the Chopin apartment, again with a select audience of music-lovers, amongst whom were Count Skarbek, Grzymała and Witwicki. It was they who reviewed the event in the press and prompted a public clamour for Chopin to make himself heard. His travel plans had again been put off. He therefore agreed to give a concert, and what is more, invited Konstancja and her fellow pupils to take part in it. This entailed obtaining permission from the Minister of the Interior, which was not difficult, and also getting Kurpiński, who had a natural right to be the conductor, to cede his place to Soliva for the evening, which was a more delicate matter. This activity woke Chopin from his lethargy, and he was now seriously planning his departure as well. 'A week after the concert at the latest I shall have left Warsaw,' he wrote to Tytus, who had agreed to accompany him.36 Chopin was, for once, decided; he had bought a trunk and clothes, and was writing out the scores he would need on his travels.

The concert which took place on 11 October 1830, his last in his native country, went off perfectly. He played his E minor Concerto and the Fantasia on Polish Airs. The concerto benefited from the conducting of Soliva, who took it slowly and did not let the over-excited Chopin get carried away. 'I was not the slightest bit nervous, and I played as I play when I'm alone,' he wrote to Tytus. Konstancja sang an aria as never before and looked seductive, the other performances were good, and the Fantasia, which he played at the end, delighted him and the audience. 'This time I understood what I was doing, the orchestra understood what they were doing, and the public understood as well,' he wrote. 'It seemed to me that I had never been so much at ease when playing with an orchestra.'37

Chopin was delighted with every aspect of the evening, but it is worth noting that the hall, with only seven hundred people in the audience, was not quite full, and that notwithstanding the deafening applause, there was only one review of the concert, and that a short one.

Chopin himself was convinced that the theatre had been full, and was probably relieved by the silence in the press. He was by now busy with the preparations for his departure, and had to pay farewell calls on all his acquaintances, many of whom gave him letters of introduction to friends and relatives in Vienna. On 25 October he called on Konstancja in order to take his leave.

At some stage in the course of the previous weeks Chopin had at last given her some intimation of his feelings, and he had apparently met with a good reception. Rings were exchanged and Chopin was allowed to write to her, through the discreet agency of Matuszyński. At this last meeting, she wrote a little verse into his album, which ended with the lines:

Others may value and reward you more.
But they can never love you more than we do.
[At some later date, Chopin added, in pencil: 'Oh yes they can!']³⁸

On the evening of 1 November, a party of friends organised a farewell dinner attended by Nicolas Chopin, Żywny, Magnuszewski, Fontana and others. They sang, danced and played late into the night, after which they walked Chopin back to his house. The next morning he made his last farewells while Ludwika finished copying some of the scores he was taking with him, and in the afternoon the family accompanied him to the coaching station. Neither the young man nor his worried family knew how long he would be away or how he would fare alone in the world.

The coach trundled away, through the dingy western suburb

of Wola, but was stopped just after passing the city gates. It was surrounded by a group of men, who turned out to be Elsner with a small male choir. To the accompaniment of a guitar, they performed a cantata which the old man had composed for the occasion. It exhorted Chopin to remember his motherland, and to keep its harmonies in his soul wherever he might find himself. There was something prophetic, both in the words and in the emotion with which Elsner embraced his pupil, as though he never expected to see him again. After the last tearful embrace, Chopin climbed back into the coach, which rolled away, bearing him off from his native land for ever.

FIVE

Vienna

Chopin was not alone for long. At Kalisz, the first halt, he was joined by Tytus, whose company quickly banished the sorrows of leave-taking. Together they went on to Breslau, where they spent four days. One afternoon they wandered idly into the Merchants' Hall to find a rehearsal for the evening's concert in progress. During a break, Chopin sat down at the piano and started showing off. The local pianist who was billed to play at the concert heard him and immediately renounced his role in terror, with the result that the unsuspecting public were that evening treated not to the Moscheles concerto advertised, but to Chopin playing two movements of his E minor Concerto as a solo.

From Breslau they travelled to Dresden, which Chopin knew already. He revisited the art gallery, its main attraction for him. 'There are pictures there at the sight of which I hear music,' he explained to his parents in one of the very few references he ever made to the other arts.[1] Chopin liked the beautiful eighteenth-century city, with its large Polish colony surviving from the days when Poland and Saxony had been united under one crown, but he was less keen on the traditional form of transport, the sedan chair, which made him feel foolish as he was carried to a soirée.

He called on the principal musical figures in the city, some of whom suggested that he give a concert before moving on.

But he refused. A concert in Dresden would have earned him some money and would certainly not have done his reputation any harm, but he was in such a sanguine frame of mind that he thought it a waste of time; he was in a hurry to reach Vienna. He felt he knew Vienna and that Vienna knew and valued him, and it was in high spirits that he arrived there on 22 November 1830.

'How happy I am to have reached Vienna, where I shall make so many interesting and useful acquaintances, and where I may even fall in love!' he wrote to Matuszyński the moment he and Tytus had settled into their rooms at the Stadt London Hotel.[2] That evening they went off to the opera to see Rossini's *Otello*, eyeing the girls in the street on the way (although Chopin did not fail to insert a pious reference to Konstancja in his letter to the go-between Matuszyński).

The next morning he received the greatest possible compliment of a visit from Hummel. Such a mark of respect from the most eminent composer left in what was still the capital of music could not have failed to encourage Chopin's boldest expectations. But these were a little clouded later that morning by the publisher Haslinger, whom he hastened to call on. Haslinger had probably lost money on the *La ci darem la mano* Variations, and had therefore not published the C minor Sonata (op.4) or the variations that Chopin had left with him on his previous visit. He declared that he had no intention of giving Chopin any money for the two concertos he had brought him. He did intimate that he might consider publishing one of them if Chopin let him have the copyright for nothing, but Chopin was determined not to let himself be exploited further. 'From now on it's: "Pay up, Animal!"' he announced in a letter to his family, explaining that he was growing wary of the 'crooks and Jews' who stood between him and making money.[3] With the reputation he had built up and the contacts he had made, he felt he could afford to be firm with them.

After a few days Chopin and Tytus moved to a cheaper hotel while they waited for the lodgings they had found to be vacated by their current tenant, an English admiral. 'An Admiral! Yes, but I shall be held in admiration, so the lodgings will lose nothing in the change!' Chopin blustered in his letter home.[4] The three spacious rooms were 'beautifully, luxuriously and elegantly furnished', the rent was low, and the landlady, a pretty young widow who professed a love for Poles and contempt for Austrians and Germans, had been to Warsaw and had heard of Chopin. But it was the position of the apartment, on the third floor of a house on the Kohlmarkt, which particularly delighted the two young men. As Chopin pointed out to his parents, it was 'right in the centre of town, with a wonderful promenade below', the music shop of Artaria on the left, and those of Mechetti and Haslinger on the right, and the opera just behind – 'what else could one possibly need?'[5] Graf, whose soft-toned pianos enchanted him, and to whose shop he had been going every afternoon in order to 'loosen [his] fingers after the journey', had promised to move an instrument into the lodgings free of charge, and this would enable Chopin to invite people to come and listen to him.[6]

His immediate preoccupation was to arrange a concert, and he duly called on musicians and others who might help him in this purpose. He looked up Nidecki, who had settled in Vienna, and the composer Czerny, who was in a tremendously good mood, having just finished writing out 'an overture for eight pianos and sixteen players'.[7] Old Würfel, now bedridden with tuberculosis, proffered advice on where the concert should be held and which of the two concertos Chopin should play. He was categorical that Chopin should under no circumstances perform free, advice which was seconded by Count Husarzewski and others who promised to help organise the event.

One of the most prominent of these was a new acquaintance, the imperial physician and erstwhile friend of Beethoven,

Dr Giovanni Malfatti, who had a somewhat unusual position both at court and in Viennese society. Chopin had a letter of introduction to Malfatti's wife, a Polish countess, and was greeted 'like a member of the family'.[8] The doctor promised to introduce him to the most notable musical personages and to arrange a concert for him at court, which was not immediately possible since this was in mourning following the recent death of the King of Naples.

'I shall be giving a concert, but where, when and how, I still cannot say,' Chopin wrote home at the end of his first week, which 'flew by'. He basked in the novelty of living in his own rooms, of eating out in the restaurants Mozart and Beethoven had frequented, of spending his days entirely as he wished and of going to the opera almost every evening. He went five times during the first week, three of them to operas he did not know – Mozart's *La Clemenza di Tito*, Auber's *Fra Diavolo* and Rossini's *Guillaume Tell*. He found the standard of singing just as high as in the previous year, and what was most welcome to him was the continual change of programme, which meant that he could rapidly improve his education in this field.[9]

Chopin was suffering from a cold, or 'swollen nose' as he put it, which is why he did not immediately call on the grander ladies to whom he had introductions. As soon as he recovered, however, he began to make up for lost time, and called on Countess Rzewuska, at whose home he expected to meet 'the cream of Viennese society', and several other Polish ladies married to Austrians. He also delivered his most important letter of introduction, from Grand Duke Constantine to Countess Tatischev, wife of the Russian ambassador. It was while he was awaiting her pleasure to receive him that, on 5 December, news arrived from Warsaw which shattered his hopes.

On 29 November, revolution had broken out in the Polish capital. The Grand Duke had narrowly escaped being assassinated in the Belvedere by a group of cadets, while the Russian troops in the city were attacked and disarmed by bands of patriots. Although the reports were far from clear, both Chopin and Tytus were well aware of what lay behind them and of what probably lay ahead – national insurrection and armed conflict with Russia. After emotional deliberations lasting all night, Tytus prepared to return to Warsaw in order to fight in the national cause, but Chopin was prevailed upon to remain in Vienna.[10]

'After Tytus left, too much suddenly fell on my shoulders,' Chopin complained.[11] He was utterly unprepared, either practically or psychologically, to cope on his own, and he naturally fretted about family and friends in Warsaw. More to the point, events taking place there had a direct bearing on his position in Vienna. Austria was one of the three powers that had dismembered and abolished the Polish state at the end of the previous century, and while a degree of cordiality reigned between Poles and Austrians at the social level, their national interests were diametrically opposed. Events taking place in Warsaw did not directly threaten anyone in Vienna, but they evoked hostility and apprehension. Although after the initial outburst the leadership of the Polish rising was assumed by Prince Adam Czartoryski, Viennese society shared Metternich's view that it was a revolution against the established order of Europe, and it was feared and disapproved of as much as the French Revolution had been. Even in the cheap trattoria where he sometimes took his dinner, Chopin overheard remarks such as 'God made a mistake in creating the Poles,' and 'Nothing worthwhile has ever come out of Poland,' which he took as personal as well as national insults.[12]

Malfatti tried to persuade him that the artist should be cosmopolitan and overcome national feeling, to which Chopin retorted that he must be a very poor artist. He had never taken any interest in politics before, but now that everyone he knew and respected in Warsaw was engaged in a fight for survival, in which defeat would entail annihilation of the world he had grown up in, he felt personally involved.

He never went near the Russian Embassy, wrote to his parents telling them to sell the diamond ring he had been given by Tsar Alexander, acquired shirt studs with Polish eagles on them, and brandished handkerchiefs embroidered with Polish motifs. He consorted with other Poles, mostly young men returning from foreign travel to join the Polish ranks who formed a rowdy element in Vienna, demonstrating their patriotic feelings at every opportunity.

The Austrian police and Russian agents kept a close watch on their comings and goings, and Chopin's sympathies were no secret to them. In consequence he never met 'the cream of Viennese society'. In fact, during his eight-month sojourn in the city he did not once play at an aristocratic gathering; all the Lichnowskys and Schwarzenbergs who were so kind to him on his previous visit do not figure in his life at all during this one. No more is heard, either, of Dr Malfatti's promises to arrange an appearance at court. Even Countess Rzewuska was on the side of law and order – not surprisingly, considering her past. At the age of four she had been torn from the arms of her mother, the beautiful twenty-four-year-old Princess Rozalia Lubomirska, who was pushed into a tumbril and sent to the guillotine in Paris during the Terror.

Chopin could not afford to keep up the spacious apartment on his own, so he sublet it to an English family, thereby making a profit, and moved up one floor in the same building. The new apartment was no garret, as Chopin hastened to assure his parents: his room was large, with three windows and handsome mirrors. It contained only a bed, a large table and the piano. It was also quiet, and suited his more subdued mood. 'How happy I am in this room!' he wrote to them. 'Before me I see a roof, beneath me I see pygmies whom I tower above. I am at my happiest when, having played long on Graf's wonderful piano, I go to bed clutching your letters, and then dream only of you . . .'[13]

He was unexpectedly joined by his friend Romuald Hube, who had returned from Italy (the trip on which Chopin had hoped to accompany him) and was stuck in Vienna, having tried and failed to cross the Polish frontier. Hube moved in with him, but the two led independent lives, he studying and arranging the notes he had made on his tour, Chopin 'always practising on the piano, usually reworking phrases, and sometimes improvising', in Hube's words.[14]

Life was pleasant, if a little uneventful. He was woken every morning by 'an insufferably stupid servant' with the morning coffee.[15] This was often drunk cold, since his first action on getting out of bed was to sit down at the piano and play, sometimes for an hour or more. His German teacher would call at nine o'clock, followed by other visitors such as Nidecki and Hummel's son, an artist. At midday Chopin would at last shed his dressing gown and get dressed to go out. After a walk on the Glacis (once part of the city fortifications, now a favoured promenade) with one or other of his friends, he would either go to lunch at someone's house or accompany friends to one of the eating houses frequented by students, and thence to one of the more fashionable coffee houses. The afternoon, or what was left of it, was spent paying calls, and at dusk he would come home to dress for the evening. There was usually a dinner, soirée or concert of some description for him to attend, but he was always back at his lodgings not later than midnight to 'play, weep, read, ponder, laugh, go to bed, put out the candle, and dream of home'.[16]

Christmas brought with it a sense of loneliness as well as the unpleasant realisation that after a whole month in Vienna he had achieved nothing. Musical success seemed more remote than ever, and his letters home reflect his listlessness. Those to Jan Matuszyński, the only others that survive from this period, are heavy with introspection and self-pity. The passage describing his visit to St Stephen's Cathedral on Christmas Eve is typical:

> *I went in. There was still nobody about . . . I stood at the foot of a gothic pillar, in the darkest corner. I cannot describe the magnificence, the sheer dimensions of those great vaults. It was quiet – only now and again the steps of a sacristan lighting lamps somewhere in the depths of this temple would break into my reverie. Tombs behind me, tombs beneath me . . . I only needed a tomb over my head . . . A gloomy harmony haunted me . . . I felt more vividly than ever my complete isolation . . .*[17]

The letter meanders on, evoking romantic visions of Chopin walking alone through the busy streets of Vienna, wrapped in his cloak and his loneliness, or returning home to 'weep out an adagio' on his piano, and dwelling on his general dissatisfaction with everything. 'Were it not for my father, to whom I should be a burden, I would return immediately,' he writes. 'I curse the day I left . . . I am bored to death by all the dinners, soirées, balls and concerts which fill my life; it is so melancholy, vacant and dreary . . . I cannot do what I please, but instead have to dress up, pull on my stockings and brush my hair; in the drawing rooms I have to affect serenity, but when I come home I thunder away on my piano.'[18] The somewhat ingenuous affectation is undermined by a puppy-like vitality: the bouts of self-pity, in which the theme of suicide crops up more than once, are followed by humorous anecdotes which he cannot resist telling.

Chopin was genuinely anxious about events in Poland, lonely without his family around him and frustrated by his lack of success, so he felt sorry for himself. Since he was twenty years old, he naturally called on images of love, death and alienation to explain his predicament. Another reason for these sombre outpourings was that Jan Matuszyński, his messenger to Konstancja, was supposed to read her passages from Chopin's letters, as well as pass on notes for her. This presumably accounts for much of the lyricism and for lines such as: 'while I still have life in me . . . until my very death . . . nay, even after my death, my ashes will strew themselves at her feet . . .' and exclamations like, 'I have not enjoyed a single moment since I arrived in Vienna!'[19]

The gap left by Tytus had been filled by 'wonderful Doctor Malfatti', who took an avuncular interest in the young pianist. He looked after Chopin's health, and even managed to 'fatten him up'. His door was always open to the young man, and he would have Polish dishes served at dinner in order to make him feel at home. Various other Polish households in the city vied with each other to care for Chopin, who now affected great contempt for 'damned Prussians' (which was supposed to denote all Germanic people). His hankering after things Polish cast a prejudice over everything Viennese. 'Everything makes me sigh and long for home, for those delicious moments I failed to value fully,' he writes elsewhere. 'The people here are nothing to me; they are kind, but not out of kindness, only out of habit; everything they do is flat, mediocre, too ordered.'[20]

Chopin's disenchantment with Vienna was not limited to the social or emotional aspects, nor indeed was it solely the result of his lack of success. He had come as a pilgrim to the city of Mozart, Haydn and Beethoven, expecting to find musical excellence. Old musicians such as Hummel shook their heads and told him Vienna was no longer what it had been, and he could only agree.

The giants of the moment were Johann Strauss the elder, Joseph Lanner and Czerny. 'Here they call waltzes works, and Strauss and Lanner who play dance-music are called Kapellmeisters!' Chopin wrote to Elsner indignantly.[21] 'Amongst the many amusements in Vienna, the favourite is the soirée at certain inns where Strauss or Lanner play waltzes during dinner,' he explained to his family. 'They are frantically applauded after each waltz, and if they play a potpourri of airs from opera, dances and songs, the audience gets completely carried away.'[22]

This was not a context in which Chopin would sparkle. Although Haslinger appreciated his talent and Mechetti thought his work brilliant, neither could afford to publish works which would not sell. Chopin's were too difficult and too cerebral for the Viennese ladies to play, while his lack of patronage did not encourage other musicians to play them. His success on his previous visit had not made a lasting impact, since his concerts had taken place during the off season, and he was now outshone by a new star that had appeared on the scene – Sigismund Thalberg.

Thalberg enjoyed high patronage, being the natural son of Count Dictrichstein, the Emperor's director of music. He had a strong, controlled and monumental style of playing. It was said of him that if he were dragged from his bed in the middle of the night and ordered to play, there would not be a note out of place, so impeccable was his technique. Chopin liked neither Thalberg nor his playing, nor his competition, judging by the bitterness lurking behind his words. 'He plays remarkably, but not to my taste,' he wrote to Matuszyński. 'He's younger than me, and the ladies like him. He plays potpourris of airs from the Mute [Auber's opera *La Muette de Portici*], gives *pianos* with the pedal and not the hand, takes tenths like I take octaves, wears diamond shirt-studs . . .'[23]

Chopin's hopes of giving a concert of his own came to nothing. On 4 April 1831 he took part in one given by the singer Madame Garcia-Vestris, appearing at the bottom of the list of performers simply as 'Herr Chopin – pianist'. He played his E minor Concerto as a piano solo and passed unnoticed. His only other public appearance in Vienna took place on 11 June, when he played the same piece. 'I feel so indifferent about it that I would not care if it never took place . . .' he wrote in his diary before the concert, for he had long before this shed his sanguine hopes of a couple of triumphal months in Vienna.[24] At least this time he was mentioned in the press, which called him a 'sincere worshipper of true art'.[25]

In the circumstances, there seemed little point in prolonging his sojourn, and he wrote to his parents asking whether he should go to Italy straight away: 'Please write and tell me what I should do.'[26] Nicolas Chopin refused to make up his son's mind for him, so after a few weeks Chopin wrote to Matuszyński. 'My parents tell me to make up my own mind, but I am afraid to,' he wrote. 'Should I go to Paris? People here advise me to wait a little longer. Should I come back? Should I stay here? Should I kill myself? Should I stop writing letters to you? You tell me what to do!'[27]

As nobody told him what to do, he lingered in Vienna. He took every opportunity to hear a new work or a new musician, went to the opera every time the programme changed, and cultivated other musicians. Amongst these were two whose acquaintance he found particularly rewarding and who undoubtedly contributed to the development of his ideas at this crucial stage.

One was Joseph Merk, the first cellist in the Imperial Orchestra and a teacher at the Vienna Conservatoire, with whom Chopin spent much time playing duets. Chopin had a particular affection for the cello, the only instrument aside from the piano for which he wrote memorable music, and with Merk's help he composed an Introduction to the Polonaise for Cello and Piano he had written at Antonin in 1829. They were published together later that year by Mechetti as op.3, dedicated to Merk.

The other friend Chopin made at this time was the violinist Josef Slavik, four years his senior and already a virtuoso. 'Apart from Paganini, I have never heard anything like it,' he wrote, 'ninety-six staccato notes with one stroke of the bow; incredible!'[28] Chopin's high opinion of his new friend was shared by Paganini himself, and had Slavik not died two years later, he would certainly have made a name for himself. Chopin and Slavik spent whole afternoons playing together, and intended to write a set of variations for piano and violin on a theme by Beethoven. Chopin is known to have been working on the Adagio at one moment, but no trace of it survives.

Chopin's output during the Vienna period was strongly marked by the uncertainties of his position. With the *Valse Brillante* (op.18), the Five Mazurkas (op.7) and other pieces which are pretty and relatively easy to play, he was probably trying to cater to the Viennese market. This does not mean that the pieces are in any sense trivial. The Mazurkas are something of a breakthrough, along with the Études he was working on, in the process of divesting himself of the more superficial characteristics of the brilliant style.

The situation in Poland also affected his output. Now that Matuszyński, Tytus, Fontana and other friends had taken the field with the Polish army, Chopin longed to unite himself with them at least in spirit. 'Oh, why can I not be with you, why can I not at least be your drummer-boy!!!' he wrote to Matuszyński after Christmas.[29] On another occasion, he spoke of trying 'somehow to grasp and capture those songs whose shattered echoes still drift here and there on the banks of the Danube – the songs that Jan's army sang'. (A reference to King Jan Sobieski's relief of Vienna in 1683.)[30]

He set more of Witwicki's poems to music, but in a letter expressing his gratitude, Witwicki suggested that Chopin make a weightier contribution to the cause by writing a national opera. The propaganda value of an opera based on some theme from Polish history being staged in European capitals would be immense, for opera at that time attracted a broader audience than any other cultural genre. 'The mountains, forests, waters and meadows have their own inner voice, though not every soul can hear it,' Witwicki wrote. 'I am convinced that a Slav opera, conceived by a true talent, by a composer who thinks and feels, will one day rise in the musical world like a brilliant new sun.'[31] Chopin was not averse to the idea in principle, and his godfather Count Skarbek had even sketched out a couple of libretti for him.

But as he struggled on with larger works – a third piano concerto, a concerto for two pianos and orchestra, the variations for piano and violin, and the *Grande Polonaise Brillante* (op.22), the last piece he ever wrote for the orchestra – he found the work increasingly taxing. At the same time he was working on his first set of Études, and on two works which belong amongst his greatest: the Scherzo in B minor (op.20) and the Ballade in G minor (op.23), the Ballade being the first piece he wrote in this form, his own invention. And it is these which announce Chopin's ultimate aim.

Although he had already composed some of the greatest music in the Romantic canon, he was still searching for a way forward. It was his work on the Études, lasting from 1829 to 1832, that, more than anything else, allowed him to develop his groundbreaking ideas, to revolutionise piano playing and to achieve new depths of sound and feeling with his instrument. He abandoned all thoughts of composing an opera and further orchestral works. He would henceforth do exactly what Witwicki suggested, but with the piano as sole medium. As he drew further away from his native land, he strove more and more to recapture its essence and that of its people in his work.

By mid-May Chopin had at last decided to continue his tour. Italy being still troubled by revolutionary unrest, Paris seemed the obvious next stop. The situation in Poland was encouraging, as the Poles had won the first round of military operations, and he no longer needed to feel anxiety for his family. Having made a firm decision to leave Vienna, however, he found himself beset by a multitude of difficulties. Quailing at the prospect of a journey on his own, Chopin had found himself a travelling companion, a young man called Norbert Kumelski, but the latter promptly fell ill and their departure was delayed by several weeks. When Kumelski had recovered, Chopin was informed by the Vienna police that his passport had been mislaid and that he must obtain a new one from the Russian Embassy (he was formally a Russian subject, and passports, both internal and external, were already obligatory in that state). After a few more weeks the police found his original passport, but the Russian Embassy would not endorse it for travel to Paris, which was considered a hotbed of revolutionary activity, so he pretended he would only be passing through on his way to London. Having successfully negotiated the Russian bureaucracy, Chopin and Kumelski now came up against the Austrian: there was a cholera epidemic sweeping through central Europe, and health certificates were required in order to travel.

Chopin took advantage of these delays to see the remaining sights and attractions of Vienna, and went on a pilgrimage to the Kahlenberg Heights where King Jan Sobieski had pitched camp and heard Mass before riding down to do battle with the Turks in 1683. He plucked a leaf from the spot and sent it to his sister Izabela for her album. The delays and the uncertainty enervated him, and his mood swung violently. 'I don't lack anything – except perhaps a little more life, more spirit; I feel weary, and then sometimes I feel as merry as I used to at home,' he wrote to his parents. 'When I feel sad I usually go to Mrs Szaszek's, where I always find several Polish ladies whose sincere and comforting words inevitably cheer me up so much that I then start mimicking Austrian generals – this is my new act. You haven't seen it yet, but those who do always fall about laughing. But then again there are days when you cannot get through to me or squeeze a word out of me. On those days I spend 30 Kreuzers on going to Heitzing or some such place in order to distract myself. I have grown side-whiskers on the right, and they're nice and bushy. You don't need them on the left, as you always have the audience on your right.'[32]

The memory of Konstancja kept cropping up in his thoughts, even during Malfatti's party in his summer residence in the hills overlooking the city, at which Chopin and others played and sang in the elegant mirrored drawing room with its french windows open onto the terrace and the smell of orange blossom in the warm night air. 'Her image is continually before my eyes,' he wrote in his diary, adding that 'sometimes I think I no longer love her, yet I cannot get her out of my head'.[33] Chopin was still a child in many ways, and showed great reluctance to grow up: when he had turned twenty in the previous year he had loaded the event with extraordinary significance, and harked back to all the things he felt he had lost irretrievably.

On 20 July 1831 Chopin and Kumelski left Vienna at last, travelling through Linz to Salzburg, where they visited Mozart's birthplace. In Munich, their next stop, Chopin discovered that the money his father had promised to forward had not arrived, and he was obliged to break his journey for a month. He soon made the acquaintance of the musicians in the city, who persuaded him to give a concert. No longer in the euphoric mood that had caused him to refuse in Dresden, he willingly agreed. The event took place in the Philharmonic Society Hall on 28 August, Chopin playing his E minor Concerto and the ever-popular Fantasia on Polish Airs, both of which were well received. The review of the concert in the local musical gazette was effusive on the subject of his 'excellent virtuosity', his 'developed technique' and 'charming delicacy of execution', and praised the works themselves.[34]

Chopin's next destination was Stuttgart, where he spent a couple of weeks, alone, since Kumelski had stayed in Munich. He was in a state of morbid depression verging on the pathological, as the very long entries in his diary reveal:

Strange! This bed I am about to lie on has probably served more than one dying person, and yet that does not worry me. Perhaps more than one corpse has lain on it – and for many days? But what makes me any better than a corpse? Like a corpse, I have no news of my father, mother, sisters, of Tytus! Nor do corpses have lovers! Corpses are pale like me, cold like my feelings. A corpse has ceased living, and I have lived long enough . . . Why does one go on living this miserable life?[35]

He looked back on his life, pointing to its worthlessness and to the fact that, cut off as he was from everything dear to him, it made no sense. There is less affectation here than in some of his letters from Vienna, and the feelings expressed have a genuine ring to them. The twenty-one-year-old composer felt lost, and anxious over his future. He was now quite alone, and further from home than he had ever been. Not the least of his worries was the fact that, while philandering in the company of Kumelski, he had caught a venereal disease.[36] If he had invested his twentieth birthday with such significance, he can hardly have regarded what may well have been his first sexual encounter, let alone its consequence, as anything but a watershed in his existence.

But he did not have time to indulge his own miseries, as only a couple of days later he received news which was to alter the course of his life dramatically – the Polish army had been defeated and Warsaw had fallen to the notoriously ruthless Russian commander General Paskievich. In his diary, Chopin wrote:

I wrote the preceding pages without knowing that the enemy had already broken in – the suburbs are destroyed, burnt down – Oh, Jaś [Matuszyński]*! Wiluś* [Kolberg] *probably died on the ramparts! I can see Marceli* [Woyciechowski] *in chains! Sowiński* [the general in whose house Chopin wrote the Fantasia on Polish Airs], *that kind old man, in the hands of those monsters! Oh God! You exist! You exist and yet You do not punish! Have You not seen enough Russian crimes? Or perhaps – maybe You are a Russian*

Yourself! My poor father! My dearest! Perhaps he has nothing left to buy my mother bread with! Perhaps my sisters have succumbed to the fury of the Russian rabble! Paskievich, that dog from Mohilev, has stormed the capital of the first monarchs of Europe! The Russian is master of the world!? Oh, father, so this is your reward in old age! Mother, suffering, gentle mother, you watched your daughter die, and now the Russian marches in over her bones to come and oppress you! . . . Did they spare her grave? They trampled it and covered it with a thousand fresh corpses! They have burnt the city! Oh, why could I not have killed at least one Russian! Oh, Tytus, Tytus! . . . What is happening to her, where is she? – unfortunate creature! – Perhaps she is in Russian hands? The Russians are pressing her, stifling, murdering, killing her! Oh my love, I am alone here, come to me, – I shall wipe away the tears and heal the wounds of the present with memories of the past . . . when there were no Russians . . . Maybe I have no mother any more, perhaps the Russians have killed her, murdered her . . . my sisters unconscious, yes, or struggling; my father in despair, helpless – no one left to pick up my dead mother. I am inactive, I sit here empty-handed, just groaning, suffering on the piano in despair . . . and what next? God, God! Move the earth – may it swallow up the people of this century. May the cruellest tortures fall on the heads of the French, who would not come to our aid! . . .[37]

Having cursed the French, Chopin set off for Paris a few days later. He was to build a new life there which suited him better than any he could have had in Warsaw, but the sense of loss sustained on that night in Stuttgart never left him. It came to embrace everything – home, country, family, friends, love and youth – and remained the fundamental inspiration for his music. As he had promised Konstancja, he would 'heal the wounds of the present with memories of the past'.

SIX

Romantic Paris

The Paris that Chopin saw for the first time in September 1831 was a formidable city. Its size, the grandeur of its buildings and monuments, the scale of its open spaces, its bustle and vitality, not to mention emblems of modernity such as the gas lighting to be seen here and there, all made Vienna look like a market town by comparison. But Paris was far more than that. 'Paris is the capital not only of France, but of the entire civilised world; it is the rendezvous of its intellectual notables,' wrote the German poet Heinrich Heine, who had exiled himself there. 'Here is assembled all that is great in love or in hate, in senti-ment as in thought, in knowledge or in power, in happiness as in misery, in the future or in the past. When one considers the collection of distinguished or famous men that one finds here, Paris appears like the Pantheon of the living. They are creating a new art here, a new religion, a new life; it is here that the creators of a new world are happily at work.'[1]

Chopin was no intellectual, and what arrested his attention first in Paris was the allure of the decadent yet vibrant capital, so very different from the strait-laced cities he was used to. It exuded a permissive atmosphere which both shocked and delighted him. Apart from the bright lights, what intrigued him most were the whores who pursued him in the street, the chorus girls who were so keen on 'duets', as he coyly put it, and the lady upstairs who suggested they share a fire on cold days.

'Here you have the greatest luxury, the greatest squalor, the greatest virtue and the greatest vice – everywhere you look there are notices about ven. disease – you simply cannot imagine the shouting, the commotion, the bustle and the dirt; one could positively lose oneself in this anthill, and the nice thing is that nobody cares what anyone else does,' he wrote to Kumelski after a few days in the city, adding that he was prevented by his ailment from 'tasting the forbidden fruit'.[2]

The other thing Chopin quickly became aware of was that Paris lay at the epicentre of European dissidence. The revolution which had swept the Bourbon Charles X off the throne in the previous year and replaced him with Louis Philippe had been incomplete, and there was continuing unrest, fuelled by the influx of defeated revolutionaries from Italy, Germany and Poland.

While Chopin was conservative by instinct, the shock of seeing his country crushed had induced a spirit of rebellion in him, and he ranged himself on the side of the enemies of the status quo, voicing subversive views on all authority. Possibly out of a desire to compensate for having failed to take part in the insurrection, he attended meetings along with other young Polish émigrés, and may even have been mixed up in some rioting.[3]

The artistic life of the French capital was as unbridled as its manners and as partisan as its politics. The progress of the Romantic revolution against the literary establishment had been marked by violent battles, as the supporters and opponents of Victor Hugo resorted to physical as well as literary weapons. This had created an atmosphere congenial to anyone with a new idea, and the city attracted artists of every kind. It was, as Heine pointed out, the artistic capital of the Western world.

'I'm delighted with what I have found here,' Chopin wrote to Kumelski. 'I have the best musicians and the best opera in the world.'[4] With Beethoven, Weber and Schubert dead, and the next generation of great composers not having yet made a significant impact (Mendelssohn was twenty-two, Schumann and Chopin twenty-one, Liszt nineteen, Verdi seventeen and Wagner eighteen), the musical establishment of Paris, consisting as it did of a handful of venerables like Cherubini (Director of the Conservatoire), Paër and Lesueur; renowned opera composers like Auber and Hérold; and above all the two lions of the moment, Rossini and Meyerbeer, was indeed the most brilliant in the world.

Paris also boasted the finest collection of performing musicians. In the concert halls, Chopin heard the pianists Herz, Liszt, Osborne and Hiller. The three orchestras – of the Conservatoire, the Academy (Opéra) and the Italian opera (the Théâtre des Italiens) – were probably the best in Europe. The singers at the two opera houses included such legendary names as Giuditta Pasta and Maria Malibran, and when he went to performances of Rossini's operas under the baton of the composer himself, Chopin felt he was hearing completely different works from those he had heard in Vienna or Warsaw. The scale of the productions overawed his critical faculty, and when he saw Meyerbeer's *Robert le Diable*, with its cast of hundreds, its pyrotechnics and stage machinery, he termed it a 'masterpiece of the new school', and declared that 'Meyerbeer has immortalised himself', strong words from someone as reserved in his praise as Chopin.[5]

Chopin had taken rooms on the fourth floor of a house in the boulevard Poissonnière, a newly built-up area on the northern fringe of the city. He soon got used to this part of Paris, and as with most things to which he got used, he would not stray far from it over the next seventeen years. 'You wouldn't believe what a nice apartment I have,' he wrote to Kumelski; 'a small room beautifully furnished in mahogany, a little balcony overlooking the boulevards, with a view stretching from Montmartre to the Pantheon and embracing this whole beautiful world.'[6] And it was not an alien world, like Vienna.

There were strong historical links between Poland and France, the most recent being those forged on battlefields all over Europe by Polish soldiers who had fought for their country under the banners of Napoleon. All but the most conservative saw the two nations as standing for the same values against the tyrannical order embodied by the Russia of Nicholas I, and French society at every level felt sympathy for the Poles and their cause.

Paris itself had long been a cultural magnet for the Poles, and there had been many living there before 1830. Some, like Countess Kisselev, a member of the Potocki family separated from her Russian husband, were well-known figures and kept salons frequented by some of the most interesting people in Paris. Others, like the Komar family or Count Ludwik Plater and his brood, had left Poland before or during the insurrection and settled in Paris. They were soon joined by others fearful of Russian reprisals or merely unwilling to live under Russian rule.

From September 1831 on, a stream of defeated insurgents began to trickle into the French capital, and Chopin was reunited with schoolfriends such as Kazimierz Wodziński, and his Conservatoire colleagues Antoni Orłowski and Julian Fontana. The latter soon left for London, where he hoped to make a living, but was to reappear in Paris a few years later. The presence of these combined with the goodwill and hospitality of the Parisians to make Chopin feel at home, and the sense of not belonging which had spoiled his stay in Vienna did not trouble him here.

When he arrived in Paris, Chopin had only a letter from Elsner to Lesueur and one from Malfatti to Paër, the master of the royal music, but the musical world of the city was so tightly knit that within a couple of weeks he had met all the most prominent musicians, including the eminent pianist Kalkbrenner, whose works he had so often played in Warsaw. Chopin could not get over the impression Kalkbrenner's playing made on him. 'You won't believe how anxious I was to hear Herz, Liszt, Hiller, etc, but they're all zeros next to Kalkbrenner,' he wrote to Tytus. 'If Paganini is perfection itself, so is Kalkbrenner, but in a totally different way. It is difficult to describe his composure, his enchanting touch – unbelievable evenness and mastery are evident in every note of his – He is a giant who tramples underfoot all the Herzes and Czernys, and, by the same token, myself.'[7]

Kalkbrenner listened while Chopin played through his E minor Concerto. He complimented him by saying that he played like Cramer with Field's touch, but declared that he 'lacked method' and would never be able to play or compose properly until he had acquired this. He also put a red pencil through the manuscript of the Adagio, arguing that it was too long and repetitive. In spite of this, and of reservations on the part of others (the forty-five-year-old Kalkbrenner, who was dubbed 'the mummy' by Heinrich Heine, was not popular with most of the younger musicians in Paris), Chopin liked him, and persisted in thinking him 'the first pianist in Europe – the only one whose shoelaces I am not worthy of untying'.[8] Kalkbrenner himself was anxious to turn Chopin into his own idea of a superior pianist and agreed to teach him, suggesting a course of three years. Chopin was minded to accept, although the length of time and the expense worried him, and he informed his parents of the plan.

The Chopins were puzzled by the idea that he still needed to learn to play, and Elsner, who was also informed, was furious. 'I can say with pride and self-congratulation that I was able to give you a few lessons in harmony and composition,' he wrote, but the idea that anyone thought they could teach Chopin to play the piano was preposterous. He saw in it a trick of Kalkbrenner's to eliminate competition. Elsner also took the opportunity to say that Chopin was too obsessed with the idea of being a pianist, which he considered to be only the first step in a musical career. He argued that Beethoven's and Mozart's piano concertos had been forgotten, while their symphonies and operas lived on, and that Chopin should seek immortality through the operatic form, which would allow him to take his place between Mozart and Meyerbeer.[9]

Chopin retorted that he could not possibly compete with anyone except as a pianist. Sudden exposure to the musical riches of Paris had intimidated him and reinforced his natural inclination to leave alone musical forms with which he was not familiar. He felt he still had much to learn. He nevertheless decided against becoming Kalkbrenner's pupil. Far from taking this amiss, the older man volunteered to help Chopin get started.

Kalkbrenner was a partner of Camille Pleyel, the son of a German composer who had established himself as a piano-maker in Paris and owned a small concert hall. Through his good offices the hall was booked for Christmas Day, and Chopin set about finding other musicians to take part in his debut. Kalkbrenner himself offered his services and those of one of his pupils, the Englishman George Osborne. Hiller too agreed to take part, while a Polish cellist settled in Paris, Ludwik Norblin, managed to assemble a quartet which included the renowned violinist Pierre Baillot. In order to avoid giving offence, Chopin also had to invite Wojciech Sowiński, a Polish pianist living in Paris, though he did not think much of his playing. The real problem was with the singers, as most of the better ones were on contract to one or other of the opera houses, and their managers were loath to let them perform in private concerts. Even with Rossini's intercession there was nothing to be done, and the concert had to be put off until 15 January 1832.

Despite these setbacks, Chopin was in good spirits. The continuing political disturbances and a cholera epidemic were keeping the aristocracy away from Paris, so there was not enough teaching work available for the numerous pianists trying to make a living in the capital. But Chopin had no diffi-culty in finding work in the émigré Polish community. He had played a couple of times at the British Embassy, and acquired a few pupils among the English colony in Paris. He had also made his mark at the other foremost embassy, the Austrian, whose musical evenings were held in the house on the rue

Saint-Dominique rented by the ambassador, Count Apponyi. The music publisher Schlesinger had asked Chopin to write some variations on a theme from *Robert le Diable*, and Chopin had reason to be confident that the concert would be a success.

Even the news of Konstancja's marriage failed to unsettle him. 'It doesn't preclude a platonic love,' he remarked in a letter to Tytus, which suggests that the thought of her had grown distant amid all the excitement of the last months.[10] Christmas, the second he had spent away from home, did plunge him into self-pity and induce feelings of alienation. 'I wish you were here – you cannot imagine how much I suffer from not being able to pour out my heart to anyone,' he complained to Tytus. 'You know how easily I make friends, how easily I can talk to anyone about blue almonds – well, I'm up to my ears in that sort of acquaintance, but I have nobody I can sigh with – when it comes to my feelings, I'm always in syncopation with others.'[11]

The discrepancy between Chopin's apparent ease with people and his fear of letting anyone approach too close, noticeable during his last years in Warsaw, had become more pronounced. When he left Poland and found himself surrounded by foreigners (and the closest English word to the one he uses is 'aliens'), he withdrew more and more into himself and became increasingly suspicious of any intimacy. Everyone was struck by this reserve, some were put off by it: after his death Liszt would echo the general feeling when he wrote that Chopin 'was prepared to give anything, but never gave himself'.[12] Liszt also noted that Chopin could hide his feelings under a cloak of composure and serenity. 'Good-natured, affable, easy in all his relationships, even and pleasant-tempered, he hardly allowed one to suspect the secret convulsions which agitated him.'[13]

Now that Tytus was no more than a distant correspondent, his role as Chopin's sole confidant was gradually assumed by the German pianist and composer Ferdinand Hiller. He was almost two years younger than Chopin, but more experienced and stronger-willed. He was also a fine musician. 'A boy with immense talent, a pupil of Hummel's,' is how Chopin described him to Tytus, '– something in the manner of Beethoven, but a man full of poetry, fire and soul.'[14]

A kind of *amitié amoureuse* sprang up between them. Hiller was fascinated by the figure of Chopin, 'as supple as a snake and full of charm in his movements', as well as by his inimitable touch on the piano. He saw Chopin every day and helped him find his bearings in Paris, and it was he who introduced him to Felix Mendelssohn, who arrived in December en route for England.[15]

Chopin and Mendelssohn took a liking to each other, and Mendelssohn agreed to take part in the concert planned by 'Sciopino', as he affectionately referred to him, for 15 January. The programmes were already printed and everything ready when Kalkbrenner suddenly fell ill. The event was postponed once again, but even while Chopin was waiting in exasperation for his Parisian debut, the first great mark of recognition as a composer was bestowed on him.

In July 1831 Robert Schumann, three months Chopin's junior, had picked up the score of the *La ci darem la mano* Variations in a Leipzig music shop, intrigued by the unfamiliar composer's name. He spent two perplexing months trying to play the Variations, and as he laboured at it, his conviction grew that here was a work of extraordinary importance, both musically and, for lack of a better word, politically. This op.2 by an unknown composer struck him as being not only brilliant, but exactly what modern music should be aiming at. He saw it as a piece of programmatic music reproducing in another medium the drama not of Mozart's opera, but of Da Ponte's libretto. He was so excited by his discovery that he wrote a review of the work for the *Allgemeine Musikalische Zeitung*, and his future father-in-law Friedrich Wisch sent a longer version to the *Revue Musicale* in Paris. Chopin was shown the manuscript, which struck him as utterly ridiculous. 'He says that in the second Variation Don Juan is running about with Leporello, that in the third he is embracing Zerlina while Mazetto is getting angry (the left hand) – and as for the fifth bar of the Adagio, he sees Don Juan kissing Zerlina on the D flat!' he wrote to Tytus. 'Plater was wondering yesterday just what part of her anatomy her D flat might be, etc.! One can but marvel at the German's fancy . . .'[16]

He begged Hiller to use his influence to prevent publication of the piece in the *Revue Musicale*, but the original did appear in the December issue of the *Allgemeine Musikalische Zeitung*. And, whatever Chopin thought of it, it constituted an impressive accolade, with its now famous concluding verdict: 'Hats off, gentlemen – a genius!' One can understand Chopin's embarrassment at the style of the piece, but it was a great deal better than the review of the same variations by Ludwig Rellstab, critic of the German musical journal *Iris*, who branded this 'vandalism perpetrated on Mozart's melody' as typical of a work originating in 'the primitive roots of the Slav nations'.[17]

Chopin's Parisian debut eventually took place on 26 February 1832 in the Salle Pleyel on the rue Cadet. The programme included Beethoven's Quintet, op.29, played by some of the best musicians in the city, led by the violinist Baillot; a couple of arias, not, it is true, by the best singers; Chopin playing his E minor Concerto as a solo and his *La ci darem la mano* Variations; and concluded with a monstrous Polonaise for six pianos specially composed by Kalkbrenner and played by himself, Chopin, Hiller, Sowiński, Osborne and Stamaty, Mendelssohn having dropped out at the last moment.

'Our dear Fryc has given a concert, which brought him a great reputation and some money,' Antoni Orłowski wrote home to his family. 'He has wiped the floor with all the pianists here; all Paris is stupefied.'[18] Osborne claims that few Parisians turned up, but his evidence is not reliable, and other sources paint a different picture.[19] There were many Poles present, as well as musicians: the two Herz brothers, Pixis, Mendelssohn and the young Liszt, who applauded furiously. Whether the whole of Paris was indeed stupefied or not, the performance was well reviewed, and it earned Chopin the immediate recognition of a number of significant people. The critic of the *Revue Musicale*, François Fétis, was in no doubt that an exceptional new talent had arrived on the scene. He was not blind to Chopin's faults, but brushed these aside as attributes of his youth, and pointed instead to the truly unique qualities he had recognised:

Here is a young man who, surrendering himself to his natural impressions and taking no model, has found, if not a complete renewal of piano music, at least a part of that which we have long sought in vain, namely an abundance of original ideas of a kind to be found nowhere else . . . I find in M. Chopin's inspirations the signs of a renewal of forms which may henceforth exercise a considerable influence upon this branch of the art.[20]

Chopin tried to follow up his success. In March he petitioned the Société des Concerts to allow him to give a concert in the Conservatoire hall, where he would have the benefit of its excellent orchestra, but this was not a privilege easily granted, and Paris was full of more renowned musicians than him. As he put it to a Polish colleague who was thinking of trying his luck there, Paris was too full of 'virtuosos, charlatans, politics and cholera'.[21]

In May he took part in a charity concert in the Conservatoire hall on behalf of the victims of the cholera epidemic, but the joy of being able to perform the first movement of his E minor Concerto with the best orchestra in Europe was diminished by the fact that his soft playing was drowned by it. The *Revue Musicale*'s critic could not hear the piano part and thought the orchestration poor.

Depressing as this must have been to Chopin, it could not have been unexpected. He was by now well aware that his manner of playing was not suited to large halls, and this sat well with his dislike of large audiences. 'I am not fit to give concerts,' he once told Liszt; 'the crowd intimidates me and I feel asphyxiated by its eager breath, paralysed by its inquisitive stare, silenced by its alien faces; but you, you are made for it, for when you cannot captivate your audience, you at least have the power to stun it.'[22] (The French word *assomer* used here has the secondary meaning of 'bore them to death'.)

This is the moment at which, according to some biographers, the penniless and starving Chopin was preparing to leave for America, where he hoped to fare better. He was supposedly saved from such a drastic expedient by a chance encounter with Prince Walenty Radziwiłł, who took him to dinner at the house of an unspecified Rothschild, where the hungry composer was allowed first to eat his fill and then to play before the assembled company, which represented the cream of the French aristocracy. The effect of his playing was such, the story goes, that not only did Chopin go home with dozens of bookings for lessons, but he became overnight the darling of *le tout Paris*.

Chopin's three closest friends in Paris at the time had no inkling of any plan to go to America. Furthermore, he was not particularly hard up.[23] During his first three months in the city he was subsisting on money received from his father, supplemented by the occasional lesson or paid soirée. In February he made some money from the concert: with the hall free of charge and the tickets at ten francs each, he would have made a handsome sum even if it had been only half-full. On the morning after the concert he was visited by a publisher who offered to buy everything Chopin had in his portfolio. He paid him cash down for the two concertos, the G minor Trio, the Grand Rondo and the Fantasia on Polish Airs, and the down-payment for so many works of that size could not have been less than substantial.[24]

As far as introductions to the world of the French aristocracy were concerned, Chopin was well provided for through his Polish connections. French society was made up of the old legitimist Bourbon aristocracy, inhabiting the Faubourg Saint-Germain; the Napoleonic nobility; and Orléanist society, made up partly of elements of the other two and partly of a new middle-class meritocracy. Families such as the Potockis and Czartoryskis had links with the first of these groups dating back to the time of the *ancien régime*. On the other hand, tens of thousands of Poles had fought in the Napoleonic armies. Dominik Dziewanowski, for instance, gave Chopin an introduction to the Duke of Montebello, the son of Marshal Lannes, with whom his uncle had served for many years. The Orléanist establishment was still easier to penetrate. Chopin played at the musical soirées of the connoisseur closely related to the King, the baron de Trémont, and one of his first pupils was having an affair with the heir to the throne, who was a frequent guest at her informal soirées, which Chopin also attended.

It is highly likely that at some stage in 1832 Chopin did get an invitation to play at the sumptuous Rothschild residence on the rue Laffitte, and was asked to give lessons to the wife of James de Rothschild, to whom he later dedicated one of his Ballades. Before he had been a year in Paris he was being invited on all sides, and the extent to which he had penetrated society can be gauged by the fact that he was usually invited not as a pianist, but as a guest. And he refused to be cowed by anyone who presumed otherwise.

'I remember how he let fly one evening at the master of a house where he had dined,' recalls Berlioz. 'Scarcely had the company taken coffee than the host, approaching Chopin, told him that the other guests who had never heard him hoped he would be so good as to sit down at the piano and play them some little trifle. Chopin excused himself from the first in a way which left not the slightest doubt as to his inclination. But when the other insisted in an almost offensive manner, like a man who knows the price and the purpose of the dinner he has just given, the artist cut the conversation short by saying

with a weak and broken voice and a fit of coughing; "Ah, sir!
... But I have only eaten very little!"'[25]

It would be wrong, however, to think of Chopin as spending
most or even a large proportion of his time with the French
aristocracy. He was just as often to be found in the homes of
humbler music-lovers, such as Thomas Albrecht, the Saxon consul
in Paris, or the banker Auguste Léo, whom he had met through
Hiller. Much of his time, too, was spent with his compatriots.

The Czartoryskis – Prince Adam, who was now the figure-
head of Poland in exile, his wife Princess Anna, and his
mother-in-law, Princess Sapieha (the one who had suggested
the nanny for Chopin's first concert) – had arrived in Paris at
the end of 1831. Chopin visited them in their humble rented
accommodation in the rue du Palais-Bourbon, where he and
other compatriots sat down to the traditional Polish Easter
dinner.[26]

The Platers, whose daughter Paulina was a pupil of Chopin's,
the Komars and a number of other Polish families also kept
open house, and a new Polish world came into existence on the
banks of the Seine, peopled by the most interesting debris of
Warsaw society. The intellectual elite was well represented by
the poet Adam Mickiewicz and a collection of other literati,
including Chopin's friend Witwicki, who turned up in the middle
of 1832.

This assemblage of beached talents could have depressing
aspects, typified by an evening at the Platers', where, according
to the poet Juliusz Słowacki, 'we sat around from ten in the
evening till two in the morning getting frightfully bored, but
thank God towards the end Chopin got drunk and started
improvising beautiful things on the piano'.[27]

But the émigré colony in Paris was no ghetto: Chopin's
French friends often accompanied him to Polish evenings, and
vice versa. 'At the house of the charming Countess Plater we
used to play while the Polish émigrés danced, and we came to

know a Mazurka so physical and full-blooded that we might have been in its native land,' Hiller later reminisced to Liszt.[28]

The fiery, extrovert Liszt had little in common with the reserved, delicate and fastidious Chopin, but he valued him for those very qualities: he admired his refinement, was in awe of his musical intelligence and envied his individuality. Liszt had been mercilessly exploited for his performing ability at the expense of all else, and he was in many respects too crude a character for Chopin's taste, but Chopin was impressed by his virtuosity, his ability to draw sound out of the piano like no one else, and his gift for playing faultlessly a piece he had never seen before straight from the score.

And it was Liszt who introduced Chopin to one who was to play a very important part in his life, an unassuming and diminutive twenty-year-old cellist called Auguste Franchomme. Chopin warmed to Franchomme, who was an instrumentalist rather than a virtuoso, a quiet man who disliked flash and exaggeration as much in people as he did in music. After their first meeting at dinner with Liszt, Franchomme accompanied Chopin back to his lodgings, listened to him play for a while, and 'immediately understood' him.

Through Liszt, too, Chopin met Heinrich Heine, and at the end of 1832 Hector Berlioz, just back from his Italian trip. Chopin now found himself in the kitchen of the Romantic movement, where the talents worked together like so many scullions, helping each other out in various ways – when Berlioz needed a piano arrangement of his *Francs-Juges* overture, it was Chopin who helped him. They would meet for dinner in a restaurant; for an evening of music at Chopin's, where the light of one candle cast great shadows in which, as Liszt put it, some of the greatest names of the next decade listened in silence; for a picnic lunch at Berlioz's; or at Liszt's for 'hours of smoky discussions' as they puffed at Turkish pipes.[29]

They could hardly have agreed on anything. Liszt had no

great fondness for Bach's work and Berlioz hated it, yet Chopin thought it the essence of music.[30] They had little time for Mozart or Haydn, Chopin's favourite composers, and they saw Beethoven as the great one, the man who had started the Romantic revolution and liberated music from its shackles. Chopin had reservations about him for that very reason, for, as he once told a friend, 'Whenever [Beethoven] is obscure and seems to lack coherence, this is not the result of the slightly savage originality with which he is credited; it is because he turns his back on eternal principles – Mozart never!'[31] According to Franchomme, Chopin had serious reservations about the great man's music, and he once told Liszt that in Beethoven 'passion too often approaches cataclysm', and for this reason he preferred Hummel.[32] He realised that Hummel was not as great a composer as Beethoven, but valued his restraint, which always prevented him from falling prey to vulgarity.

Chopin did not appreciate any of the more modern composers; he was lukewarm towards Weber, never bothered to pass comment on Schubert, thought little of Mendelssohn's music, and less still of Schumann's. Admire as he might the clever pianist in Liszt, he could not bring himself to like his compositions, and between Chopin and Berlioz there was mutual incomprehension. Berlioz found his Polish friend's music lacking in drama, as well as rhythm and cadence. The story of Chopin illustrating Berlioz's method of composition by dipping a pen in ink, bending it back and then flicking it at a piece of lined paper, is almost certainly apocryphal, but a more reliable source records Chopin saying that 'Berlioz puts down a lot of chords and then fills in the intervals as best he can.'[33]

The differences of opinion went deeper than liking or disliking each other's compositions, and had more to do with how these young men saw themselves and their careers. The Romantic movement was a revolution against the eighteenth-century role of the arts as an amenity and of the artist as an artisan. The artist had come to be regarded as a seer who had the divine gift of understanding and interpreting the universal truths that governed the world of those who no longer believed in the God of the Bible. Victor Hugo represented himself alternately as Zoroaster, Moses and Christ, somewhere between a prophet and a god.

The movement which in music began with Beethoven was to make a new position for music at the apex of the arts and for the musician as the quintessential artist, and therefore inherently divine. Chopin was to benefit from this. But he did not fit easily into the Romantic movement, because he saw himself more as a craftsman than an artist, and his instinctive reticence shied away from the arrogance implicit in the modern artist's role.

The Romantic movement insisted on functions. In order to be great, music too had to have a function, the only argument being as to whether that function should be cathartic, spiritual or political. And if art had a function, then the artist had a mission. Chopin's music had no function, and he could never take himself seriously enough to see himself as having a mission. As with Bach, music for him was an exercise in which form and development were the all-important factors, and while it was indeed a form of self-expression, it remained a personal one. 'Music has its own language and its own purpose, and one has to learn to reach the depths of the listener's soul,' he explained to a colleague.[34] As he once told Hiller, he would like to be considered a lyric poet, 'something like your Uhland'.[35]

Chopin nevertheless feasted on all the musical riches Paris had to offer that winter season of 1832–33, his second in the French capital. Berlioz marked his return to France by giving a performance of his *Symphonie Fantastique* at the Conservatoire. But in the symphonic genre, Chopin was more excited by the performance by the same orchestra with full choir of Beethoven's Ninth Symphony, which neither he nor Paris had heard before. Chopin's erstwhile idol John Field, the inventor of the Nocturne form, also gave three concerts, but Chopin had already heard him play during the summer, and had been disappointed by the crudeness and lack of fluency of his style.

After the New Year, which he saw in at a party at the Austrian Embassy, where he played along with Rossini, Liszt and Kalkbrenner, Chopin gave a concert himself. Although he did not make much money out of it, he was satisfied with his own performance and with its reception. At the beginning of April he played a duet with Liszt at a concert given by Berlioz to raise money for Harriet Smithson, the English actress he was in love with, after she had broken her ankle, and a few days later joined Liszt in another concert, at the Hôtel de Ville.

Chopin had made up his mind to spend at least three years in Paris, and consequently asked Paër to obtain a permit for him (the French government was trying to resettle impecunious Polish refugees in distant and less inflammable areas of the country). The Tsar, eager to isolate the real exiles, had offered an amnesty to those who had not played a leading role in the insurrection. Chopin could easily have availed himself of this, which would have allowed him to return to Poland whenever he wished, but did not do so, and thereby burnt his boats. In his case being a refugee did not present serious problems, as his French parentage and his contacts saved him from the more irritating inconveniences such as having to register with the police, not being allowed to live where he wanted, or needing permission before moving about France or leaving it. It was nevertheless a momentous decision on his part, and he made it consciously. As he wrote to Tytus: 'One breathes sweetly here.'[36]

SEVEN

Pianist à la Mode

'If I had a friend (a friend with a big, crooked nose, because that's the one I mean) who several years ago had played with me in Szafarnia, who had always loved me with conviction, and my father and aunt with gratitude, and if he, having left the country, had not written a word to me, I should think the worst of him, and however much he begged and snivelled, I should never forgive him – and yet I, Fryc, still have the effrontery actually to try to excuse my negligence, and I write, after a long time of sitting tight like a beetle which only raises its head above the water when nobody has asked it to,' was how Chopin opened a long-put-off letter to Dominik Dziewanowski. The rest of the letter decidedly gainsays the penitent tone:

> But I shall not try to make excuses, I prefer to own up to my guilt, which may loom larger from afar than it does here, for I have been torn apart by people in all directions. I have made an entry into the highest society, I sit next to ambassadors, ministers, princes; and I don't really know how it happened, because I didn't push myself. At the moment this is very important to me, because that is apparently where good taste is dictated; you immediately have great talent if you have been heard in the English or Austrian embassy, you play better if the Princesse de Vaudemont patronised you – I cannot write patronises, since the woman died a week ago . . . (she had a multitude of black and white dogs,

canaries, parrots, and was the owner of the most amusing monkey in Paris, which used to bite other countesses at her soirées). Amongst artists I have friendship and respect; I wouldn't write this to you if I hadn't been here over a year, but their respect is proved by the fact that people with great reputations dedicate their works to me before I have similarly honoured them; Pixis dedicated his new Variations with a Military Band to me, and they also compose variations on my themes; Kalkbrenner has written variations on one of my Mazurkas. Pupils of the Conservatoire, pupils of Moscheles, Herz, Kalkbrenner, in a word, accomplished artists, take lessons from me, place my name under Field's – in fact, if I were even more stupid than I am, I would think that I had reached the peak of my career; but I can see how much I still have before me, I can see it all the more clearly as I live very close to the first artists, and I can see their shortcomings. But I'm ashamed of writing all this rubbish; I have been boasting like a child; I would cross it all out, but I haven't got time to write another letter, and anyway, perhaps you still haven't forgotten my character, and if you do remember it you'll see that I haven't changed much, with the exception that I have one side-whisker – the other won't, simply won't grow. Today I have to give five lessons; you may think I'll make a fortune, but a cabriolet and white gloves cost more, and without them you wouldn't have <u>ton</u>. – I love the Carlists, hate the Philippists, and I'm a revolutionary myself, so I don't take any notice of money, only of friendship, for which I beg you.[1]

The tone of this letter betrays a degree of euphoria which, given Chopin's character, could only mean that he was sure of himself and his future. He had achieved a distinctive reputation, and by the beginning of 1833 was considered one of the brightest stars of the Parisian firmament. The reason for his success in carving out a niche for himself among so many better-known artists was that he had something unique to offer, and offered it in such a way that he did not challenge or threaten any of his fellow musicians.

His piano-playing had developed greatly over the last couple of years, and was now quite unlike any other's. Those who heard him play in the right circumstances were immediately captivated. Charles Hallé, a German pianist who came to Paris, was 'fascinated beyond expression' when he first heard Chopin. 'I sat entranced, filled with wonderment, and if the room had suddenly been peopled with fairies I should not have been astonished,' he wrote. 'The marvellous charm, the poetry and originality, the perfect freedom and absolute lucidity of Chopin's playing at that time cannot be described. It was perfection in every sense . . . I could have dropped to my knees to worship him.'[2]

The first thing that struck people about Chopin's playing was the elegance and control he displayed. There was no apparent exertion, no difficulty, no exaggerated movement, his fingers moving quite effortlessly over the keys. 'His delicate and slender hands cover wide stretches and skip with fabulous lightness,' observed another pianist.[3] He could play rapid trills or legato like nobody else, producing the effect of strings of pearls or, as Hiller put it, the flight of a swallow. Perhaps Chopin's most distinctive characteristic was his touch: he could play the same note in various ways, producing a whole range of nuances. This was why he was so fond of Pleyel's pianos, which were the most sensitive. He heightened these nuances with his revolutionary use of the sustaining pedal, but above all with his application of *tempo rubato*: while his left hand played in strict time, his right would just hint at the anticipation of a phrase, or else reluctance to begin it. 'Let your left hand be your conductor and keep strict time,' he would tell his pupils.[4] According to Hiller, 'Rhythmic precision in his case was linked with a freedom in his leading of a melody, which gave the impression of improvisation.'[5]

Combined with the look of harmonious concentration on

his face – no knitted brows or passion, just an expression of deep thought – this always gave the impression that what he was playing was spontaneous creation, whether it was indeed an improvisation or a written work. 'The whole man seemed to vibrate, while under his fingers the piano came to life with its own intensity,' wrote another pianist. 'It was so magnificent that it caused shivers of delight.'[6]

The idea of spontaneity fascinated the Romantics, and Chopin's strongly developed gift for improvisation – sitting down at the piano and creating music out of nothing for an hour or two – held people spellbound, not merely by the beauty of the music, but also by the consciousness of something extraordinary taking place. This surely was communion with the gods, heaven speaking to mere mortals through the inspired agency of the divine interpreter, and it fitted perfectly the Romantic vision of the artist's place in the scheme of things. It was as an expression of this concept that the poet Hyacinthe de la Touche always spoke with reverence of Chopin as 'that pallid Pole who holds the Heavens open'.[7]

Chopin's person was in complete harmony with the way he played. The frail, thin body suggested something ephemeral, while the more commanding head, with its abundant and fine dark blond hair, its pronounced nose, its tender and intelligent eyes and slightly fussy mouth, seemed to suggest superiority with an element of mocking irony. His movements and deport- ment were graceful, his whole figure emanated a sense of harmony and elegance. 'His bearing had so much distinction,' according to Liszt, 'and his manners such a cachet of good breeding that one naturally treated him as a prince.'[8] After his first meeting with Chopin, the critic Ernest Legouvé commented that 'he looked like the natural son Weber might have had with a duchess'.[9]

This gave Chopin an enormous advantage in Parisian society. Before the July Revolution of 1830, musicians, even such as

Liszt or Rossini, were generally let in by the back door, listened to and then sent out to be paid by the butler. After 1830 the agent of divinity could no longer be treated as a tradesman. The musician would more often be invited to the soirée as a guest, politely asked to play, and a gift or money would be discreetly forwarded to his address the following day. Chopin, who had learnt to sit at table at the Blue Palace and the Belvedere, and had been on easy terms with the most exalted from an early age, was both welcome and at ease in such circumstances. As a result, he was invited on all sides, and the invitation would often contain some such proviso as: 'It is, of course, understood that you may leave your fingers at home.'[10]

Another consequence of his unique combination of musical and social gifts was that he had no shortage of pupils who could pay a high fee for lessons, and he soon became the most sought-after teacher in Paris. There are letters in which aristocratic ladies beg him in the most deferential terms to take on their daughters; in another, a marquess interceding on behalf of the daughter of the comte de Castellane concludes: 'Liszt desperately wants to give lessons to Madame de Contades, and she to take them from you.'[11] His popularity, moreover, did not merely embrace the aristocracy; Chopin was also giving lessons to Conservatoire students and professional musicians.

By the beginning of 1833 he was giving up to five lessons a day at twenty francs a time, which meant that he could earn six hundred francs a week from this source alone. When one considers that a cab fare was one franc, the best seats at the opera about ten, and the most expensive tailor would make a frock-coat for under 150, it is clear that Chopin was doing extremely well financially. On top of this there was the sporadic but substantial income from the publication of his music.

In December 1831 the publisher Schlesinger had commissioned Chopin to write something on a theme from the popular opera by Meyerbeer, *Robert le Diable*. With the help of Franchomme,

Chopin had produced a Grand Duo Concertante for Piano and Cello, which appeared in print early in 1833. Following Chopin's Paris debut in February 1832, Jacques Farrenc, a publisher of no great standing, bought the rights to all his larger works, paying a cash deposit while the scores were being copied for the printers. But Chopin, 'out of indolence and a complete lack of interest in his affairs', as Farrenc put it, failed to produce any fair copies as the months went by.[12]

He had taken the money from Farrenc because he needed it, but he was aware that there were better publishers about, notably Schlesinger in Paris and Probst in Leipzig, who had already written to him in Vienna enquiring about rights.[13] While living off Farrenc's advance, Chopin negotiated with them, and by the autumn of 1832 had reached a long-term agreement with Schlesinger. In November, Farrenc, exasperated with the 'lazy and utterly eccentric' Chopin who had still produced no clean copies, lost his temper and tore up the contract.[14] One can only speculate as to whether he got his advance back.

For all his apparent insouciance in matters of money, Chopin had grown canny and highly suspicious of all entrepreneurs. He had rightly assessed Farrenc as a poor businessman, simply for the reason that he was proposing to publish a whole series of grand works for piano and orchestra by an unknown composer. Schlesinger, on the other hand, bought the rights to all the large works Farrenc had wanted, but also acquired those for three Nocturnes, eight Mazurkas and twelve Études. These were what he intended to publish first, knowing that they would sell easily and would pave the way for the others. He also farmed out the German rights to Probst in Leipzig. By April 1833 Nicolas Chopin wrote to his son that the Leipzig edition of the Nocturnes and Mazurkas had reached the music shops in Warsaw and sold out in a matter of days.

As Chopin's financial situation improved, his father's letters began to dwell persistently on the subject of putting aside some money, but in contradiction to his ever-dutiful answers, Chopin did nothing of the sort. He moved into an elegant apartment on the rue de la Chaussée d'Antin, more central than, though not far from, his previous home. Although the higher rent was taken care of by his taking a lodger, a young Polish acquaintance, Dr Hoffmann, he indulged every temptation to spend money. He dressed at the best tailors, bought expensive furniture and drove everywhere in a hired cabriolet rather than a normal cab. He was continually buying presents for people and unnecessary luxuries for himself, and he spent a great deal of money on filling his rooms with flowers. He was always lending cash to impecunious Poles, and even seems to have lent Berlioz's fiancée Harriet Smithson a generous sum when she broke her ankle.[15]

Chopin was busy, carefree, and seldom alone for long enough to worry about anything. He was healthier and stronger than he had been for years, and had apparently built up a resistance to the sort of ailments that had regularly laid him low hitherto. 'Chopin is well and strong,' wrote Antoni Orłowski. 'He is turning the heads of all the ladies and making all the husbands jealous. He is in fashion. Soon we shall all be wearing gloves à la Chopin.'[16] Who these ladies may have been, and what grounds for jealousy their husbands may have had, is impossible to tell in the absence of evidence.

Distressed to find a sexual blank in Chopin's first six years in Paris, many biographers have seized on the person of one of his pupils, Countess Delfina Potocka, to fill it. Chopin could certainly not have made her husband jealous. Having been married off at an early age to the brutal Mieczysław Potocki, Countess Delfina subsequently left him to live with her parents, the Komars, who had moved to Paris. It was then, in November 1831, that Chopin started giving lessons to her and her two younger sisters. Her husband visited her in Paris several times, but it proved impossible to patch up the marriage, so he went back to his Ukrainian estates. She set up house on her own and began to enjoy life on the princely allowance he sent her. During the early 1830s she had a series of affairs, some of which, like the concurrent ones with the duc d'Orléans and Talleyrand's natural son the comte de Flahaut, became notorious.

'The Great Sinner', as she was dubbed by Adam Mickiewicz, was three years Chopin's senior. She had no trouble in indulging her epic sexual appetite, as her great beauty was enhanced by a seductive manner and one of the finest singing voices in Europe. It is more than likely that Chopin, who saw her often during his first years in Paris, and who valued highly both her talent for the piano and her voice, was under her spell. Gossips assumed a romantic liaison. Some biographers have gone on to assert the existence of an affair, and some to describe what they believe to have been its deeply carnal nature.

There are only two pieces of what might be termed evidence to support the existence of such a liaison. One is a letter from a Pole in Paris to his wife, in which he censures Countess Delfina's conduct, and lists Chopin as one of her many lovers. It was, however, written after the composer's death by someone who did not know him, and is at best a good specimen of contemporary gossip.[17] The other is the information given to an early biographer by the widow of the Dr Hoffmann who shared Chopin's apartment for a few months in 1833.

According to her, her husband had stated that Countess Delfina often came to the apartment late at night in order to play, sing and sleep with Chopin, and that he occasionally returned the courtesy at her house. But Mrs Hoffmann's evidence is not as reliable as it might appear. She only married Hoffmann some ten years after the putative events, and related them fifty years after that to one who was determined to prove the existence of an affair, and almost certainly prompted her memory. She is also unreliable on points of detail, stating, for instance, that her husband had lived with Chopin for many years. She would even have us believe that the worthy doctor had helped Chopin with his compositions, suggesting alternative harmonies which were eagerly seized on.[18]

The possibility of a liaison between Chopin and Countess Delfina was dismissed by most serious biographers, but it was given a new lease of life by the appearance of what purported to be copies of his letters to her. These were produced in 1945 by someone who suggested various provenances, but could not be pinned down to a single version of where the originals were and where she had seen them. In the muddled conditions of post-war Poland, nobody paid much attention to such inconsistencies, and the texts were accepted by many as being authentic. The style in which they are written seems Chopinesque enough – too much so, on closer examination – but the texts reveal an entirely new Chopin. The reticent man who never made significant statements about music, who recoiled from making judgements on other musicians, and who rarely mentioned his own compositions, is seen here expatiating on the theory of music, making crude and merciless criticisms of Liszt and Schumann, and explaining the meaning of his own works. Moreover, the collection of texts includes two love letters full of extraordinarily earthy eroticism, which accords ill with what is known of Chopin's character, style of conduct and tastes. They also feature words that were not current at the time, and use others, whose meaning has changed, in their modern sense. The texts have since been subjected to thorough examination and dismissed as forgeries (for a more detailed discussion of the texts and their history, see Appendix B). The fact is that, possible, likely or probable as the affair might seem, there is not one shred of real evidence for its existence.

All the evidence of a reliable nature points in a different direction. Konstancja's marriage had not significantly altered Chopin's passion for her. She had been little more than a piece of romantic furniture in his heart, and although its position had shifted somewhat, it was still there. As can be seen from Chopin's letters to Tytus and to his sister Ludwika, he still regarded Konstancja as the now unworthy object of his affections, and her image remained a conveniently disembodied focus for surplus emotion and effusions of sentiment. This did not prevent him from being aware of other women, as his letters to Tytus bear out, but both the degree of his interest and his bashfulness can be gauged from an episode which he recounted in one of them.

The pianist Johann Peter Pixis, whom Chopin had first met in Stuttgart, arrived in Paris accompanied by a fifteen-year-old 'pupil', whom he kept securely locked away, with the intention of marrying her in due course. Chopin went to call on Pixis one day and, finding him absent, was just explaining the object of his visit to the young lady when her ageing beau came panting up the stairs. Pixis was convulsed with jealousy, much to the amusement of Chopin, who was astonished that 'anyone could think me capable of such a thing!', which suggests that he did not see himself as being capable of it. 'Me – a seducer!' He could not get over the drollness of the idea.[19]

Whatever turning of ladies' heads there was seems to have remained on a fairly innocent level, as indeed Orłowski's remark suggests. Chopin had had physical relations with at least one woman before reaching Paris, and may well have availed himself of the opportunities afforded by the chorus girls and the whores he mentions, but five years later, when he found himself on the point of consummating his love for a woman, he would recoil at the thought of transposing his emotions onto the physical plane.[20] This strongly suggests that he had never, up to that point, taken an affection to its physical conclusion. This was not particularly surprising in his case, as his natural reticence was reinforced by his code of behaviour, which in turn was dictated by his position and career.

Chopin was invited to sit with exalted company and to teach

young ladies from the most aristocratic families precisely because he knew how to behave and no whiff of scandal regarding a pupil attached itself to his person. His natural inclination was to avoid unseemliness in all things, and he was growing more fastidious than ever. As Liszt points out, he always wore an air of chastity, and winced as much at a crude word as he did at a muddy shoe or a speck of dust on his frock-coat.[21] He loved the company of women, but he liked them well-bred, well-dressed and unattainable, and the resulting flirtations were little more than an understated game which enlivened his lessons and his social life.

Fond as he was of this kind of company, Chopin did not take up the invitation from Liszt's mistress, the comtesse d'Agoult, to pass the summer on her estate. Instead, he spent it with Franchomme's family near Tours. He was just as happy being looked after and fattened up by his friend's family, who were of very humble standing, as staying in any château, and when he returned to Paris, he wrote that 'when I look back on it all, it seems such a charming dream that I wish I could be still dreaming it'.[22]

Franchomme had become a close friend, and hardly a day passed without his calling on Chopin, often accompanied by Liszt. A typical afternoon is evoked by a letter from Chopin to Hiller, who was on holiday in Frankfurt. 'I am writing without knowing what my pen is scribbling, because Liszt is playing my Études and banishing all other thoughts from my head,' he wrote, adding wistfully: 'I wish I could rob him of the way he plays my Études.' This provoked a few scribbled lines of modesty from Liszt, and a few words by Franchomme. Liszt wrote that the Études were 'magnificent', which was followed by more modesty from Chopin, and tuttings from Liszt, interspersed with comments such as 'by the way, I bumped into Heine yesterday, who told me to hug you cordially', and 'Berlioz sends his love'.[23] Berlioz was less in evidence since he had married

Harriet Smithson and moved to the village of Montmartre, but even there he would sometimes organise picnics for Liszt, Hiller, Chopin, the poet Alfred de Vigny and others, at whom he would prattle on about 'art, poetry, thought, music, drama; in a word, everything that makes up life'.[24]

While he clearly enjoyed this extraordinary concentration of artistic talents, Chopin was happier with his less bombastic and more reflective friends, such as Franchomme and Hiller. And they both played an important role in his life. 'I think I can say that Chopin loved me, but I was in love with him,' explained Hiller.[25] It was he who introduced Chopin to Vincenzo Bellini, who came to Paris in the autumn of 1833, and whom Chopin adored, both for his person and his music. They would congregate in the small apartment on the boulevard Saint-Germain of the singer Lina Freppa. 'We used to chatter about music, sing and play; chatter, sing and play,' records Hiller. 'Chopin and Madame Freppa would take turns at the piano – I would also do my best to play a part – and Bellini would make observations, accompanying himself in one of his cantilenas, rather to illustrate what he was saying, than to show off to his listeners.'[26]

It was largely thanks to friendships such as these that Chopin's yearning for family and home began to recede. He still suffered from bouts of homesickness, but there was no lack of antidotes. There were households, like the Czartoryskis', now installed in a spacious apartment on the rue du Faubourg du Roule, or the Platers', where he could go whenever he wanted. There was the Polish Club, around the corner from him in the rue Godot de Mauroy, with its collection of old generals and scruffy young poets, where he could have a cheap dinner or play billiards. Above all, he now had a few Polish friends settled in Paris, such as his Conservatoire colleague Fontana, who had failed to make a living in England, and Albert Grzymała.

Grzymała, a remarkable man in many respects, had led an eventful life which on two occasions led him into Russian jails,

once in 1812 as a prisoner of war, once in 1826 for his connections with the Russian Decembrists. He had held high office in
the Polish Treasury and during the insurrection had been sent
to London to negotiate a loan. After staying there for a couple
of years he had come to Paris, where he made a living from
dealing on the Stock Exchange. His magnificent looks and zest
for life involved him in a succession of affairs, and he soon
became a well-known, even notorious, figure in Parisian society.
He was a cultivated man with a wide range of artistic and
musical interests. The forty-year-old Grzymała exuded strength
and resilience, and gradually began to fulfil the role of elder
brother in Chopin's life, becoming his confidant and adviser
in all matters.

Finally, at the beginning of 1834, Jan Matuszyński, whose
medical studies were interrupted by the insurrection and who
had been obliged to finish them in Germany, turned up in
Paris to take a teaching post at the École de Médecine. 'My
first thought was to call on Chopin,' he wrote to his brother-
in-law. 'I cannot tell you what joy it was to meet again after
five years of separation. He has grown tall and strong, and I
hardly recognised him.'[27] Chopin was so delighted to see his
friend again that he persuaded him to come and share his
lodgings (Dr Hoffmann's addiction to his pipe had irritated
Chopin so much that he had got rid of him). According to
Hiller, 'Even when Chopin stayed in of an evening playing the
piano, he had to have at least one friend with him.'[28] He now
had all the friends he could wish for.

Considering how he had settled down in Paris, it may appear
strange that during the 1833–34 season Chopin did not, as far
as is known, give a single concert. Paradoxically, this was a mark
of his success: he no longer needed to perform. He appeared
in public once, on 15 December, at Hiller's concert, when he
played a Bach Adagio with Liszt and Hiller, 'with an understanding of its character and perfect delicacy', according to the

Revue Musicale.[29] (True Romantics were appalled. 'It was heart-rending, I swear,' wrote Berlioz, 'to watch three astonishing talents, full of energy, glittering with youth and vitality, apply themselves to the execution of this absurd and ridiculous psalmody.'[30])

Chopin did not mind taking part in a friend's programme, but from now on he avoided giving concerts himself, as he could not stand the strain of putting together a programme, selecting other musicians and dealing with the arrangements. More to the point, he disliked what he saw as the tyranny of the concert form. He loved playing to people, but he liked to do it in an atmosphere of free association, as though a group of like-minded friends had come together. He wanted to be surrounded by people who understood what he was doing, who empathised with him.

His financial independence and his ability to steer his own artistic course were also reinforced by the growth of his reputation as a composer, following the publication of a greater number of his works. It is difficult to gauge the extent of his reputation solely from the reviews, as a partisan spirit prevailed in many quarters. In France, the *Gazette Musicale*, founded by Chopin's publisher, Schlesinger, was consistently favourable, while the rival *France Musicale* passed his first works over in silence. This does not mean, however, that the opinions expressed were insincere. The *Gazette* indeed consistently pointed to his importance as a composer, but admitted that to many, even his most fervent admirers, Chopin was an 'inexplicable phenomenon', in the sense that he did not seem to belong to any tradition.[31] In Germany, Schumann continued to champion him, reviewing every work as it came out in more or less ecstatic terms in his own paper, the *Neue Zeitschrift für Musik*. While most other German critics were also generous in their praise, Rellstab simply could not bring himself to regard Chopin with anything but horror. Having accused the *La ci darem la mano* Variations of being Slavic vandalism, he attacked the Nocturnes no less vehemently, stating that if one were to hold Field's 'charming romances' (his Nocturnes) up to a concave distorting mirror, one would see Chopin's coarse new works reflected. When reviewing the Études op.10, he strongly advised anyone attempting to play them to have a surgeon in attendance, as permanent finger damage was likely.[32]

Whatever the critics wrote, the works sold and were played. The Nocturnes, Waltzes and Mazurkas were ideally suited to the home or the small gathering, which were by now dominated by the piano, thanks to the rapid technical development of the instrument. Throughout Europe the rise of a large middle class with cultural aspirations turned it into a kind of household altar at which culture was worshipped. By the 1830s there was a piano in every middle-class home, particularly in countries such as Germany, and where there was a piano there were scores of Chopin's music.

When, in the spring of 1834, Hiller suggested that Chopin accompany him to the Lower Rhine Music Festival organised by Ferdinand Ries and Mendelssohn at Aachen, he agreed. It must have been in a spirit tinged with triumph that he set off to revisit Germany, which he had passed through only three years before as an unknown pianist. Mendelssohn was overjoyed to see them and offered them his box for the concerts. 'They have both developed their technique,' he wrote to his family, 'and Chopin is now as a pianist one of the very best – he astonishes one with novelties, like Paganini on the violin, and introduces wonderful things which one would have thought impossible.' At the same time he complained that 'They both suffer a little from the Parisian love of despair and emotional exaggeration, too often losing sight of time and sobriety and of true musical thought.' He confessed to being deficient in this respect himself, and to feeling 'like an old schoolmaster faced by a couple of "mirliflores" or "incroyables".'[33]

After the festival, Chopin and Hiller followed Mendelssohn back to Düsseldorf, where the exchange of virtuosity continued. Hiller recorded what was apparently a fairly typical occasion, in this case at the house of the painter Friedrich Wilhelm Schadow:

There we met several of the most promising young painters, and a lively conversation was struck up. Everything would have been fine but for poor old Chopin, whose reticence kept him in the corner, unnoticed. Both Mendelssohn and I knew that he would get his own back on us for this, and we waited in happy antici-pation. Eventually, the piano was opened and I played for a while, followed by Mendelssohn. But when we asked Chopin to play something too, everyone looked around in surprise. He had only played a few bars when everyone, especially Schadow, began to look at him in a very different way – they had never heard anything like it before. In wild enthusiasm they begged him to play again and again.[34]

At the end of May they took a steamer up the Rhine, Mendelssohn accompanying them as far as Cologne, and Chopin and Hiller sailing on up to Koblenz. 'Today I feel like the steam from our boat,' Chopin wrote to Hiller's mother. 'I evaporate into the air and feel one half of me wafting off towards my country and my people, the other towards Paris and you.'[35] A few days later he followed the second half back to Paris.

EIGHT

Second Love

'Chopin is all sadness,' Liszt wrote to his mistress in September 1834. 'Furniture is a little more expensive than he had thought, so now we're in for a whole month of worry and nerves.'[1] It was true. At the end of the summer he had decided to move to a more elegant apartment in the same street, the rue de la Chaussée d'Antin, not far from where the Opéra now stands. The rent was high and the furnishings he selected were in keeping with his reputation as the most elegant musician in Paris.

Chopin's slightly precious and unconventional taste manifested itself strongly in his choice of décor. The fashion of the times was for heavy fabrics, deep colours and ornamented furniture, but he covered his walls with pale grey paper, his chairs with plain dove-coloured material, and the windows and bed were curtained in voluminous swathes of white muslin and silk. There was not much furniture, but what there was tended to be fussy, and while there were few pictures, there was a collection of exquisite objects and bibelots of one sort or another distributed around the rooms. A young English girl who visited him thought his drawing room 'such a *bijou* of a room'.[2] One of his pupils commented, rather less flatteringly, that 'he lived like a woman, almost like a cocotte'.[3] Matuszyński, who had moved with him, made a contribution to the rent, but his new apartment's size shows that Chopin was by now earning a great deal of money, mainly from teaching.

This might appear curious, given that he had never had regular instruction from a proper piano teacher. Yet just as he was a born pianist, so he turned out to be a born teacher. 'It was with real joy that he devoted all his strength to teaching for several hours a day,' remembered Karol Mikuli, one of his professional pupils; 'a holy artistic zeal inflamed him, and then every word from his lips was a stimulation and a source of enthusiasm.'[4]

He took great pleasure in teaching pretty young ladies, but he never taught talentless aristocrats; he was in a position to accept only genuinely gifted pupils, and he enjoyed leading them along towards the discovery of their own talent. 'Liszt cannot equal Chopin as a teacher,' wrote one pupil. 'I do not mean that Liszt is not an excellent teacher; he is the best possible until one has had the good fortune of knowing Chopin, who is, in terms of method, far ahead of all other artists.'[5]

This method was idiosyncratic. Where others advocated a long apprenticeship, and gave their pupils arduous exercises to develop their technique, Chopin strove in the first place to open the world of music to them, regarding technique as no more than a means of unlocking their powers of expression.

In theory, his lessons lasted between forty-five minutes and an hour, but in practice they often ran on to a couple of hours with the most gifted pupils. Chopin would spend most of that time speaking and illustrating what he meant. The pupil would sit at the Pleyel grand piano, while Chopin either stood or sat making remarks or corrections, sometimes going over to the upright in the same room to demonstrate or accompany. He insisted on what, by the standard of most of his contemporaries, was a low seat, the elbows level with the white keys. He wanted the player to be able to reach all the notes at the extremities of the keyboard without leaning or moving his elbows; the complete antithesis of Liszt's way of playing, which gave observers the impression that his whole body was climbing over the keyboard.

Chopin taught that all suppleness and intelligence should be concentrated in the fingers themselves. He believed that every finger had different attributes, and that these must be developed to the full. All possible finger movements were permissible – passing one finger over the other, and playing the black keys with the thumb included. The whole point of this method was to develop the touch, which to him was the beginning and end of piano-playing. Fingers should fall, not strike, and caress rather than hit the keys. And the same key should be touched in different ways in order to produce a variety of tones. That was why he favoured the Pleyel piano. An Érard produced a perfect rounded note when a key was struck, but the Pleyel required coaxing and caressing, and was therefore more capable of nuance if played well. He discouraged the use of the pedal until a pupil's touch had been perfected, for he believed that tone must be created through the fingers, and not by the artificial agency of the pedal, which could then be used to additional effect.

For him, the key to expression was phrasing – for music was only a language. He likened poor phrasing to someone reciting a poem he knows by heart in a language he does not understand. According to Chopin, some musicians betrayed through their playing that music was not their native language, merely a skill they had picked up. 'One should sing with the fingers!' he used to say.[6] The style in which they should sing was that of the Italian *bel canto*, and when pupils did not understand what he was driving at, he used to tell them to go to the Italian opera and listen to the Italians using their voices – his ultimate model in this respect was the soprano Giuditta Pasta.[7] 'You must sing if you wish to play the piano,' he told one pupil, and he actually made another take singing lessons.[8] He discouraged them from practising very much, but he was strict on questions such as time: he always used a metronome himself, and told his pupils to do likewise.

Chopin taught his pupils to analyse a work for its inner structure, and to understand its logic and meaning before attempting to play it. He did not mind if they played it differently from himself; he gave his own works a different expression each time he played them. 'Forget that anyone is listening to you,' he said to one pupil, 'and always listen to yourself.'[9] The choice of music he made them play was dictated by this insistence on their learning to recognise the inner structure of a work: Bach Fugues; Clementi's *Gradus ad Parnassum*, Preludes and Exercises; and works by Cramer, Handel, Scarlatti, Hummel and Mozart. He did sometimes set more modern works by Beethoven, Weber, Field or Moscheles, but on the whole avoided those of Mendelssohn, Schumann and Schubert.

Chopin enjoyed teaching, and he was usually patient, gentle and polite with his pupils, but his mood could change, particularly if he was feeling unwell. He could become highly irritable, and then he would pace the room breaking pencils or nervously tugging at his hair. He was even known to fling scores across the room, and once broke a chair in his irritation.[10] This sort of behaviour was usually limited to his professional pupils; he demanded more of them and they were more prepared to take it from him than his aristocratic young ladies.

Chopin was not lucky with his professional pupils. His first, Caroline Hartmann, died in 1834. In the same year he took in another, Adolf Gutmann, who was to become a lifelong favourite, but never struck anyone else as having a great talent. Karl Filtsch and Paul Gunsberg also died young, while Emilie von Gretsch and Friederike Streicher gave up playing professionally. The only pupils who made any kind of career were Thomas Tellefsen, Georges Mathias and Karol Mikuli. Some of the best pianists he left behind him were in fact aristocratic amateurs.

Chopin was so busy with lessons that he had little time for composing. He therefore dug into his stock of manuscripts and pulled out the Grande Polonaise for Piano and Orchestra and the G minor Ballade, both of which he had written in Vienna. He now wrote an Andante Spianato to precede the first of these and sold it to Schlesinger, and polished up the Ballade. But he did manage to write four new Mazurkas (op.24), two Polonaises (op.26) and two Nocturnes (op.27), and was working on the second set of Études and some of the Preludes.

He had now created the forms which would permit him to fulfil his aims. The two Polonaises of op.26, for instance, effectively brought into being a new genre distinct from that of the earlier Polonaises, one that allowed him to make the more political patriotic statements he felt impelled towards now he was in exile.

While his days were heavily booked with lessons, his evenings, particularly with the start of the season, were taken up with social or musical events of one sort or another. On 1 December 1834 there was a private concert given by Delfina Potocka. On 7 December he played a movement of his E minor Concerto and the new Andante Spianato sandwiched in between *Harold in Italy* and the *King Lear* Overture at Berlioz's concert in the Conservatoire. On 25 December he joined Liszt at the Salle Pleyel to create what must have been a unique musical experience: the two pianists sat down together and played a Moscheles duo for four hands and then one by Liszt.

Beside these public performances, he also played at many private soirées. He would usually hold back from playing, only to be seduced into doing so very late. 'A small circle of select listeners, whose real desire to hear him was beyond doubt, could alone determine him to approach the piano,' recalls Berlioz. 'What emotions he would then call forth! In what ardent and melancholy reveries he loved to pour out his soul! It was usually towards midnight that he gave himself up with the greatest abandon, when the big butterflies of the salon had left, when the political questions of the day had been discussed at length, when all the gossips had exhausted their supply of stories, when all the snares were set, all the perfidies consummated, when one was thoroughly tired of prose, then, obedient to the mute petition of some beautiful, intelligent eyes, he became a poet and sang the Ossianic loves of the heroes of his dreams, their

Justyna Chopin, portrait by Ambroży Mieroszewski in 1829, now lost.

Nicolas Chopin, by Ambroży Mieroszewski.

The house at Żelazowa Wola in which the composer was born. The porch is a later addition.

Ludwika Chopin, by
Ambroży Mieroszewski.

Izabela Chopin, by
Ambroży Mieroszewski.

Below: The Warsaw Lycée.
The Chopin family lived
in the building on the
left from 1817 to 1827.
Chopin would have
worn a uniform similar
to that of the young men
in the picture.

Left: Emilia Chopin,
a miniature by an
unknown artist.

The Church of the Holy Cross in Warsaw.
In 1827 the Chopin family moved into an
apartment on the second floor of the
building on the extreme right.

Wojciech Żywny, by
Ambroży Mieroszewski.

The drawing room of the
Chopin apartment.

Tytus Woyciechowski. A photograph taken in the 1870s.

Józef Elsner, by an unknown artist.

Chopin at the piano, drawn by Eliza Radziwiłł during his stay at Antonin in 1826.

Chopin at the age of twenty, by Ambroży Mieroszewski.

Above: Konstancja Gładkowska, a portrait, now lost, painted some ten years after the time of her relationship with Chopin.

Left: Jan Matuszyński, watercolour by an unknown artist painted in Paris in the late 1830s.

Left: Chopin, portrait by an unknown artist painted in the early 1830s.

Above: Hector Berlioz, copy of a portrait by Émile Signol, 1832.

Left: Franz Liszt, copy of a portrait by Luigi Calamatta.

Felix Mendelssohn, watercolour by an unknown artist.

Above: Hiller and Chopin, a contemporary medal.

Vincenzo Bellini, portrait by an unknown artist.

Chopin in the mid-1830s, lithograph by Englemann.

Below: Delfina Potocka, drawing by Paul Delaroche.

Below: Chopin's apartment on the rue de la Chaussée d'Antin.

chivalrous joys and the sorrows of the absent fatherland, his dear Poland.'[11]

Chopin was highly sensitive to atmosphere, and if there was someone vulgar or irritating in the corner of the room, he could only play shorter works such as Waltzes and Nocturnes. He needed concentration to start on one of his improvisations, and this did not come until the company had dwindled to a select few. As Legouvé records, Chopin was a good pianist until midnight, when he became sublime.[12]

Sublime it clearly was, but the physical strain of playing, and particularly of improvising, was immense. In spite of Matuszyński's attempts to keep him at home in the evenings that winter, Chopin managed to exhaust himself thoroughly. In March 1835 he caught the influenza which had half of Paris in bed, developed bronchitis, and by the middle of the month was coughing up blood. Matuszyński was worried about Chopin's lungs and prescribed the waters and baths of Enghien, just north of the capital, followed by waters in Germany in the summer. But before he could think of his health, Chopin had to pull himself together for three end-of-season events.

One was the Herz brothers' concert at the Salle Pleyel on 22 March, which he and Hiller had promised to take part in. Another was a Polish charity concert to be held on 5 April. He had suggested this as a means of raising money for the Benevolent Association of the Polish Ladies in Paris, founded in the previous year by Princess Czartoryska, of which Grzymała, Matuszyński and the Platers were active members. He now found himself lumbered with the task of organising it.

As usual when Chopin tried to arrange something, everything started going wrong, particularly when it came to finding singers, but after concerted efforts and some help from Grzymała and a musical friend of theirs called Aleksander Jełowicki, the programme at the Théâtre des Italiens was one that many a charity could envy.

Habeneck conducted, while Chopin played one of his rare

performances of the E minor Concerto with full orchestra.[13] The renowned tenor Adolphe Nourrit sang Schubert *lieder* and duets with Madame Falcon, who also performed a couple of Rossini arias. Hiller played a piece of his own, and the evening ended with a duet played by Liszt and Chopin on two pianos. It appears that Chopin's playing of his concerto was poorly received, but the event was a financial success; even after Liszt and Hiller had been presented with diamond rings, Habeneck and Nourrit with snuff-boxes and tie-pins and Madame Falcon with a bracelet, the profits were considerable.[14]

Hardly had he recovered from the exertion and nervous strain of this performance than Chopin had to return the favour to Habeneck and take part in a concert at the Conservatoire on 26 April, where he played the Andante Spianato and Grande Polonaise. The reviews made no mention of his playing, which suggests that he failed to shine on this occasion as well. He must have felt so himself, as this appearance marks the end of his career as a concert pianist.[15]

Whether Chopin did take the waters of Enghien that summer is not known, but fate led him to a different spa just as it was drawing to a close. He received a letter from his parents saying they had left for Karlsbad (Karlovy Vary), and, grasping the chance to see them again, decided with uncharacteristic speed to join them there. After a few days and nights spent in the mail coach, he arrived in Karlsbad on 15 August. It was late in the evening, and since cursory enquiries informed him that his parents had not arrived yet, he went to bed. At four o'clock in the morning he was woken by Nicolas and Justyna, who had been there all along and had learnt of his arrival. They fell into each other's arms, and later that morning wrote a joint letter to the rest of the family in Warsaw. 'Our joy is indescribable!' wrote Chopin. 'We don't stop telling each other how many times we have been thinking of one another.'[16]

They spent a month together in the fashionable spa, and

Chopin eagerly absorbed all the parental affection he had missed so much. 'We drink, eat together, hug each other, reproach each other; I am at the height of my happiness!' he wrote. But they did not entirely ignore other people. The little town was full of Poles, and there were other acquaintances, such as Count Franz Thun-Hohenstein with his two sons, who had taken lessons from Chopin in the previous year. The time passed in walks through the surrounding hills, picnics, soirées and musical evenings, in which Chopin was joined by the cellist and composer Jozef Dessauer, who was also staying in Karlsbad.

The Thuns were insistent that Chopin should come and stay with them when they returned to their castle at Tetschen on the Elbe, particularly as Josephine, one of the Count's daughters and also a former pupil of Chopin, was pining to see him and hear him play again. Since Tetschen was vaguely on the way back to Warsaw, he decided to take up the invitation and accompany his parents thus far on their homeward journey. They left Karlsbad in the second week of September, and after a few days at Tetschen, Nicolas and Justyna departed for Warsaw, leaving their son to stay on in the picturesque castle. But much as Chopin enjoyed the surroundings, as well as the company of his former pupil Josephine, to whom he gave the manuscript of a Waltz, he was eager to get back to Paris, and on 19 September he left, accompanied by one of the young counts who was going to Dresden.

Alighting from the mail coach that evening in Dresden, Chopin unexpectedly met a former boarder of his father's, Feliks Wodziński, who was staying there with his family. Politeness demanded that Chopin call to pay his respects, and when he did so, the pleasure of renewing an old acquaintance was completely overshadowed by the effect the eldest daughter, Maria, made on him. He had last seen her as an eleven-year-old girl in Warsaw, and now beheld a striking young woman of sixteen with a slightly swarthy complexion, black hair and magnificent eyes which had already set more than one heart on fire.

Instead of hurrying back to Paris as he had intended, Chopin spent two weeks in Dresden, mainly in the company of the Wodzińskis. Maria was a very good pianist, with an enchanting touch, but she was no beauty – the poet Juliusz Słowacki, who had met her the previous year, described her as 'very ugly' before going on to fall in love with her.[17] Chopin copied a waltz into her album and gave her a little card bearing the first bars of one of his Nocturnes and the inscription '*soyez heureuse*', hardly signs of passion. Yet, according to some of the other Poles in Dresden, it was obvious that he was in love.[18]

What Maria felt can only be deduced from the letter she wrote after he had left Dresden on 3 October, in which she let a certain amount of feeling slip through the bounds imposed by convention. 'On Saturday, when you had left us, we all wandered about sadly, our eyes filled with tears,' she wrote, going on to describe just how sad first one brother, then the other, then her father, and finally her mother had been, her mother who was missing her 'fourth son Fryderyk'.[19]

Chopin had promised Mendelssohn that he would stop in Leipzig for a few days on his way back to Paris. Mendelssohn had alerted Schumann, who was staying in Leipzig with his future in-laws, the Wiecks, and they all awaited him avidly. 'Tomorrow or the day after, Chopin is arriving here from Dresden, but he will most likely not appear in a concert, for he is a great idler,' wrote Wieck, who was deeply suspicious of all the praise he had heard of him.[20]

Chopin reached Leipzig on 4 October. 'He did not want to stay for more than a day, so we spent it together, without parting, and made music,' Mendelssohn wrote to his sister. His reaction to Chopin's compositions had originally been one of bewilderment and slight distaste. Only in February that year he had told Moscheles in London that 'a new book of Mazurkas by Chopin and other new pieces of his are so mannered they are hard to stand', and a couple of weeks before Chopin's arrival he had written again denigrating his playing.[21] But now he was impressed by the mastery Chopin had attained, and was 'glad to be with a perfect musician again'. While he acknowledged the fundamental differences between them, he claimed that he could 'understand Chopin perfectly'. 'It was an unusual evening, that Sunday,' he reminisced. 'I played my Oratorio at his request while curious Leipzigers silently slipped in, eager to see Chopin; and when, between the first and second parts, he played his new Études and his new concerto in very quick time to the astonished Leipzigers, and I followed with the rest of my [oratorio] St Paul, it must have sounded to them as though an Iroquois had met up with a Kaffir for conversation.'[22]

Having made Mendelssohn change his mind, Chopin then managed to placate the irate Wieck, who had spent the whole day at home waiting for him with Schumann. He played himself, to Schumann's and Clara Wieck's delight, and then listened to her play. Afterwards he declared her to be the only woman in Germany who could play his compositions properly.

After promising Mendelssohn that he would be back in Germany in the spring (he had already made plans to join the Wodzińskis then), Chopin set off on the next day for Heidelberg. But the travelling and the autumn weather, not to mention the excitements and exertions of the last two months, told on his health, and he fell ill on arrival. The severe bronchitis of that spring had been a warning he felt he could ignore, and indeed people like Matuszyński and his parents, who had not seen him since, all found him stronger and healthier than when he had left Poland. If he did indeed have tuberculosis, he had been in a state of remission since 1827, with only one partial relapse, in Vienna in 1831. But this second attack, which was so severe it started a rumour in Germany that he had died, suggests that the exertions of the last year had undone all the previous years' success in building up his constitution.

Chopin limped back to Paris at the end of October. He had

to look to both his health and his finances, which was not made any easier by the arrival of Maria Wodzińska's elder brother Antoni, a scatterbrained and restless character whom both mother and sister begged Chopin to look after. 'Antoni is thoroughly good-natured, in fact too much so, for he is always being taken in by others,' wrote Maria. 'Besides he is careless and never gives a thought to anything, or at least very rarely . . .'[23] Mainly out of a desire to earn some credit with the Wodzińskis, Chopin acquitted himself honourably, taking Antoni from opera to theatre to concert, and giving him dinner in the finest restaurants.

He had only just finished playing host to Antoni Wodziński when he found himself obliged to help the violinist Karol Lipiński, who had come to Paris in the course of a concert tour of Europe. He was a fine virtuoso, and Chopin willingly arranged a musical soirée and introduced him to the right people. But Lipiński had a difficult character, prone to intrigue, and they quarrelled when the violinist refused to help Chopin with a Polish charity event.[24]

This included a ball and a small concert, and, just before Christmas, a charity bazaar, which gave Chopin a good deal of trouble.[25] He was better placed than most to collect 'jumble', as he knew most of the artists in Paris and could also ask his lady pupils to give or make things for the sale. The result was a collection of books, drawings, pictures, embroidered purses and knick-knacks, with the odd manuscript by Chopin and Liszt thrown in. This was sold in an elegant shop lent by an obliging tradesman in the Chausée d'Antin, on stalls served by a pride of princesses and duchesses, while Chopin played the piano for hours at a time during the three evenings of the sale. Not surprisingly, the whole of Paris had to be there, and the jumble sale made an enormous profit.[26]

Notwithstanding Matuszyński's protests, Chopin rarely passed up an invitation and was out every evening, while his friend's attempts to make him wear thick boots during the winter were thwarted by his dandyism. Nicolas Chopin's admonitions on the same subject, heavily larded with hints that if he did not look after his health and his pocket, his plans regarding 'certain persons' would come to nothing, were not heeded either, and in March 1836 Chopin again fell ill.

The rumour of his death occasioned by his illness in Heidelberg had reached Warsaw at the beginning of December 1835, and persisted in spite of various mentions of his appearances in the Paris press, so much so that the Warsaw papers had to publish a denial of it at the beginning of January.[27] It had, amongst other things, brought a worried Mr Wodziński to pay an apparently casual call on the Chopins in Warsaw. Although nothing had been stated openly, Chopin's parents knew that their son was in love with Maria and intended to meet the Wodzińskis in Dresden that summer. He had even suggested that Justyna accompany him to Dresden. While they remained non-committal, the Wodzińskis paid several calls on the Chopins in Warsaw and gave every sign of encouraging the familiarity.

For some reason, Chopin abandoned his original plan of going to Germany in the spring. This is the more surprising, in that Paris quietened down considerably with the end of the season. In March, Hiller had left in order to settle in Frankfurt, Berlioz had gone off earlier, and Liszt was in Switzerland with his mistress. Antoni Wodziński had gone to Spain to fight in the Carlist War, and Delfina Potocka was selling up in Paris, having decided to go back to her husband in Poland. At Easter, which came early in April, Chopin gave the traditional Polish dinner for a group of compatriots at his own apartment, and then went to stay at Enghien. Whether this was dictated by his health, and with whom he was staying, are questions it is impossible to answer. They are the more tantalising, as a year later, when driving past the place with Chopin, a friend recalled: 'He turned my attention to the wide lake, and, on its edge, the little villa in which he had spent the previous summer. His face became suffused with the pleasantness of the memory; it must have been a very happy period in his life.'[28]

One person who made him welcome in that part of the world was the marquis de Custine, whom he had met at the Czartoryskis' and elsewhere during that season. Custine was the last scion of an ancient family. His father, a distinguished Revolutionary general, and his grandfather had both been guillotined during the Terror. His mother, the celebrated Delphine de Sabran, had lived on to become the mistress of Chateaubriand, father of the French Romantic movement. Custine had been brought up by her in exile, and after his return to France in 1815 had married and had a child, but the death of both wife and child had precipitated a crisis which brought to the surface his latent homosexuality. In 1824 he had been beaten up and dumped in a ditch, naked and half dead, by a group of soldiers, with one of whose comrades he had arranged a tryst. This affair had resulted in his banishment from the boulevard Saint-Germain and had forced him to create a world of his own, based on his literary and artistic interests.

The new order ushered in by the Revolution of 1830 made such social incongruity more acceptable and his position on the Parisian scene unassailable. The dinners he gave at his apartment in the rue de la Rochefoucauld were among the most exclusive in the city, and apart from the old habitués like General Junot's widow the duchesse d'Abrantès (who wanted to marry him), and his uncle the old comte de Sabran (an *ancien-régime* leftover of poetry and wit of whom Chopin was particularly fond), regular guests included Chateaubriand, Madame Récamier, Heinrich Heine, Victor Hugo, Alphonse de Lamartine, Meyerbeer and Berlioz.

Custine's Paris apartment was only a *pied-à-terre*; his main residence was at Saint-Gratien, on the other side of the lake of Enghien, where he had 'a beautiful Florentine Villa arranged in the English manner', filled with exotic objects collected on his travels, and furnished in a taste rather similar to Chopin's, with white predominating.[29] The house stood in a fine park bordering the lake, and was one of the most informal residences in France, its doors permanently open to a chosen group of intimates. 'Perfect house. Delightful room,' wrote Stendhal after his visit; 'everything that is most perfect about the country at only 1¾ hours from the Opera.'[30] The literary critic Charles Augustin Sainte-Beuve took a different view, describing the house as 'a perfect Sodom and Gomorrah'.[31]

Custine did live with a young Englishman, and had recently extended his protection to the eighteen-year-old Count Ignacy Gurowski, but he was no rampant homosexual. A large man of forty-five with a plump, somewhat womanish face, his manners were impeccable, his conversation witty and full of charm. He had an emotional nature and cultivated deep and enduring friendships with persons of both sexes. His loyalty towards people like Gurowski, even after he got married, was exemplary.

Chopin became the object of some of these sentiments, but there is no reason to believe that they went beyond a deep appreciation of him and his music and the same avuncular tenderness which Chopin sought and encouraged in others. 'You know that you are the only person who can come whenever he likes, knowing that you will always give pleasure,' Custine wrote to him in March. 'Once and for all then, do not ever ask whether you can come, just come when you feel like it.'[32] Chopin certainly availed himself of the invitation that spring and summer.

He loved the area to the north of Paris and spent many happy days on excursions to Chantilly and Ermenonville, and in the park of Montmorency, just outside which lived the old poet Julian Niemcewicz. Niemcewicz's diary records one occasion on which Chopin arrived for lunch with him and the Napoleonic veteran General Kniaziewicz, who lived with him. They were unexpectedly joined by the poet Adam Mickiewicz, and after lunch, during which Chopin had everyone in stitches with his impersonations, they went off to the village of Montmorency and joined in a country festival.[33] It was a perfect antidote to the sometimes overpowering intensity of the artist's life in Paris.

At the end of May Liszt turned up in Paris, hoping to catch Thalberg, who had given a couple of concerts and been acclaimed as the greatest pianist in Europe, for he longed to challenge his rival and defeat him. Thalberg had left, but Liszt nevertheless gave a concert in which he impressed Chopin by the progress he had made in the past year. Liszt then gave a dinner, at which the guests included Meyerbeer, the tenor Adolphe Nourrit and the painter Eugène Delacroix, whom Chopin had not met before.[34] At the beginning of June Liszt returned to his mistress in Switzerland and Chopin went back to Enghien, to await news of the Wodzińskis' movements.

In the first days of July he heard that they were in Marienbad and promptly set off himself, arriving there at the end of the month to find Mrs Wodzińska alone with her two daughters. He put up at the same hotel and settled down to spend the month of August with them. He must have been deeply in love with Maria, to spend so much time in one place doing very little, considering how restless he was by nature. The Wodzińskis and their Marienbad acquaintances were not the most exciting people to be with for one used to the company Chopin kept in Paris. As Custine, who turned up with Gurowski in mid-August, remarked, apart from Chopin 'there was nobody in Marienbad', except for 'a few very second-rate Poles'.[35]

The benefits of taking the Enghien cure had been offset by the exertion of his comings and goings, and Chopin was in poor shape. There were fewer picnics and walks in the hills that year, and more sitting around with the Wodzińskis at the hotel. He taught Maria to play his new Étude and composed a song for her to a poem by Witwicki, while she painted a watercolour portrait of him and sat embroidering a pair of slippers. Nothing was said, although it was obvious to all around that the two were in love. Before the end of the month the Wodzińskis travelled to Dresden, on their way back to Poland, and Chopin went with them. After putting it off from day to day for two weeks, he proposed to Maria at the 'grey hour' of dusk on his last day in the city. Maria seems to have been delighted, and her mother was immediately informed. It could have come as no surprise: allowing her daughter to spend six weeks almost entirely in the company of a young man who was visibly in love with her was tantamount to encouraging him.

On the next morning, before his departure, Chopin talked the matter over with Mrs Wodzińska, who was slightly absent-minded and suffering from toothache, and could therefore not 'give sufficient attention to the subject of the grey hour', which had already become the code phrase for the proposal. What she did say was that, without her husband present, she could not promise anything definite; for the time being the matter must remain secret. She enjoined Chopin to look after his health. 'Everything depends on that,' she wrote, and added, after instructions about going to bed early and wearing warm socks, that 'you must realise that this is a trial period'.[36]

Chopin left Dresden that afternoon, and arrived in Leipzig on 12 September, to the astonishment of Schumann, who had just written a letter to him and did not expect to see him walk through the door. 'My joy was great,' Schumann wrote to a friend, and described how Chopin presented him with a copy of his new G minor Ballade, saying that of all his own works it was the one closest to his heart. As for Chopin's playing, Schumann declared that it was 'complete perfection, mastery which does not even seem to be aware of its own worth'.[37] 'Imagine an aeolian harp that had all the scales, and that these were jumbled together by the hand of an artist into all sorts of fantastic ornaments, but in such a manner that a deeper funda-mental tone and a softly singing higher part were always audible, and you have an approximate idea of his playing,' he wrote after hearing Chopin play his Études.[38]

Schumann's fanciful yet solemn approach, and his evident consciousness of undergoing an artistic experience, annoyed Chopin as much as his review of the *La ci darem la mano* Variations had done four years earlier. Schumann kept trying to explain his works and place them in context. In his review of the F minor Concerto earlier that year, he had written that it was obvious Chopin had been principally inspired by Beethoven, which was clearly not the case. He claimed him as a truly Romantic composer, seeing rebellion in his work, and had recently written that 'if the powerful autocrat of the North [the Tsar] knew what a dangerous enemy threatens him in the works of Chopin, in the simple melodies of those Mazurkas, he would banish this music. The works of Chopin are like cannons hidden beneath flowers.'[39]

The two musicians later called on Wieck – Mendelssohn was away from Leipzig – and then on Henriette Voigt, a pianist much admired by Schumann, for whom Chopin played.[40] On this occasion Schumann complained of Chopin's 'dreadful habit of passing one finger quickly over the whizzing keyboard at the end of each piece, as though to get rid of his dream by force'.[41] As he is the only person ever to have mentioned this habit, one is led to suspect that Chopin did it on purpose to annoy the ponderous enthusiast.

On his return to Paris, Chopin found a letter from Mrs Wodzińska confirming what she had said and reminding him of his promise to look after himself. The slippers embroidered by Maria had also arrived – one size too big, so he would have to wear thick socks with them. Chopin settled down to observe the rules he had set himself: working in the morning, giving lessons all afternoon, dining at six, then going out, but always coming home by eleven, and above all 'playing of the grey hour'.

Letters were now coursing regularly between Chopin and

Maria and her mother. Maria spoke of her sadness at parting and her longing to see him again in 'May or June at the latest', and although her letters are rather naïve and non-committal, and a little too full of requests for music, novels and for a Pleyel piano he had promised to choose and ship for her, there is no doubt that she was committed to the idea of becoming his wife.

The surviving correspondence yields no hint that she might be considering a move to Paris. It is difficult to see how Chopin could have supported the two of them there, not to mention possible children and a marital ménage, on his earnings – and whatever dowry she might come with would not have sufficed. It seems rather that what was being contemplated was his return to Poland, which raises the question of how he envisaged this. In the heady atmosphere of Marienbad he would not have given it too much thought, but back in Paris he could not have failed to ponder the issue.

Despite his French parentage, Chopin never thought of himself as a Frenchman. He was entirely Polish in his outlook, he identified with the Poles, and his letters and behaviour make it quite clear that he saw himself as living in a foreign land. But he loved Paris as a city, he loved it for the quality of his life there, and he loved it for being the musical capital of Europe. A move to Warsaw, let alone the Polish countryside, would have spelt misery for him, and it is hard to believe that he ever considered the possibility seriously. It is more likely that he did what he usually did when faced with a dilemma: that he avoided confronting the issue and transposed it onto a theoretical plane. He probably even dwelt on the pleasant or romantic aspects of a return to his homeland, and conjured visions of birch trees shimmering in the summer breeze. But it is tempting to suspect that he was subconsciously undermining his own plans: his good resolutions about staying in at night and looking after himself did not last.

NINE

Art and Politics

Liszt had spent the past year in Switzerland with his mistress, the comtesse d'Agoult. She was an aristocratic bluestocking who had rebelled against convention and left her husband in order to live with the man she viewed as a great artist, and therefore a kind of god. They had been leading a quiet existence, insofar as the celebrity and style of Liszt would allow, and she was hoping to steer him away from the life of a virtuoso pianist towards that of the Olympian composer. But it was not to be. That summer, while Chopin was in Marienbad, they had been joined by a friend and admirer of Liszt, the novelist George Sand.

George Sand, or rather Aurore Dupin, was one of the most famous and certainly one of the most notorious women of the time. Fatherless since the age of four and rejected by her mother, she had spent much of her childhood and adolescence in a convent, and escaped from a loveless home into a loveless marriage, to the baron Dudevant. Unable to stand it any longer, she left him and went to Paris, where she led a precarious existence trying to survive on journalism. She had written a novel in collaboration with another journalist, Jules Sandeau, which was published under his name and proved a success. Sandeau realised that the merit was hers and backed out of the partnership, leaving her to write her next book on her own. The upshot was the feminist novel *Indiana*, which came out in 1832 under her new pseudonym of George Sand and made her famous overnight.

She continued writing, and her fame spread, helped along by the titillating ambiguities that surrounded her person. Her masculine pen-name sat uneasily with the feminine Aurore, and she was apparently happy to be referred to as Madame Sand, the baronne Dudevant or plain George. As a child, she had worn boys' clothes in order to go riding, and when she settled in Paris she took to dressing as a man, both because it was cheaper and more practical, and because it allowed her to go to the theatre alone without fear of being molested. 'Madame Sand was very small, and was made to look smaller still by the men's clothes that she wore with ease and not without a certain youthful virile grace,' recorded Marie d'Agoult. 'Neither the swelling of her bust nor the protrusion of her hips betrayed her sex.'[1]

In the circumstances, it would have been surprising if George Sand had not been a little confused about her own identity, and her books convey a perplexity of messages that both delights and disappoints feminists. Not surprisingly, this 'hermaphrodite genius', as Alexandre Dumas called her, fascinated her contemporaries. What is more surprising to anyone who reads her works today is that they took her very seriously; she was looked up to with respect by most of the progressive intellects of Europe.[2]

In 1833, the same year as she met Liszt, George Sand had fallen in love with Alfred de Musset, the *enfant terrible* of French Romantic literature, and they proceeded to have a tempestuous and destructive affair. Its high point came with their 'honeymoon' in Venice, where he fell ill and she took off with the doctor called to his bedside, whom she brought back to Paris. After Musset's return to Paris the affair went through several more convulsions of extraordinary violence, and finally burnt itself out in a blaze of sadomasochistic passion. George Sand then had to face her husband, and managed, by the beginning of 1836, to obtain a legal separation, to reclaim her dowry and her small country estate, and to get custody of her two children, with whom she now arrived in Switzerland.

The little group roamed Switzerland, behaving, with the exception of Marie d'Agoult, like a gang of students on holiday. In one hotel register, Liszt filled in the questionnaire as follows: *Place of birth:* 'Parnassus', *Occupation:* 'Musician-Philosopher', *Coming from:* 'Doubt', *Going to:* 'Truth'. They dressed to shock, and provoked respectable travellers by setting up what must have looked like a gypsy encampment in their hotel rooms. An English tourist, horrified to see himself sitting opposite a long-haired, strangely clad, gesticulating youth, asked his neighbour who that 'fellow' might be, and thenceforth Liszt and his countess were 'the Fellows', while George Sand gave herself a sobriquet based on the slang word for nose, *pif*, with a Swiss twist to it: Piffoël.

There could hardly be a greater contrast between the noisy, flamboyant and often childish behaviour of the Fellows and Piffoël on their holiday and Chopin's ingenuous courtship in Marienbad. And while Chopin returned to Paris to work, look after his health and dream of the 'grey hour', Liszt and particularly his lady had very different ideas on how they were going to spend their next few months. Having forfeited her place in Parisian society by running off with her pianist, Marie d'Agoult was determined to create a new position for herself, as hostess of an artistic salon.

When she returned to Paris in the first week of October 1836, she took an apartment with a large reception room in the Hôtel de France on the rue Lafitte and sent Liszt out to haul in the celebrities. The coterie he mustered included Meyerbeer, Berlioz, Chopin, Adolphe Nourrit and various other musicians, the poets Heinrich Heine and Adam Mickiewicz, and representatives of some of the more interesting ideological movements of the time: the famous renegade Catholic priest and editor of *Le Monde* the abbé de Lamennais; the baron d'Eckstein, a converted Jew who had become a militant Catholic; and the Saint-Simonian philosopher Pierre Leroux. In October 1836 this company was swelled by George Sand, who moved into a small room at the Hôtel de France, attended by her latest lover, the Swiss poet Charles Didier.

Chopin did not much like Marie d'Agoult and was no longer very friendly with Liszt, whose style, both musical and social, irritated him. Liszt had transgressed against his code when one day he had used his apartment to make love to Marie Pleyel, the celebrated pianist and wife of Chopin's favourite piano-maker and friend.[3] The atmosphere at the Hôtel de France was hardly calculated to appeal to Chopin. Sainte-Beuve described it as 'a mass of affectation, vanities, pretentiousness, of bombast and uproar of every kind', produced by people whose talent was 'out of control'.[4] 'We wanted to reform everything . . . the theatre, poetry, music, religion and society,' Marie d'Agoult later wrote.[5]

Music and philosophy were strongly represented, and the inevitable consequence was much talk of the social and political relevance of music. Liszt yearned to recapture 'the political, philosophical and religious power' that he imagined music had in ancient times.[6] The outcome was a woolly theory of 'humanitarian art', which involved Nourrit and others going off to the slums of Paris and conducting choirs of hundreds of workers as they sang hymns to words by Lamartine. Nourrit lamented the fact that he had become a singer, affirming that if he had concentrated on other studies, he 'would have directed humanity along the path of progress'.[7] This 'Humanitarian Parnassus' was nicely parodied by Musset in the press:

Inspiration descends, the eye of the God [Liszt] *lights up, his hair shudders, his fingers arch and pound the keys with fury. He plays with his hands, his elbows, his chin, his nose. Everything that can strike hammers away . . . 'Sublime!' they exclaim. 'That'll cost me twenty francs in repairs!' moans the Divinity of the House* [Marie d'Agoult].[8]

Even Berlioz was later forced to admit that 'we talked too much ... We did not listen, we philosophised.'[9] But Marie d'Agoult defended their enthusiasm. 'It was all very febrile and sickly, but it was generous.' It stemmed from 'a love of the people, of the poor, of the suffering, from a Christianity that would not wait for the afterlife'.[10]

It was a symptom of the times and the place, for Paris was a breeding ground of new pseudo-religions seeking to fill the void left by the retreat of the Catholic Church. Some of the Hôtel de France regulars were adepts of the *nouveau christianisme* of the Saint-Simonians, which predicated a highly spiritual materialist system for the reorganisation of the world and the regeneration of mankind. Others subscribed to a variety of similar cults, which veered perilously between the comic and the scandalous.

Chopin found most of this ridiculous, but he did frequent the Hôtel de France, and it was there that he met George Sand for the first time, probably in the last week of October 1836. A few days later, on 5 November, he entertained her, Liszt and his countess, Mickiewicz, Grzymała and the writer and traveller Ferdinand Denis at his own apartment. Denis noted that Liszt played magnificently, making a great effect on George Sand, who 'really felt that powerful music', but that the host merely clowned about on the piano.[11] On 9 November, Chopin went to dinner at the house of Count Marliani (an expatriate Italian who was the Spanish consul in Paris), where he again spent the evening in the company of George Sand, Liszt and his countess. The following day the three dined at Chopin's. On 13 December, Józef Brzowski, a visiting composer from Warsaw, received a card from Chopin which ran:

Today I shall have a few guests, Madame Sand amongst them; Liszt will play, Nourrit will sing. If this pleases Mr Brzowski I await him this evening.[12]

Brzowski was more than pleased, and he duly arrived to find a dazzling array of people. There was the effervescent, long-haired Liszt; the huge, scruffy Custine with his regal manner; the plump and gentle Nourrit; the staid middle-aged legitimist deputy Pierre Antoine Berryer, in impeccable white tie and tails; the seedy pianist Pixis, whose nose Heine described as 'one of the curiosities of the musical world'; the splendidly mus-tachioed Grzymała; the fashionable playwright Eugène Sue; the republican journalist Victor Schoelcher; Włodzimierz Potocki, nephew of Delfina's husband; Heinrich Heine; Jan Matuszyński; Ferdinand Denis and Bernard Potocki, son of the author of *The Manuscript Found in Saragossa*.

There were only two women present. 'Both of them, though close in sympathy, were striking by their apparent diversity,' recorded Brzowski. 'The Countess, blonde, lively, attractive, with a humorous and graceful manner, dressed with exquisite taste, was a typical high-class Parisian lady. George Sand was quite the opposite, dark-haired, solemn and cold, not at all French, with regular features and a calm, rather dead physiognomy, in which one could read only intelligence, thought and pride; her dress was fantastic, and betrayed a desire to show off. Her white smock was bound by a wide crimson sash, her little white tunic of strange cut had crimson facings and buttons. Her black hair, parted evenly in the middle, fell on either side of her face in curls and was tied with a gold band across her forehead.'[13]

'While the Comtesse d'Agoult was entertaining the guests with her sparkling, witty and enchanting conversation, and a sweet smile lit up her face framed by blonde locks *à l'Anglaise*,' continues Brzowski, 'George Sand ensconced herself on the little sofa placed diagonally before the fireplace, and, lightly puffing out clouds of smoke from her cigar, replied sparingly and solemnly to the questions of the men who sat down beside her.'[14] Liszt drew attention to himself, prowling about, gesticu-lating and trying to start a philosophical debate, which Chopin deflated with cynical observations. When a bored Brzowski asked Chopin if he would make Liszt play, Chopin suggested a Moscheles sonata for four hands. The two sat down side by side, Chopin as always taking the bass part, while Pixis turned the pages, occasionally looking up to cast glances of profound admiration in the direction of Brzowski, who had never heard anything like this.

After the sonata, Chopin served ices to his guests, followed by tea which was poured by Marie d'Agoult, while George Sand remained 'nailed to her sofa and did not leave her cigar', as the diarist records. 'She would occasionally cast a glance at the person talking to her, but mostly just stared into the fireplace at the dancing flames.'[15] Accompanied on the piano by Liszt, Nourrit then sang several Schubert *lieder*, but Liszt, whom Brzowski so much wanted to hear on his own, got involved in a heated philosophical discussion with Bernard Potocki. At length the tedious talk irritated Chopin, spoiled Marie d'Agoult's temper and even bored George Sand, who normally loved such conversations.

In a period of under six weeks, Chopin had spent the evening in the company of George Sand at least as many times, but while he had no objection to being in the same room as Europe's most celebrated woman writer, he was not impressed by her. Quite apart from the fact that his heart was set on Maria Wodzińska, George Sand did not answer to Chopin's ideal of womanhood. 'What an unattractive person La Sand is,' he commented to Hiller as they walked home from the Hôtel de France one evening, 'but is she really a woman?'[16] He echoed these sentiments in a letter to his parents, adding that there was something verging on the repellent about her.[17]

He was not the only one to have reservations. Heine thought that her body was too short and plump, her eyes rather dull, and that 'her slightly hanging lower lip seems to suggest exhaustion of the senses'.[18] Marie d'Agoult dwelt on her eyes, which 'seemed to see without looking, and although they were powerful, did not emit anything; a calm which made one anxious, something cold as one imagines the Sphinx of antiquity'.[19]

George Sand was far too dazzled by some of the other people in the group to take much notice of Chopin. Liszt had alerted her to Chopin's genius, which is why she bothered with him at all, but she herself could not see it. Musically, she was more impressed by the breathtaking acrobatics of Liszt, whose talent was more evident; by Meyerbeer, whose spectacular operas were all the rage at the time; by Berlioz with his romantic ebullience; and by Nourrit's philanthropy. To be Polish in Paris at that time was glamorous in itself, but even here Chopin was outshone in her eyes by Mickiewicz, the elemental bard who seemed to speak and suffer for his nation.[20] She was fascinated by the poet's ability to work himself into a kind of trance and improvise verse for an hour or two before collapsing in a fit of exhaustion, and his interest in the interrelation between religion, culture and politics fitted with the ideological climate at the Hôtel de France. In Grzymała, whom she had dubbed her 'dear exile', George Sand saw the archetype of the defeated Polish patriot, and found a kindred soul in a more personal sense.

The reticent, refined Chopin, who avoided philosophical or political discussion, who refused to compete with Liszt, who hid his genius behind a façade of irony and jest, was eclipsed by this galaxy. And while Heine, Hiller, Custine and Liszt himself considered Chopin the greater artist, the more politically minded of the group, including Mickiewicz and Grzymała, rated him as a salon musician, and lavished their admiration instead on Liszt, in whom they saw a political force.

Soon after the soirée described by Brzowski, George Sand returned to her country estate and the Hôtel de France circle was gradually eclipsed in Chopin's life by the usual demands of the Paris season. At the end of the month there was a joint concert given by Liszt and Berlioz, there was the annual Polish Ladies' jumble sale, there were dinners and dances, while

Christmas Eve was spent at the house of an émigré Polish publisher. The guests included Aleksander Jełowicki, Mickiewicz and old Julian Niemcewicz, who got drunk and kept them up till one o'clock with reminiscences of eighteenth-century Poland. Afterwards, Chopin played, and 'everyone was so taken up by his playing and the good cheer that nobody had noticed it had dawned half an hour before'.[21]

This was hardly the way to heed Mrs Wodzińska's instructions, and although Chopin kept writing to her protesting his good behaviour, she was aware of the life he was leading through the gossip of other Poles in Paris. Chopin wrote letters, sent presents to mother and daughter, and complained: 'Why is it not true about those mirrors in which one can see everything, about those magic rings which can transport one to the place in which one's thoughts would like to wander . . .'[22] He also went to see a fortune teller, who predicted the happy fulfilment of all his marital dreams, but this turned out to be a poor prediction.

Since her return to Poland in October, Mrs Wodzińska had had ample time to talk the matter over with her husband and let Chopin know whether his suit had been accepted. But Christmas came and went with no news, while the tone of the letters Chopin was receiving altered as time passed. Mrs Wodzińska's now made no mention of 'the grey hour' and, although full of references to the Chopin family, whom she had seen once or twice in Warsaw, grew more impersonal. Maria's were even more revealing. 'Adieu, mio carissimo maestro, do not forget Dresden, or, soon, Poland. Adieu, au revoir . . . Au revoir, au revoir, au revoir! It gives one hope,' she had ended a letter in October 1836.[23] By the end of January 1837, however, the references to 'May or June at the latest' had been dropped, and replaced by a forlorn 'when we meet again'. And a couple of months later, she was signing off: 'Adieu, I hope you will not forget us.'[24] The Wodzińskis were stalling.

The reason usually adduced is that the aristocratic Wodzińskis (who are graced with a title in most biographies of Chopin) thought too highly of themselves to give their daughter away to a commoner, however famous. This is based on a misunderstanding. The Wodzińskis were no more distinguished by birth than Chopin's mother, and could have had no grounds for comparison with his father, a foreigner of some standing in Warsaw whose origins were kept scrupulously quiet. They were, it is true, much wealthier, but they would not have been remotely disgraced by marrying their daughter to the artist who was everywhere proclaimed as one of Poland's greatest geniuses and had the entrée to the houses of the Czartoryskis and the Radziwiłłs, before whom people of the standing of the Wodzińskis bowed low. Moreover, when Maria had returned to Poland that autumn, there had been a conspicuous lack of interesting suitors.

The circumstances point to other reasons, such as Chopin's poor health, his refusal to take care of himself, the gossip reaching Poland about his contacts and possible relations with 'scandalous' women such as Marie d'Agoult and George Sand, the obvious conflict between his life in Paris and theirs in Poland, and a general feeling that a match with a country neighbour would be less fraught with problems. Mrs Wodzińska, who had encouraged the whole project, was now in an awkward position, particularly as she genuinely liked Chopin. She let the matter drift, no doubt hoping it would die a natural death.

Chopin certainly had plenty to distract him from his broodings, as a veritable musical duel unfolded in Paris. His old Viennese rival Sigismund Thalberg had turned up at the beginning of 1837, and Liszt published a vitriolic attack on the pianist and his repertoire, which he judged facile, in the *Revue et Gazette Musicale* on 8 January. He followed this up by turning up late at his rival's concert, coming in noisily while Thalberg was playing and making mocking asides throughout the performance. He then announced a series of concerts he would give at the Salle Érard in order to teach the Parisian public what real music was.

The first of these took place on 28 January, with a programme including Beethoven Trios hitherto not heard in Paris, Schubert *lieder* sung by Nourrit, and Liszt himself playing some Beethoven, Chopin's new Études and several pieces of his own. The next three were equally impressive, both in the repertoire and its performance. Thalberg admitted defeat, saying publicly that if he possessed a tenth of Liszt's talent, he would consider himself a great artist. But Liszt was not satisfied, and was only just dissuaded by Marie d'Agoult from writing another article rubbing the point in. Thalberg proceeded with his programme and gave a concert at the Conservatoire on 12 March, the success of which annoyed Liszt so much that he booked the large Conservatoire hall on a Sunday and managed to fill it at short notice for a magnificent performance. But the affair was not to rest there.

The flamboyant Italian revolutionary Princess Cristina Belgiojoso, now an expatriate in Paris where she held a notable position in society, had asked Liszt, Thalberg, Pixis, Chopin, Czerny and Herz to help her collect money for refugee Italian patriots. The event was to take place in her Pompeian music room, and they were all to improvise on themes from Bellini's opera *I Puritani*. Even at the staggering price of forty francs a seat the room was full to bursting on 30 March for this duel which only needed weapons to become deadly.[25]

Liszt's playing was by all accounts stupendous, and Heine was appalled at the effect it had on the audience, which was hypnotised. Princess Belgiojoso declared him the only pianist in Europe. The victor shook hands with his rival and invited him to dinner, but with such hauteur that Thalberg left Paris the next morning.

Chopin had been happy enough to see Thalberg brought down a peg, for the memory of Vienna still rankled, but Liszt's vicious persecution of the man horrified him. According to Brzowski, he did not mince his words when he reproached Liszt for it after Thalberg's departure.[26] It was typical of everything that Chopin disliked about Liszt. Chopin had been confined to his bed several times during the last couple of months, but never seriously, and it is difficult to tell whether the plea of illness which he invoked as an excuse for not taking part in Liszt's concert a few days later, on 9 April, was genuine or not.

But as Chopin cooled towards Liszt and his countess, they grew increasingly eager to draw him into their coterie. While he sat in Paris, 'coughing with infinite grace', as Marie d'Agoult put it, and waiting for news from the Wodzińskis, great efforts were being made to drag him down to Nohant, George Sand's estate. She was now living there, enjoying a stormy physical relationship with Michel de Bourges, a left-wing lawyer from a neighbouring town, alongside her affair with Charles Didier, and trying to help Liszt by keeping Marie d'Agoult in the country while he performed in Paris.

In the interests of keeping her happy, George Sand was prepared to have anyone down to stay, though she herself hoped for Mickiewicz, whom she had promised to help with the French translation of one of his works. When, at the beginning of April, Marie d'Agoult had gone to Paris to assist at Liszt's concert and then bring him down to Nohant, George Sand wrote: 'Tell Mick. (non-compromising manner of spelling Polish names) that my pen and my house are at his disposal and only too happy to be so, tell Grzzz . . . that I adore him, Chopin that I idolise him, all whom you love that I love them, and that they will be welcome if brought by you.' On the next day she added: 'I want the Fellows, I want them as soon and for as long as possible. I want them madly. I also want Chopin and all the Mickiewiczes and Grzymałas on earth. I even want [Eugène] Sue, if you like. What else would I not want, if it was your whim? Even M. de Suzannet or Victor Schoelcher – anything, except another lover!'[27]

But, as Marie d'Agoult pointed out, 'Chopin is irresolute; with him only his cough is dependable.'[28] Although Chopin wrote to a friend that he might go to Nohant, he never did, much to the disappointment of the Countess, who seems to have conceived a plan to pair him off with George Sand. His thoughts were elsewhere. It was now April, and 'May and June at the latest' were approaching without his having heard a word from the Wodzińskis about their plans for the summer in Germany. At the beginning of June he heard that Antoni Wodziński had been wounded in Spain, and although Chopin kept the wound secret from Antoni's mother, hoping to be able to break the news gently when he saw her, this gave him an excuse to write again, as Antoni needed money. In his letter he dropped heavy hints about not knowing what he was going to do that summer. Mrs Wodzińska's reply was cordial and chatty, but made no mention of any plans. Nor was there the usual postscript from Maria.

Chopin's physical condition was not good, and the nervous agitation caused by the baffling behaviour of the Wodzińskis made things worse. 'You are at the limit between the torments of the mind and sickness of the body,' Custine wrote to him that spring, advising him to spend a couple of months quietly at Saint-Gratien, at the same time offering to lend him money for a journey to the waters in Germany. Chopin did avail himself of Custine's invitation to Saint-Gratien several times, but the visits were hardly calculated to restore his health.[29]

Brzowski's diary describes one such excursion, on a Sunday at the beginning of June.[30] It was a fine day, and Brzowski admired the countryside as they rolled out of Paris through the Porte de Clichy in their hired cabriolet and then drove through Saint-Denis to Saint-Gratien, where they were met by Custine and a lady, as well as his two catamites, Edward Saint-Barbe and Ignacy Gurowski. Having arranged to meet Gurowski for dinner at Enghien at six and then return to Saint-Gratien for the evening, Chopin and Brzowski set off for Montmorency, a small village which was full of trippers from Paris come to spend the day in the beautiful adjoining park.

After a copious breakfast of bread, butter and fresh milk, they went to hire donkeys, the accepted conveyance for visiting the countryside. Chopin was immediately accosted by two young girls who remembered him from the previous year, and they and their donkeys were duly hired. They set off, each mounted on his ass with the two girls on foot leading them. Brzowski was taken up by 'the May green of the trees, the delicious smell of the forest, the unexpected vistas between trees or along valleys', while Chopin was engaged in flirtatious conversation with the girl leading his donkey. At length they reached the Hermitage, where they were shown Rousseau's work room, the desk on which he had written *La Nouvelle Héloise* and the decrepit piano on which Grétry had composed.

On their return journey they were caught by a sudden downpour and had to hurry back, Chopin expertly trotting along on his donkey and laughing at the disconsolate Parisian ladies in their flowery dresses. Back at Montmorency, they took their leave of donkeys and girls and climbed back into their cabriolet, which made for Enghien and the inn where Gurowski should have been waiting. There was no Gurowski in sight, and Chopin wanted to while away the time at the piano which stood in the corner, but the landlady refused to unlock it, fearing that the long-haired gentleman from Paris might damage it.

Gurowski eventually showed up, driving a carriage himself, and insisted that since it was such a fine evening they must go and call on a rich Englishman who lived by the lake. They drove over to the place, only to find that the Englishman was out in a boat. When at length he rowed back to the shore, Gurowski decided to go boating himself, so it was some time before they got back to the inn and sat down to dinner. As they were all in high spirits and hungry, they ate well and put down several bottles of champagne, some good hock and fine claret. It was a completely drunk Gurowski who drove them back to Saint-Gratien at breakneck speed, sending other vehicles rolling off the road. Custine was annoyed at their lateness, as he had arranged a musical evening and everyone was waiting.

After a change of clothes and an attempt to sober up a little, they came down and entered the drawing room, whose white walls, decorated with large flowers, were hung not with pictures but with two huge mirrors in heavy gilt frames. Comfortable sofas and armchairs covered in white brocade to match the curtains were scattered informally around the room, and the only touch of colour was lent by the Oriental vases standing on the white marble fireplace and the Pleyel grand piano. The assembled company included the duchesse d'Abrantès, the social journalist Sophie Gay, the comtesse Merlin, Berlioz and his wife Harriet, the tenor Louis Duprez and his wife, and several others, including one Brzowski termed 'an old writer', who was almost certainly Chateaubriand. Victor Hugo and his wife were expected but failed to appear. The whole group clustered around Chopin, who found it difficult to hide his lingering intoxication, and after a while the music started.

First Duprez and his wife sang a duet from a Donizetti opera. Duprez had recently arrived from Italy and quickly supplanted Nourrit as the leading tenor in Paris, with the result that Nourrit had to quit the capital. Duprez then sang a duet from one of Bellini's operas with the comtesse Merlin. She was a perfect fit for the Custine salon – born in Havana, she had escaped from a convent and led a tempestuous life. Beautiful, clever and cultivated, she was an excellent musician who gave concerts and presided over a musical salon of her own.

When they had finished, Custine invited Chopin, who played a couple of new Études and his second Ballade. Then everyone begged him for a Mazurka, and he obliged, after which, 'like some kind of prophet inspired', he started on a warlike improvisation.[31]

The company then adjourned to the dining room for supper, after which some of the guests left. The remainder begged the comtesse Merlin to sing some Spanish songs. Custine dug up some castanets, Chopin sat down at the piano and began to improvise on the melody and tempo she gave him, and the Countess was soon dancing around the room as she sang. When she had finished, Custine insisted that it was 'the magician, the Sylph of Saint Gratien' who must round off the evening, and Chopin once more launched into a long improvisation. It was well after midnight when the last notes died away, and in spite of being pressed by Custine to stay the night, the two Poles climbed back into their cabriolet and returned to Paris. Chopin could not have been in bed before two.

Before Brzowski left for Warsaw in June, Chopin took him and Matuszyński out to dinner, typically at one of the grandest restaurants in Paris, the Rocher de Cancale in the rue de Montorgeuil. The occasion was meticulously recorded by Brzowski:

One climbs to the first floor, and already on the stairs leading out of the lower room there are relays of garçons, one of whom counts how many there are in the party and shouts to the others to prepare a room suitable for the number. So we found ourselves in a cabinet for three in which we settled ourselves comfortably. On the table in the centre of the room lay a book listing the dishes, a sheet of clean paper, and pen and ink. The elegant, slim but comprehensive volume, listing everything most refined that Paris can offer the gourmet, became the object of our scrutiny and discussion. Finally we gave complete freedom of choice to Chopin. He wrote out what we wished to eat and the waiting garçon was handed the note. We were soon served. We started with oysters – excellent! Next came soup, a cream of game – wonderful! Next they served us Matelot [probably a matelotte, a fish stew]. This dish, equal only to nectar, by its wonderful texture and exquisite taste seemed to be trying to proclaim with pride that we were indeed dining at the Rocher de Cancale. The next dish was asparagus – beyond all praise. Then came other savoury dishes, and the whole repast was noisily accompanied

*by the most magical champagne . . . With cigars in our teeth we
set off for coffee at Tortoni's.*[32]

Although he still bandied about names like Ems and Wiesbaden
in a note to Mrs Wodzińska, fishing for a response, Chopin
remained in Paris, or rather, hopped about between Paris and
Enghien. In mid-June Custine tried to take him along when he
left for Wiesbaden, while Marie d'Agoult encouraged him to
'come and create a new motherland at Nohant' with Mickiewicz
and Grzymała, but Chopin refused to stir from Paris. Then,
suddenly, he made a decision. It was, from the point of view
of his health, the worst he could have made, and one cannot
help feeling that he made it to spite himself. His friend the
piano-maker Camille Pleyel was going to London for a couple
of weeks, and Chopin elected to join him.

They arrived on 7 July 1837. Fontana had told Chopin that
England had an 'Italian sky' in the summer, but Chopin found
it grey and sooty and was soon racked by fits of coughing. Yet
while London assaulted his senses, it also fascinated him. 'The
English women, the horses, the palaces, the carriages, the wealth,
the luxury, the space, the trees, everything, from the soap to the
razors – everything is wonderful – everything ordered, everything cultivated, everything well-scrubbed,' he wrote to Fontana.[33]

He took up residence in Bryanston Square, and as his guide
he took Stanisław Koźmian, a London-based friend of Fontana.
'Chopin has been here for two weeks incognito,' Koźmian related
to his brother. 'He knows nobody and wishes to see nobody but
me. I spend the whole day with him, and sometimes even the
whole night, like yesterday. He is here with Pleyel, famous for his
pianos and his wife's adventures . . . They have come to "do"
London. They have put up at one of the best hotels, they keep a
carriage; they are simply looking for ways of spending money.
One day we go to Windsor, another to Blackwall, another to
Richmond.' This hectic activity was presumably dictated by

Chopin's need to obliterate mortifying reflection on his marital plans.[34]

He did not call on Moscheles, which was rude to say the least, as the older composer was bound to (and did) find out that he had been in London. He was not very good at maintaining his incognito. On one evening that Pleyel spent with his English counterpart, the piano-maker James Broadwood, Chopin accompanied him, but insisted on being introduced as 'Mr Fritz'. But after everyone had played the piano a little, he could not resist the urge himself, and, sitting down at the instrument, had everyone gaping in astonishment after a few bars, and the truth was out. Nobody else played like that.[35]

After almost three weeks of frenetic activity, Pleyel and Chopin left London, reaching Paris in the last week of July. While in London, Chopin had received a letter from Mrs Wodzińska which informed him that the family were not going to Germany or anywhere else that summer. The letter has not survived, and it is possible that it contained something more definite, for when he wrote back to her on 14 August (he now had to inform her of Antoni's wound), the final paragraph suggests that he had understood. 'Your last letter reached me in London, where I whiled away the past month,' he wrote. 'I had thought that from there I might travel through Holland to Germany . . . I returned home, the season is getting on, and for me it will probably come to an end in my room – I await a less sad letter from you than the last. Perhaps my next will only be a postscript to Antoni's.'[36]

The season did indeed end for Chopin in his rooms, in the middle of a deserted Paris, with Custine in Germany, the Czartoryskis in Brittany, Liszt and his countess in Italy. George Sand spent most of the summer in Paris looking after her dying mother, but then returned to Nohant in a gloomy state of mind. Looking back over the past few years, she felt horrified by her own emotional as well as physical promiscuity, doubtful of her ability to feel or sustain real love, and prematurely spent.[37] She decided to remain in the country and work, took a tutor for her children who doubled as her lover, and settled down to 'no longer count the bad days or look forward to better ones'.[38]

The autumn of 1837 was a time of reflection for Chopin too. He was smarting from the dénouement of the Wodziński affair, and did not get over it for a long time. He made a packet of all Maria's letters and on the envelope wrote two words which can only be translated as 'my tragedy'. But this was not enough to bury the episode, and he kept Maria firmly in his mind just as he had Konstancja, as an image and an object for emotional self-indulgence.

His finances too must have been in a pitiful state, for his lifestyle had lately become regal. At some point he had engaged a servant, he entertained often in his rooms, and he was always buying people expensive presents. The chaotic summer must have made it impossible for him to give lessons regularly, and the trip to London proved expensive. He now had to work hard at the lessons and also to sell a few compositions.

His life during most of that year had been far too hectic to permit the concentration he needed in order to write. He had been working on the Preludes and had written some Mazurkas and Nocturnes, but it was only in the autumn that he could concentrate enough to polish up some of them for publication. Of the longer works produced that summer and autumn, the most important are the famous Funeral March, which he did not publish then but later included in a sonata, and the B flat minor Scherzo, op.31. Both of these are highly dramatic, though restrained, pieces, and they provide a good example of the direction in which he was moving.

Chopin's position in Parisian artistic and social life was, by 1837, unassailable. But the price paid for this had been high; his health had given way, and as he approached his twenty-eighth birthday he felt rudderless and isolated. Playing the part of the fashionable, cosmopolitan artist had been something of a failure. He had little in common with Berlioz and Liszt, less still with their intellectual friends. As for the French aristocracy, he realised better than anyone that his relationship with it was on the most superficial level. The few exceptions, such as Custine or the King's Director of Music the comte de Perthuis, could not obscure this fact. He had one or two humbler French friends, such as the journalist Legouvé and the cellist Franchomme, and a few sincere admirers like the banker Auguste Léo, the Hanoverian ambassador Stockhausen, and the wine merchant and Saxon consul Thomas Albrecht, perhaps the closest of all his non-Polish friends, to whose daughter he had stood godfather.

Chopin was not a self-sufficient person, and this collection of friends did not constitute the 'family' that he needed. What is more, they could not speak Polish, which was more important than one might suppose. Chopin's French was not good: he spoke haltingly and with a strong accent, while his letters reveal that he could neither spell nor construct his sentences properly in that language. He found speaking French continually a strain, and needed to resort to his mother tongue for a relaxed chat. The style of his letters to Polish friends like Grzymała or Fontana is effortless and allusive: sentences often lack an ending, thoughts are not carried through or explained, and layers of meaning are hinted at. With friends like these, he did not need to develop his thoughts or feelings, and the same was to some extent true of all Poles. It was with them that he preferred to spend the evening when he was tired or depressed. As he explained to one French lady, 'One's greatest solace in a foreign land is to have someone who carries one's thoughts back to the homeland every time one looks at him, talks to him or listens to his words.'[39]

Chopin was not as committed to the Polish cause in the political sense as many of his countrymen would have liked. Most of them were cut off not only from their country, but also from their position in society and their means of livelihood. This tended to make their patriotism more visceral, and drove many of them, particularly the intellectuals, towards mysticism of one sort or another. Gripped by the tyranny of the national cult, and having no option but to sacrifice themselves to it, they saw the world, and life itself, as a national Gehenna. Chopin was cut off from home and family through his own choice, and he would almost certainly have spent most of his life in Paris whether the insurrection had taken place or not. The poets Mickiewicz and Słowacki used to reproach him for wasting his talent 'caressing the nerves of the French aristocracy' instead of sowing rebellion with his music.[40]

His patriotism was never in question: he gave generously to all Polish charities and never failed to offer his services to the cause. But he also gave lessons to members of the Russian aristocracy passing through Paris, and he could not be accused of chauvinism. His patriotism and nostalgia for Poland were metaphysical. They remained the primary inspiration for most of his music, but they did not translate into political action. He was an exile certainly, but in the sense in which every artist of the Romantic movement saw it: he was an exile from Arcadia.

The rude awakening from the dreams woven round his love for Maria Wodzińska forced him to face up to the fact that he would never return to some kind of 'normal' life in Poland. The end of his fifth year in Paris also brought home a number of truths. He had come to see that he had to stand on his own, with only his art to support him. And just as he rejected the exclusive and narrow patriotism of some of his compatriots, he also rejected the political tendencies of the French Romantics, and with them the concert platform, in favour of a spiritual ascent, and a more intimate communion with his listeners.

Shortly before Christmas that year there was another Polish bazaar for Chopin to help with, and it was a busy season for him in other respects. Musical attractions included the first performance, on 5 December, of Berlioz's Requiem at the

Invalides. In the last days of February 1838, Chopin was called to the Tuileries to play before the royal family. Each time he did this he was presented with a gift: a silver-gilt tea set for one performance, a pair of Sèvres vases for another, and a dinner service for a third, all inscribed '*Louis Philippe, Roi des Français, à Frédéric Chopin*'. A few days later, on 5 March, he took part in a concert given by the young pianist Charles Morhange, who had adopted the pseudonym Alkan. Chopin, Zimmermann, Gutmann and Alkan played Alkan's arrangement of Beethoven's Seventh Symphony for eight hands on two pianos, a typically publicity-oriented concert piece. Later that month Chopin travelled down to Rouen, to help his friend Antoni Orłowski, who had settled there and needed to make his mark by giving a concert. What Chopin had not anticipated was that all the Paris music critics would go to Rouen as well for the occasion. The result was that Orłowski was the Cinderella of the evening. 'Here is an event which is not without importance in the musical world,' wrote Legouvé in the *Revue et Gazette Musicale* of 25 March. Chopin played at length before an audience of five hundred, who were 'penetrated, moved, enraptured'. The review concluded with the exhortation:

> *Forward then, Chopin! Forward! Let this triumph decide you; do not be selfish, give your talent to all; consent to pass for what you are; put an end to the great debate which divides the artists; and when it shall be asked who is the greatest pianist in Europe, Liszt or Thalberg, let all the world reply, like those who have heard you: It is Chopin!*[41]

Instead of persuading him to return to the life of a performing pianist, this seems to have put Chopin off for good. His appearance in Rouen was his last in public for a long time. This was not the result of laziness, reticence or even of his proverbial dislike of having to take on responsibility for organising the events. It was because he could not communicate with an indiscriminate audience in such an atmosphere. That was why he had not shone at the Hôtel de France – not because he was overshadowed by Liszt, but because he did not feel the atmosphere or the audience to be appropriate. When it was, he responded quite differently, and literally gave of himself. In November 1836, at the very time that he was clowning about before Marie d'Agoult and George Sand, Chopin played before Charles Hallé, a dedicated young musician who had just arrived from Germany. 'Chopin! He is no man, he is an angel, a god (or what can I say more?),' Hallé wrote home to his parents. 'There is nothing to remind one that it is a human being who produces this music. It seems to descend from heaven – so pure, and clear, and spiritual.'[42]

'Concerts never create real music,' Chopin later confided in one pupil, 'they are a form which one has to renounce in order to be able to hear what is most beautiful in art.'[43] Heinrich Heine, who had written an article on Chopin just before the Rouen concert, had understood his feelings and his intention better than Legouvé. 'Chopin does not derive his satisfaction from the fact that his hands are applauded by other hands for their agile dexterity,' he wrote. 'He aspires to a greater success; his fingers are the servants of his soul, and his soul is applauded by those who do not merely listen with their ears, but also with their souls.'[44]

TEN

Love Above All

In the spring of 1838 Chopin was often to be seen at the soirées of Countess Charlotte Marliani, whom he had met a couple of years before. She was an undistinguished but affable Frenchwoman who had married the Spanish consul in Paris. He was an exiled Italian revolutionary, and since there was mutual sympathy between the Polish and Italian exiles, his wife's salon was a meeting place for members of both groups. The regular guests included Grzymała, Mickiewicz and the Czartoryskis, as well as notable Italian expatriates such as Princess Belgiojoso.

Although she was no intellectual, Countess Marliani had also opened her doors to some of the debris of Marie d'Agoult's 'humanitarian' salon of the previous year. As a result, her apartment in the rue de la Grange Batelière was cosmopolitan and artistic in atmosphere, and it was here that George Sand decided to stay when she came to Paris on business for two weeks in the middle of April. Liszt had some time before written to her from Italy, urging her to 'see Chopin a little', but he need not have bothered, for the two inevitably met once again.[1]

They had both changed a great deal during the fifteen months since they had last seen each other. In the autumn of 1836, the happy, carefree Chopin who was hoping to marry Maria Wodzińska had turned his nose up at the Hôtel de France set, rarely played the piano, and usually clowned about or parodied Liszt when he did. George Sand was put off by his apparent frivolity and snobbishness, and was herself in an intellectually assertive mood. Now Chopin was sad and more serious; George Sand was weary and reflective. The surroundings in which they saw each other were more conducive to a reappraisal of each other's qualities. In the homely atmosphere of the Marliani apartment Chopin played often and played at his best. At Custine's, where they both had dinner on 8 May, George Sand could see him in his element. The guests, who included the duchesse d'Abrantès, the comtesse Merlin, the Victor Hugos, Jules Janin, Sophie Gay and the poets Charles Nodier and Lamartine, listened to Duprez singing Gluck arias, Franchomme playing his cello, and finally to Chopin. It was a warm evening and the scent of the garden wafted in through the open french windows of the dining room where they sat. Chopin improvised for hours in the semi-darkness, with only a 'magic glow' lighting up the large painting covering the wall behind him.[2]

George Sand fell in love with Chopin. 'I must say that I was confused and amazed at the effect this little creature wrought on me,' she wrote some two weeks later. 'I have still not recovered from my astonishment, and if I were a proud person I should be feeling humiliated at having been carried away by my emotions at a moment in my life when I had thought that I had settled down for good.'[3]

She was only thirty-three years old, less than six years older than Chopin, but she had lived with such intensity and packed so much experience into those years that she felt played out. This had not affected her physically, as Balzac noted. 'She hasn't a single grey hair, in spite of the terrible experiences she has been through. Her swarthy complexion has not altered; her lovely eyes are as lustrous as ever. She always looks stupid when sunk in thought, for, as I told her after studying her a while, all her expression is concentrated in the eyes.'[4]

Those eyes were now devouring Chopin, who soon found himself gazing back into them and realising that the cavalier, cigar-smoking image George Sand projected in public was a mask behind which she hid her vulnerability. Those sphinx-like eyes exercised an immense power of silent attraction, and it was not long before Chopin was irresistibly drawn towards her. He was bewildered and anxious, and called on Grzymała for support. 'My dearest, I must see you urgently today, even at night, at 12 or 1,' he wrote to him. 'Don't fear any embarrassment for yourself, my dearest, you know I have always valued your good heart. It's a question of advice for me.'[5]

Having spent the last two years dreaming of a love affair in which every move forward, every step in intimacy was drawn out over a period of months, Chopin was knocked off balance by this new development and the rapidity with which it was taking place. After only a couple of weeks he was on the brink of sexual consummation, and at this point he hesitated. George Sand had to return to Nohant as her son Maurice had fallen ill, and on her last evening in Paris, 14 May, she was at Grzymała's with Delacroix, listening to Chopin playing into the small hours. At the moment of parting, Chopin grew embarrassed, as he sensed that it was incumbent on him to make a physical advance. He shied away, with a remark about 'not spoiling the memory' of the past three weeks. This suddenly revealed to her that he still thought of love-making as somehow shameful, an attitude that could not fail to jar with her, who had slept with almost every man she had ever loved.

She returned to Nohant perplexed and worried. 'We allowed ourselves to be swept along by a passing wind,' she reasoned, but found that reasoning got her nowhere.[6] While she was wondering what to do next, Chopin was doing the same in Paris. The image of Maria suddenly loomed, presumably as a sort of counterbalance of respectable purity to the frighteningly real sexual possibilities of the situation in hand. His chronic irresolution played its part too, and he went running to 'Uncle Albert' Grzymała. The upshot of this was that Grzymała wrote to George Sand (it is unclear whether Chopin knew of this or not) discussing the matter at some length and apparently warning her not to trifle with Chopin. He also told her that Chopin still cherished the memory of someone else, at the same time expressing misgivings as to whether he could ever be happy in marriage.

George Sand replied with a very long letter, in which she laid bare her thoughts and begged Grzymała to form a judgement, by which she swore to abide. The two had become intimate in the last couple of years, and admired each other greatly (it is possible that Grzymała briefly enjoyed her favours as a lover). So she laid before him the main issues as she saw them with remarkable candour. 'This person, whom he wants to or feels himself bound to love, will she make him happy?' she speculated. 'Or will she increase his sufferings and his sadness? I don't ask whether he loves, whether he is loved by her, whether it is more or less intense than with me. I know more or less what is happening inside me, and what must be happening inside him. I want to know which of us two he must forget or abandon for his own peace of mind, for his own happiness, for his life even, which seems to me too fragile and unstable to be able to resist unhappiness.'

Having said this, and having stressed that she did not wish to play the part of a wicked angel and sniff 'the incense intended for another altar', she rambled on incoherently. She pointed out that 'there is a being, excellent, perfect from the point of view of his heart and his honour, whom I shall never leave', by which she meant her children's tutor, the playwright Félicien Mallefille. But a page or so further on she admitted that Mallefille's caresses had become a good deal less welcome since she had fallen in love with Chopin. She declared that Mallefille was as malleable as wax, and that he would not stand in the way of any decision she made. She had been horrified at Chopin's deficient or unhappy sexual experience, and appeared to see it as her duty to sort him out. Recoiling from this, however, she put forward another solution, which appealed to her image of herself as a reasonable, grown-up person in control of her destiny. 'I think that our love can only last in the conditions in which it was born,' she wrote, 'that is to say only from time to time, when a good wind brings us together, when we can take a trip to the stars, after which we can part in order to walk on earth.'

Stripped to essentials, this meant that she would keep Mallefille as her lover, that Chopin could adore as many Polish ladies as he wished, and that she would 'chastely press him in my arms when the celestial wind deigns to snatch and waft us up into the heavens'. (It is one of the failings of Sand's prose style that when she hits upon a convenient metaphor she labours it to death.) The letter rambled on in quest of a solution. 'If he is happy or will be happy through her, let him be,' she summed up. 'If he will be unhappy, stop him. If I can make him happy without spoiling his happiness with her, I can arrange my life accordingly. If he can only be happy with me by ruining his chances of happiness through her, we must avoid each other and he must forget me. There is no avoiding these four points.'[7]

But there was a fifth 'point': she was in love with Chopin and no longer wanted Mallefille. George Sand was a curious mixture of eighteenth-century rationalism and Romantic impulse, and, having reasoned everything out on paper, she proceeded to act in complete contradiction to her conclusions. It is not known whether Grzymała ever replied to her letter, or what he wrote if he did, but having laid the whole matter in his lap, she now took it firmly back into her own hands, and dashed off a note to him saying:

My affairs are calling me back. I shall be in Paris on Thursday. Come to see me and try to keep it a secret from the Little One. We shall give him a surprise. Yours, dearest, G.S. – I shall, as usual, be staying with Mme Marliani.[8]

Grzymała promptly warned Chopin of the surprise that lay in store for him, and received the following answer:

*My dearest! I cannot be surprised, because yesterday I saw
Marliani, who told me she was coming. I shall be at home till
five, giving lessons, rottenly (I'm just finishing my second). What
will come of all this, God only knows. I feel really awful. I've been
calling on you every day to give you a hug. Let's have dinner
together somewhere.*[9]

When George Sand arrived in Paris on 6 June, reason and
scruples quickly gave way before natural instinct, and the two
became lovers. The affair was only slightly complicated by the
arrival in Paris of Mallefille, who still considered himself to
be the official lover and accompanied George Sand much of
the time. She took a little garret room not far from the Marlianis',
ostensibly so that she could get on with her work, and thereby
guaranteed herself some freedom. Evenings were usually spent
at the Marlianis', where the deception was possible as the group
of friends who gathered there, Delacroix, Grzymała and
Mickiewicz, were in on the secret. Like the others, Mallefille
was entranced by Chopin's playing. 'Hidden in the darkest
corner of the room, I wept while following in my mind the
desolate images you conjured up,' he wrote, little realising that
he had more urgent cause for tears.[10] While he sat down and
wrote a poem exalting Chopin and his country, Chopin was
sitting in Delacroix's studio on the Left Bank with George Sand,
posing for a joint portrait. A Pleyel piano had been moved into
the studio in June, and Delacroix painted Chopin playing it,
with George Sand sitting just behind in an ecstatic pose.

In August she sent Mallefille off with her son on a trip around
Normandy, and was at last able to see Chopin whenever she
wanted. A month of bliss followed. George Sand wrote to
Delacroix of 'the delicious exhaustion of a fulfilled love', and in
September she was 'still in the state of intoxication in which
you last saw me'. 'There has not been the slightest cloud in our
clear sky, not a grain of sand in our lake. I am beginning to

think that there are angels disguised as men.'[11] Being George Sand, she had to explain to herself and others that her love was 'neither a preconceived decision, nor a substitute, nor an illusion born of boredom and solitude, nor a caprice, nor any of those things with which one deceives oneself by deceiving others'.

She began by refuting all that she had written and decided in the past year, bombarding the unfortunate Delacroix with her arguments and conclusions. 'Love above all, don't you agree?' she wrote to him. 'Love above all when one's star is in the ascendant, art above all when the star is in decline!'[12] The ponderous philosophical novel she was halfway through was put aside, and she embarked on a musical-philosophical drama entitled *Les Sept Cordes de la Lyre*, in which the Spirit of the Lyre, a symbolic Chopin, exclaims: 'Listen to the voice that sings love and not to the voice that explains it.'[13]

At the beginning of September, however, the 'celestial wind' theory came into sharp conflict with reality, for Chopin was getting possessive, and George Sand could not face carrying on with Mallefille, who was back in Paris. As a result, the man she would 'never leave' was unceremoniously dismissed. He proved to be a good deal less malleable than she had thought, and when he realised what lay behind his dismissal, he grew violent.

There are two versions of what happened. One is that Mallefille posted himself outside Chopin's apartment in the rue de la Chaussée d'Antin and tried to seize George Sand as she emerged, she taking advantage of a heavy goods wagon which rolled between them to leap into a passing cab. The other version is that, after nearly breaking down Chopin's door one night, he attempted to strangle the composer and was only stopped by the timely intervention of Grzymała. Whichever is closer to the truth, Mallefille was certainly wandering around Paris uttering wild threats, and the two lovers had to be careful throughout September, during which they did not go out much together.

George Sand had for some time been planning to spend that

autumn and winter in Italy on account of the delicate health of her fifteen-year-old son Maurice, and Mallefille's threats made such a plan still more expedient. For some reason, Italy was dropped in favour of Majorca, which was presumably suggested by some of the Spaniards who frequented the Marlianis. One of these, the Marquess of Valldemosa, though a Majorcan himself, seems to have known the place but vaguely, and threw out a few optimistic remarks about the beneficial climate. Without further ado, or a thought for the fact that Spain was in the throes of civil war, George Sand made up her mind and started to make preparations.

She assumed that Chopin would go with her, but he hesitated as he always did before a decision. Grzymała expressed misgivings about the advisability of his accompanying her on the journey, and the prospect of leaving Paris for some six months for an unknown destination did not fill Chopin with enthusiasm. On the other hand he could not resign himself to letting this woman who meant so much to him go off and leave him alone, so he borrowed money, pre-sold the almost completed set of Preludes, and arranged for Pleyel to have a piano shipped out.

On 18 October, George Sand left with her two children and a maid, travelling by easy stages. Chopin was to meet them en route, and began to say his farewells in Paris. On 20 October he went to Saint-Gratien for the day, and made a painful impression on Custine, who wrote:

He is leaving for Valencia in Spain, that is to say for the other world. You simply cannot imagine what Madame Sand has managed to do with him in the space of one summer! Consumption has taken possession of that face, making it a soul without a body. He played to us a farewell, with the expression that you know. First a Polonaise, which he had just written, magnificent by its force and verve. It is a joyous riot. Then he played the Polish prayer. Then, at the end, a funeral march, which made me burst into tears in spite of myself. It was the procession taking him to his last resting place; and when I reflected that perhaps I would never see him again on this earth, my heart bled. The unfortunate creature cannot see that the woman has the love of a vampire! He is following her to Spain, whither she is preceding him. He will never leave that country. He did not dare tell me he was going; he only spoke of his need for a good climate and for rest! Rest! – with a Ghoul as travelling companion![14]

Chopin left Paris on 25 October, in the company of the brother of the Spanish minister Mendizabal, travelling night and day in order to catch up with George Sand at Perpignan. They arrived there on 30 October, Chopin 'fresh as a rose and pink as a turnip, looking well and having borne heroically the four nights in the mail coach'.[15] The next day they took ship from Port-Vendres and reached Barcelona on 2 November. They had to spend five days there, awaiting the departure of the weekly packet to Palma, during which they made the acquaintance of the French consul, dined aboard a French navy brig anchored in the roads, and even went on a long excursion into the surrounding countryside. In spite of the civil war, of which they were continually reminded by bursts of distant gunfire, the city was thronged with people pretending that nothing out of the ordinary was going on, and the warm evenings were dominated by the sound of guitars and merry-making.

On the evening of 7 November the party embarked on the *Mallorquin*, the steamer which plied between Majorca and Barcelona, and after a warm and perfectly calm night crossing, sailed into Palma harbour in the late morning under a blazing sun. While Chopin and the children remained on the quayside being stared at by the locals, George Sand set off in search of a hotel, only to return a few hours later having discovered that there were none in Palma, and that such rented accommodation as there was had been taken by refugees from the mainland.

She eventually found a couple of squalid rooms in a noisy and poor area of the city, where they camped for the night, and on the next day went in search of better lodgings, trusting in the introductions she had brought to people in Palma. She had letters to the Canut family, the foremost bankers in the town, to that of the Marquess of Valldemosa, and to various other members of Palma society, but while some of them were pleasant enough, most were guarded in their behaviour, and none offered any help.

As Madame de Canut points out in her memoirs, the Majorcans were taken aback by the arrival on the scene of an unattached woman who wrote books and smoked cigars, accompanied by two long-haired boys and a little girl who wore boys' clothes, none of whom went to church, and whose manner exuded a strong odour of immorality.[16] This of course excited the local rakes, and on the one evening that she went to the opera with the Canuts, George Sand was stared out of existence with either disapproving or lecherous looks. She therefore left Majorcan society to itself, and turned for help to the more congenial French consul in Palma, Monsieur Flury.

With his help, she tracked down a Mr Gomez who was prepared to rent her his little villa at Establiments, a couple of miles from Palma. They moved in on 15 November, and were delighted with the primitively furnished but picturesque house called 'S'on Vent'. 'My dearest, I am at Palma, surrounded by palms, cedars, cactuses, olives, oranges, lemons, aloes, figs, pomegranates, etc.; everything the Jardin des Plantes has in its hothouses,' Chopin wrote to Fontana the very same day. 'The sky is like turquoise, the sea like lapis lazuli, the hills like emeralds, the air like in heaven. During the daytime it is sunny and hot, and everyone walks about in summer clothes; at night you hear guitars and singing for hours. Huge balconies overhung with vines; moorish battlements. Everything looks out towards Africa, like the town itself. In a word, this is the most wonderful life.'[17]

George Sand too was delighted with the place, which she

described as 'a green Switzerland under a Calabrian sky, with the solemnity and the silence of the Orient', and declared to a friend in Paris that she would 'never leave Majorca'.[18] Both Chopin and Maurice went for long walks, and their health improved. But after one longer expedition, during which the weather changed suddenly, Chopin had an attack of bronchitis. This would not have been serious had the weather remained fine, but it deteriorated dramatically. Torrential rain and a drop in temperature quickly turned the charming villa with its pane-less windows, thin walls and chimneyless braziers into a 'cold, damp, smoky hole'. Chopin's bronchitis grew worse, and by the end of November he was racked by fits of coughing. George Sand was so alarmed that she called in a doctor, who brought a couple of colleagues, each of whom examined Chopin. 'The first sniffed at what I had coughed up, the second tapped at the place I had coughed it up from, the third poked about and listened while I coughed,' Chopin wrote to Fontana. 'The first said that I was dead, the second that I was dying, the third that I was about to die.'[19]

The doctors departed and Chopin's condition improved in-dependently of them. This was largely thanks to the way George Sand looked after him, cooking special meals for him and at last managing to get an artisan to build her a stove, which meant the room could be heated without attendant fumigation. Although she was irritated by the fact that 'instead of making literature, I am making the food', as she wrote to Grzymała, she kept her spirits up and continued to write enthusiastic letters to her friends in Paris.[20] Chopin, who had been 'dreaming of music, but could not make any' since the Pleyel had not arrived yet, managed to rent a piano locally and get down to work on the remaining Preludes, and even wrote a new Mazurka (no.1 of op.41).[21]

Just as things were beginning to look up a little, the weather deteriorated further, the walls of the house swelled with mois-ture like a sponge, and Chopin's health took another plunge.

In mid-December he wrote to Fontana that 'my manuscripts lie dormant, while I cannot sleep – I can only cough and, covered in poultices, lie here waiting for the spring, or something else . . .'[22]

The doctors who had caused such amusement had in fact diagnosed tuberculosis, and they had done what was demanded by Spanish law in such cases: reported it to the authorities. As soon as he heard of this, Mr Gomez told the party to decamp forthwith and to pay for the whitewashing of the house and for new furniture, as by law all effects touched by a tuberculotic had to be burnt.

George Sand had been thinking of moving anyway. On a sightseeing excursion at the beginning of their stay they had visited the former Carthusian monastery of Valldemosa, which she thought 'the most romantic spot on earth'.[23] After its dissolution, the monastery had been taken over by the government, which rented out the monks' cells to anyone who wished to stay there. She had immediately taken one, with the notion of going there to write. When they were overcome by the dampness of Palma, she began to consider moving to the higher ground of Valldemosa, but was put off by the difficulty of furnishing the cell. However, just as Mr Gomez told her to vacate his house, a family which was moving out of Valldemosa offered to sell her theirs. So, on 15 December, the little party loaded up the rented piano, the stove and all the effects they could take, and set off up the mountainside. This was no easy undertaking, for there was no proper road up to the monastery. 'Many times I have travelled from Palma to this place, always with the same carter, always by a different route,' Chopin later wrote to Fontana. 'The roads are created by streams, repaired by avalanches; today you cannot get through here because it has been ploughed up, tomorrow only a mule can get through – and you should see the local carts!!!'[24]

The monastery nestled in the mountains and enjoyed a magnificent view over the surrounding countryside and the sea, 'one of those views which overcome one, because they leave nothing to be desired, nothing to be imagined', as George Sand put it. 'Everything the poet and the painter might have dreamt up has been created in this place by nature.'[25] The cell which they moved into consisted of three large chambers reached from a communal passage. The furniture consisted of camp beds, rickety tables, rush chairs and a white-wood settee. The clay floor was covered with rush matting and white sheepskins. Chopin described their new home thus:

> *Valldemosa, between the mountains and the sea, a huge aban-*
> *doned Carthusian monastery, where, in a cell with doors larger*
> *than any pair of gates in Paris, you can imagine me, my hair*
> *uncurled, without white gloves, pale as ever. The cell is in the*
> *shape of a tall coffin, with a great dusty vault, a small window,*
> *and, outside, oranges, palms, cypresses. Opposite the window, my*
> *bed of straps, under a Moorish filigree rose. Next to my bed there*
> *is a hopeless square desk I can hardly write on, on it a leaden*
> *candlestick (a luxury here) with a candle in it, my Bach, my own*
> *scrawls, someone else's papers . . . silence . . . you can yell . . . silence*
> *still. In a word, it is a strange place I am writing from.*[26]

Amongst the other inhabitants of the monastery were a local apothecary; the guardian of the place; an old former servant of the monks; and a woman from the mainland who offered to help George Sand with the cooking and domestic work. The sense of isolation felt by the little party, which was heightened by the fact that they had still not received a single letter from Paris, was not unpleasant to them at first.

Although he had recovered slightly from the crisis of the first weeks of December, Chopin was still 'very weak and feeble' at the end of the month, and every time the weather took a turn for the worse his health did too. The combination of illness and surroundings even induced a hallucinatory state, which alarmed George Sand. It was only after spending a couple of weeks at

Valldemosa that she discovered why the whole of Palma did not retire to the mountains during the winter. 'There are rainstorms here that you can have no idea of anywhere else,' she reported to Charlotte Marliani. 'It is a terrifying deluge. The air is so damp that one feels utterly exhausted. I am a mass of rheumatic pains.'[27]

Whenever he was not actually laid out by illness, Chopin worked on the Preludes, writing, as he put it to Fontana, 'in the cell of an old monk, who may have had more fire in his soul than I, but stifled it, stifled and doused it, for he had it in vain'.[28] While there were a thousand irritations and problems to complain about, he felt that 'it all pales into insignificance next to this sky, the poetry with which everything here breathes, next to the colour of these beautiful places still unfathomed by any human eye'.[29] The only thing that did afflict him seriously, as he explained to Grzymała, was to see George Sand 'continually anxious, nursing me (Lord preserve us from the local doctors), making my bed, sweeping my room, brewing infusions, denying herself everything for my sake, with children needing her constant attention . . .'[30] A decade later she wrote that 'the poor great artist was a detestable patient' and claimed he was 'completely demoralised',[31] but at the time she wrote to Charlotte Marliani from the monastery: 'If you knew him as I have got to know him, you would love him even more, my dear,' and called him 'an angel of patience, gentleness and goodness'.[32]

George Sand had taken on great responsibilities. She had to spend part of each day looking to the education of her children, and she had to go on churning out quantities of prose for her expectant editor, as well as catering to all the practical needs of the little group. The maid she had brought with her seems to have been of little use, while the woman who had offered her services, and who had subsequently been joined in this by another local woman and a little girl, turned out to be taking her due (having refused any payment) by scrounging shamelessly, which was particularly galling in view of the difficulty of obtaining victuals.

If the ladies of Palma had decided that the Chopin-Sand party was a little unorthodox, the peasants of Valldemosa found it deeply immoral. As the local *alcalde*, or magistrate, told a Polish traveller who happened to drop in on Valldemosa in January 1839, the foreigners never talked to anyone and never went to church, the young boy went about sketching all day long and the little girl was dressed as a boy. The locals had heard that George Sand herself slept much of the day and spent the nights writing, drinking endless cups of coffee and smoking cigarettes. All this added up to godlessness in their eyes, and her manner was not calculated to breach their prejudice.

Combining financial considerations with those of principle, they began to charge her more for food. She made the mistake of thinking that she could bargain and play one off against the other. Their solidarity proved equal to the test, and they raised their prices to ridiculous levels, refusing to do business except on their own terms. George Sand would never forgive them for the humiliation. In the end she had to buy her own goat in order to have a supply of milk, and dispatched frantic messages to Flury in Palma, who would send his cook out with provisions.

Apart from the irritation, she must have been deeply anxious at finding herself saddled with responsibility for a sick man and two children in an increasingly hostile place, particularly as her financial reserves were dwindling rapidly. Nothing had been cheap on this holiday; even the doctors called in to see Chopin had charged more than the best in Paris. George Sand had soon spent all the money she had brought, and was drawing ever more heavily on her credit at the Canut bank. Chopin's cash too had been whittled away, and to cap it all, the Majorcan customs demanded a duty equivalent to half its value when the Pleyel piano finally arrived in Palma harbour on 21 December.

It took three weeks to strike a bargain with the customs, who finally let it go for half the amount.

The arrival of the piano in mid-January coincided with the sudden appearance of spring, and spirits rose all round. George Sand and her children again went for long walks, while Chopin could sit out in the garden and breathe more easily. Above all he could now get down to work seriously. All but four of the twenty-four Preludes had been more or less finished before his arrival in Palma, and he had somehow managed to write those four (nos 2, 4, 10, 21) using the locally-bought piano, but he could not polish up or revise any of them until he heard them on the Pleyel. A few days after this arrived he was able to send the completed manuscripts off to Fontana. He then finished the Mazurka he had started at S'on Vent, wrote two new Polonaises (op.40) and the F major Ballade, op.38, all of which he sent off before two weeks had elapsed, and started on a new Scherzo (C sharp minor, op.39). Such activity, unusual in Chopin at the best of times, is eloquent evidence of his good spirits.

Just as they were beginning to enjoy life again, and soon after George Sand had written to Charlotte Marliani saying that they had no particular urge or plans to leave, they suddenly made up their minds to go, and go as soon as possible. The reason for this sudden and unwise move remains obscure, as later accounts by George Sand are conflicting.[33] On 11 February 1839, after fifty-six days at the monastery of Valldemosa, they left for Palma, but even on this first lap of the journey its inadvisability became obvious. George Sand had tried to borrow a sprung carriage for the journey down the mountainside, but nobody wished to have to burn theirs after its use by a tuberculotic, with the result that they had to make the nine-mile journey in great heat on a rough cart. On arrival at the lodgings of Flury, who had offered them accommodation while they waited for the *Mallorquin* to sail, Chopin was convulsed with coughing and was spitting blood. After a good night's rest he seemed better, and waited patiently for the next stage of the journey.

George Sand now discovered that the Pleyel piano was liable to draconian export duty, and decided to sell it in Palma. This was no easy matter, for nobody wished to touch an infected piano. Finally the French-born Madame de Canut sold her own and took in Chopin's. Having settled that, they could finally leave, and on 13 February they boarded the *Mallorquin*, only to have another unpleasant surprise. On the passage from Barcelona they had been able to wander about the deck in happy ignorance of the fact that this was reserved, on the return journeys, for the island's principal export – live pigs. Now the party was taken to their cabin and told to remain below deck throughout the voyage. It was a warm night and the airless cabin in which Chopin gasped for breath was filled with the stench of the pigs. There was no question of sleep as the animals had a tendency to seasickness if allowed to remain still, and were therefore periodically chased about the deck.

By the time they sailed into Barcelona, Chopin was haemorrhaging and coughing up 'bowlfuls of blood'. George Sand wanted to take him ashore immediately, but the captain refused to give her one of the boats, which were needed to unload the precious porcine cargo. In despair she tossed a coin and a note to a passing fisherman, begging him to row over to the French brig the *Méléagre*, which was still at anchor in the bay. The captain of the *Méléagre* himself came over in his launch and took the party off the *Mallorquin* to his own ship, whose doctor staunched Chopin's haemorrhaging and sedated him. Before they were put ashore, the doctor examined him thoroughly and diagnosed no disease and no perceptible damage to the lungs, merely stressing that Chopin had a delicate chest which should never be put under undue strain.

In Barcelona, they stayed at a hotel, and it was again necessary to go through the rigmarole of paying in advance for bedding and effects which would have to be destroyed, notwithstanding the French doctor's clean bill of health. Chopin's condition improved markedly during the week they spent there, and on 21 February the whole party was able to board a French ship bound for Marseille. George Sand and her children shouted '*Vive la France!*' as they climbed aboard.[34]

It was not merely the expression of a happy homecoming; a few days before, George Sand had written to Charlotte Marliani that 'one would have to write ten volumes if one wanted to give some idea of the baseness, the bad faith, the egotism, the stupidity and the wickedness of this dumb, thieving and bigoted race'.[35] Even taking into account the possibility that she and Chopin had been trying to keep up their morale while in Majorca, the letters they both wrote from the island tell a very different story from the ones she began writing now. 'Another month in Spain and we should have perished there, Chopin and I; he of melancholy and disgust, I of fury and indignation,' she wrote to Charlotte Marliani. The last week, during which the problems of getting away had culminated in Chopin's seeming brush with death, had made her cup overflow. 'They wounded me in the most sensitive spot in my heart, under my very eyes they pierced a suffering person with pinpricks. I shall never forgive them, and if I ever write about them it shall be with venom.'[36] She was as good as her word. The accounts of the holiday she included in two different books are vitriolic in their description of the Majorcans and wildly exaggerate the conditions on the island.[37]

On 24 February, after a calm passage, their ship docked at Marseille. Chopin was deposited in the competent hands of Dr Cauvière, a friend of the Marlianis', a doctor whose skill and wisdom were further enhanced in George Sand's eyes by the fact that he was an ardent republican. He began with a thorough examination of the sick man, but could find no 'lesions', no 'cavities' and no serious illness of any kind. 'He is nursing him like his own child,' George Sand wrote, 'visits him every morning and every evening, takes him for walks, panders to him and is full of little attentions.'[38]

Chopin's health improved rapidly, but Cauvière made George Sand abandon her original intention, which had been to move out of Marseille and take a house in the country, and later to go to Italy for a couple of months. The doctor insisted that what Chopin needed was a long rest, as his constitution had been weakened by the continuous travelling. So they settled into a hotel close to Cauvière's house, and now George Sand herself found that she was not well at all, for the strain of the last months was beginning to tell. As a result she was quite happy to sit quietly with her 'little Chop'.

After two weeks, Chopin was writing to Grzymała that his health was better: 'vesicatories, diet, pills, baths and the incomparable care of my Angel are slowly putting me back on my feet'.[39] 'I'm much better,' he wrote to Fontana a couple of weeks later. 'I'm starting to play, eat, walk and talk like everyone else.'[40] While George Sand began work on a new novel, Chopin got back to the C sharp minor Scherzo, and to sorting out his finances, which were in a terrible mess. The resulting correspondence affords an insight into the petulant and frequently childish way in which he conducted his financial affairs, and the racial stereotyping to which he was prone.

Before leaving Paris, Chopin had pre-sold the Preludes to Pleyel for 2,000 francs, of which he was advanced five hundred. The agreement included the shipping out of the piano, worth between 1,200 and 1,400 francs. He had also borrowed a thousand francs from Auguste Léo, and another thousand from an unidentified person. The loan from Léo was only supposed to be a short-term one, repayable from the remaining 1,500 to be delivered by Pleyel on receipt of the completed Preludes, which should have reached him long before Christmas. But the delays in finding suitable lodgings and the late arrival of the piano, not to mention Chopin's illness, had wrought havoc with these plans. Léo started clamouring for his money, which elicited the following reaction from Chopin in his letter to Fontana at the end of December:

> *Leo's a Jew! I cannot send you the Preludes, as they're not ready; but I'm better now and will hurry up, and I'll write the Jew a nice letter thanking him, so he feels awful (he can feel what he likes as far as I'm concerned). The crook! And to think that I called on him specially on the eve of my departure... Schlesinger is an even worse dog, to include my Waltzes in an album! and to sell them to Probst* [for Germany] *when out of kindness I had let him have* [the German rights] *for his own father in Berlin – but all these lice don't worry me now. Let Leo rage!*[41]*

By the end of January, Chopin had sent Fontana the completed Preludes, for which Fontana was to collect, after copying them neatly, the remaining 1,500 francs from Pleyel. With this money Fontana was to repay the anonymous creditor and the landlord at the rue de la Chaussée d'Antin. He was then to sell the German rights to Probst for a thousand francs, with which he was to repay Léo. Unfortunately, Pleyel seems to have felt that the 1,500 was in some measure surety for the piano, for which Canut had not yet forwarded the money, and he refused to pay up. This news reached Chopin in Marseille. 'I had not expected such Jewish behaviour from Pleyel,' he wrote to Fontana, and urged him to try to sell the French and English rights to the new Ballade to Pleyel for a thousand francs, and the universal rights to the two Polonaises he had just finished for 1,500 francs.

---

*Chopin's expletives are typical of the unguarded way he wrote to his close friends, and should certainly not be taken, as they might be today, to denote anti-Semitism: the 'Jew' Léo remained one of his closest friends to the end, as did other Jews such as Thomas Albrecht, Meyerbeer, Mendelssohn, Moscheles and so on.

If this could not be done, Fontana was to take the two works to Schlesinger, and not Probst, as Chopin explained:

If we must deal with Jews, let's at least stick to the Orthodox ones. Probst could play some filthy German trick on me – there's no holding him. Schlesinger has always been slippery, but he's made enough money out of me, so he won't refuse to make more; but be polite with him, because the Jew likes to cut a good figure. So, if Pleyel starts making the slightest difficulties, go to Schlesinger and tell him I'll give him the Ballade for France and England for 800, and the Polonaises for France, England and Germany for 1500 (and if he balks at that, let him have them for 1400, 1300, or even 1200). If he mentions the Preludes (I'm sure Probst will have told him about those), tell him that I promised them to Pleyel a long time ago, as he wanted to publish them and begged me before my departure, which was indeed the case. You see, my dearest; I could afford to break with Pleyel for Schlesinger's sake, but not for Probst's . . .[42]

Chopin was upset by the behaviour of Pleyel, who he sensed, rightly, had heard rumours of his illness and wondered whether he would ever return to Paris. 'I'll come back all right, and both he and Leo will get their thanks!' he wrote to Fontana.[43] In the meantime he pinned his hopes on Schlesinger, his usual publisher, a little optimistically as it happened. In a letter to Fontana at the end of March, when everything should have been sorted out, he wrote:

My dearest, since they're such a band of Jews – hold everything, till my return. The Preludes are sold to Pleyel (so far I've received only 500 Frs), so he can wipe the other end of his stomach with them if he chooses, but as for the Ballade and the Polonaises, don't sell them to Schlesinger or Probst.[44]

What Schlesinger had done is not known, but the fact is that the next eight major works by Chopin to appear in Paris (with the exception of the Preludes) were published not by Schlesinger, but by a new publisher called Troupenas, and it was two more years before Schlesinger once again became Chopin's publisher. In the meantime, Chopin had to borrow money from Grzymała and to allow his apartment in the rue de la Chaussée d'Antin to be re-let, and all he could do was rage at people who owed him money, mostly Poles such as Antoni Wodziński.

These were, however, only minor irritations, and they did not manage to cloud the happiness of the months spent in Marseille. The tribulations George Sand and Chopin had been through had served to bring them closer together. Chopin was all admiration for his 'angel', and wrote to Grzymała: 'You would love her even more if you knew her as I now know her.'[45] She, for her part, might easily have grown dissatisfied with the situation, for she was not used to spending so much time with one man. She was also a very physical person who could not have had much satisfaction from Chopin since they had left Paris in the autumn: both his illness and the continual presence of the children would have made intimacy difficult. Yet she found, for the first time in years, that she could still be in love once the initial passion had subsided, and she remained fascinated by this creature, so different from herself.

'Chopin is an angel,' she wrote to Charlotte Marliani. 'His goodness, his tenderness and his patience sometimes make me anxious; I feel that he is too fine, too exquisite, too perfect to live long in this crude and heavy earthly world. In Majorca, when he was mortally ill, he made music which smelt of paradise. But I have grown so used to seeing him in heaven that I do not think life or death means anything to him. He does not really know himself which planet he is on. He has no idea of life as we think of it and as we feel it.'[46] At the same time she sketched out the plan for a new novel, *Gabriel*, whose subject-matter is suggestive – it is about a Renaissance princess brought up as a man, who is in some sphere of the imagination an angel as well as a man and a woman.

It was almost certainly something to do with their relationship that made Chopin write, in a letter to Fontana on 7 March: 'I told you that in my desk, in the first drawer on the side of the door, there was a little note which you, or Jaś, or Grz could open; I now ask you to take it and burn it without breaking the seal or reading it – I beg you on our friendship to do this – the note is now unnecessary.'[47] The fact that the next thought in the characteristically rambling and chaotic letter concerns Antoni Wodziński suggests that the note had something to do with his sister, or at least a subject linked with the thought of her. It looks very much as though Chopin were now definitely burying the past and settling for a life with his new companion.

It was a quiet life, since Chopin was still being kept in by Dr Cauvière and was anyway not tempted by Marseille, which he found ugly. He had to admit to Grzymała that he was a little bored. Another reason for staying at home was the fact that their arrival was something of an event in the life of the city, and they were besieged by 'enthusiasts of literature and music'. Apart from a few of George Sand's friends and a Polish poet who lived nearby, they admitted nobody, but, in the words of George Sand, 'luckily Chop, with his piano, dispels the boredom and brings poetry back into our lodgings'.[48]

While they were still in Marseille, news reached them that Adolphe Nourrit, who had gone to try his luck in Naples after falling from grace with the Paris public, had committed suicide there. This afflicted Chopin deeply, as apart from his friendship for Nourrit, he always responded badly to news of deaths. George Sand tried to make him believe it was just a rumour, but when, a few days later, Madame Nourrit turned up in Marseille with her husband's body, her six children and a seventh in her womb, reality could not be avoided. While she was arranging the funeral service to be held in the cathedral, she asked Chopin if he would play the organ. When this became known, many people turned up in the hope, as George Sand put it, of seeing herself sitting astride the coffin smoking a cigar and of hearing Chopin make the organ explode. They were disappointed, for not only was the organ in poor condition, but Chopin restricted his contribution to one of the Schubert *lieder* the singer had done so much to popularise, 'not with the exalted and glorious tone Nourrit used to lend it, but in a plaintive, soft tone, like the distant echo from another world'.[49]

By the beginning of May Chopin was quite recovered, and as he was getting restless, Cauvière decided that an excursion to Italy was now practicable. The party consequently set off for Genoa, where they spent a couple of weeks sightseeing. Chopin felt well and energetic throughout, and even weathered 'with valour' the storm that caught their ship on the return journey.

After a couple of days at Marseille they set off for George Sand's country house at Nohant, travelling by ferryboat up the Rhône as far as Arles, and thence by easy stages in a carriage. They arrived on 2 June, and Chopin received his first impression of this place which was to play such a large part in his life over the next years. 'We arrived safely,' he wrote to Grzymała, 'lovely countryside, nightingales, larks . . .'[50] 'I hope that a few months of Nohant will have good results,' wrote George Sand, 'and he seems to want to stay here as long as possible. But I shall take him at his word only as long as I see that this place is truly beneficial to him.'[51]

ELEVEN

Conjugal Life

George Sand had inherited Nohant from her father, a Napoleonic cavalry officer descended from an illegitimate daughter of the Maréchal de Saxe, himself a bastard of one of the Saxon kings of Poland. It was a comfortable rather than stylish eighteenth-century manor house standing on the edge of a village, with its own park stretching away on the other side. Not far away the river Indre flowed lazily through the flat landscape, which was beautiful, if a little melancholy.

Chopin was given a sunny room on the first floor with red and blue Chinese wallpaper and windows onto the garden. On one side a door led into a small book-lined study, beyond which was George Sand's bedroom. On the other side of Chopin's bedroom was a small room into which he later moved an upright piano. Life at Nohant was informal and there were no fixed hours. Guests could get up when they liked and have whatever breakfast they wished brought to their room, after which they were free to do as they chose until the bell called them to dinner at six o'clock.

George Sand would spend the night writing. She went to bed at five or six in the morning, and never got up before eleven or noon. She would pay no attention to her guests until dinner, after which she would sit with them until they retired, and then go back to work. Chopin on the other hand was always up early in the morning in order to work, and went to bed early.

'We dine out in the open,' wrote George Sand, 'friends come over, first one, then another, we smoke and talk, and in the evening, when they have gone, Chopin plays to me in the dusk, after which he falls asleep like a child.'[1] Not surprisingly, after only a couple of weeks of this regime, she was able to write to Charlotte Marliani: 'his health improving mightily at Nohant. This life at least seems to be good for him.'[2]

Soon after they arrived, George Sand had called in one of her oldest friends, Dr Papet, to examine Chopin thoroughly. His verdict was that there was no evidence of tuberculosis, only a chronic infection of the larynx, and he was of the opinion that a steady diet, fresh air and a regular, restful life could repair Chopin's constitution, echoing what the doctor on the *Méléagre* and Cauvière had said.

Chopin's medical history has recently absorbed the attention of a number of experts, who have pointed out a glaringly obvious fact hitherto ignored by biographers – namely that not every lapse in the artist's health must be related to one underlying chronic malady. It is, for instance, clear that he suffered from gastro-intestinal problems from an early age. He appears to have been put on a high carbohydrate diet for this reason, and it has been suggested that much of the vomiting on Majorca may have been provoked by his inability to keep down local foods, such as the staple pork. From an early age too, he was subject to severe toothaches, probably caused by abscesses. It has also been suggested that he suffered from various allergies, and a case has been made for his having cystic fibrosis. Given his weak constitution, he would have been prone to every kind of viral infection, and some of his coughing fits were probably just the result of a bad cold.[3]

The lack of consensus about his condition at the time is explained by the existence of two discrete schools of thought on the subject. The southern school, which included Spain, believed, rightly as it happened, in the contagiousness of tuberculosis and diagnosed the disease on the first telling symptoms, which Chopin's condition certainly bore. The other school, which governed French medicine at the time, did not believe in the theory of contagion, and would not accept a diagnosis of tuberculosis until damage to the lungs was detectable. Chopin's appeared to be in good condition. The doctors who examined him did all, however, spot a weakness in the larynx, which seemed to be the main problem at this stage.

There is a strong likelihood that Chopin did have tuberculosis, probably contracted in childhood. At the time, tuberculosis, or pulmonary consumption as it was then generally known, affected one in four of the population in most parts of Europe. It principally attacks the lungs, larynx and glands, but it can take other forms, and is often accompanied by other ailments. It progresses by stages, punctuated by periods of remission during which the patient can appear to have shaken it off entirely. If he did indeed have tuberculosis, Chopin enjoyed a long spell of remission between 1827 and 1835, and although subsequent intervals were usually much shorter, particularly in the later stages, they could still produce quite dramatic improvements. This would explain the disparities in contemporary accounts of his supposed condition – he could appear to be at death's door one moment, and perfectly healthy a few weeks later.

Consumption has a profound effect on the character and behaviour of those it attacks, and has been known to change their nature over a period of time. It tends in the first place to cut them off from others and make them egocentric, sometimes to the point of paranoia. It heightens their sensitivity and sometimes their sexual awareness and appetite. It distorts their mental balance, leading to delusions and violent swings of mood, between depression and euphoria, apathy and excitement, laziness and feverish bouts of work. The outward symptoms include irritability, anxiety, mania and fits of rage. The disease also

179

sometimes compensates for its own depredations, by inducing a state of hallucinatory intoxication at times of great physical suffering, and intensive bursts of creative energy at moments when the patient comes close to death.

It is important to keep all this in mind, for it has direct bearing on a problem which faces the biographer at this point. A couple of weeks after the couple's arrival at Nohant, on 19 June 1839, George Sand took a knife and carved the date on the panelling of her bedroom. In the absence of any similar graffiti, one is led to assume that the date was a significant one from her point of view, and while it could have been something to do with her personal spiritual life, her books or even the date of planting a tree, it has usually been associated with Chopin, and often with the subject of sex. It has been pointed out, quite plausibly, that this could be the anniversary of the consummation of their love – the date would indeed seem to fit. This is no more than speculation, but it is the most reasonable explanation, for this was the first affair she had had which had lasted for a full year without going sour, and it looked like continuing happily for some time to come.

But there is another explanation often put forward: that on this day she decided to stop having sexual relations with Chopin. This is based on her assertion, first made in a letter to Grzymała written many years later, when she was breaking up with Chopin, and reiterated in her *Histoire de ma Vie* (much of which was written under the influence of her son, who did his utmost to expunge everything relating to Chopin from her life), that she stopped having sexual relations with Chopin on account of his poor health, and that their cohabitation over the next eight years was entirely chaste. Neither of these sources can be treated as impartial, and both contain a good many untruths.[4]

Whether Chopin and George Sand did or did not continue to make love, and when, is not something one can pronounce on with any authority. It seems most unlikely that they should have stopped so early in their relationship, and even more so that it should have been done in such a categorical way. The theory that she feared the occasional love-making might kill him holds no water, in view of her own assessment of his health. She believed passionately in natural remedies, and would have been the first to prescribe a healthy bout of sexual activity for the nervous tension and frustration which she held responsible for all his ills.

In *Histoire de ma Vie* she suggests that their relationship was over, and that the last thing she wanted after their return from Majorca was to have Chopin hanging around her. She claims she went along with his wishes out of fear that he might have a breakdown and die if she left him to himself. These sentiments accord ill with her treatment of Musset, whom she dumped in a foreign country while he was dangerously ill in order to run off with his doctor, and of various other lovers before and since. It is absurd to argue that any woman, let alone a woman like George Sand, would allow herself to be blackmailed into the role of titular mistress as well as mother and nurse for eight years to a man she did not love.

At Nohant they settled to a routine which did not allow for much passion, since they were two creative artists absorbed by their work. George Sand was frantically writing new books in order to patch up her finances, while Chopin quickly got down to composing. 'He has already produced some beautiful things since his arrival here,' she wrote in mid-July.[5] Apart from polishing up a few pieces, such as the Mazurka he had written in Palma, he now composed the Scherzo and finale of the B flat minor Sonata, op.35 (the third movement, the famous Funeral March, had been written in 1837), one of his greatest works and a major landmark. He also wrote three new Mazurkas (op.41) and two Nocturnes (op.37). He was pleased with his work, and particularly with the three Mazurkas, 'which I think are pretty, as all new children appear to their ageing parents', as he put it to Fontana.[6] In the afternoons, when he had nothing better to do, he would give piano lessons to Solange, George Sand's eleven-year-old daughter, or else read the score of Bach's *Well-Tempered Clavier*, correcting his edition – 'not just the engraver's mistakes, but also passages accepted by those who claim to understand Bach (not because I pretend to understand him better, but from a feeling that perhaps I can sometimes guess right)'.[7]

In August, Chopin wrote to Fontana that he would not be returning to Paris until the weather changed, as the country air was doing him good. But the moment he felt better, he began to get bored. George Sand saw this coming, and put greater urgency into her invitation to Grzymała to join them. Some relief was provided by the visit of Witwicki, who was spending the summer not far away, but this only lasted a few days. Some of the neighbours who dropped in occasionally provided entertainment, particularly George Sand's half-brother, Hippolyte Châtiron, a rowdy and bibulous country bumpkin whom Chopin took a liking to, but they could not make up for his need of close friends and of Paris.

'Your little one is fair to middling,' George Sand wrote to Grzymała in mid-August. 'I think he needs a little less of the calm, solitude and regularity which country life entails. Who knows, perhaps he needs a little outing to Paris. I am ready to make any sacrifice rather than see him consume himself with melancholy. Come and take the pulse of his morale. Who will ever define the limit between physical illness and moral languor? It is not to me that he will want to admit he is bored. But I think I can guess it.'[8]

Grzymała did come down for a few days at the end of the month, and Chopin cheered up visibly, but after his departure he resumed his former state, 'always a little better or a little worse, never decidedly well nor decidedly ill', as George Sand described it. This does not seem to have been such a bad state, however, for 'when he feels a little stronger he becomes very merry, and when he is feeling melancholy he goes to his piano and composes beautiful pages'.[9] The pages in question were the F sharp major Impromptu, op.36.

In September, George Sand decided that she would have to spend that winter in Paris, since a play of hers had been accepted at the Comédie Française and she wished to supervise its production. It had also become evident that she could no longer go on providing her children's education herself, and this could best be seen to in Paris. Chopin was already looking forward to getting back, because, as George Sand put it, Paris 'is good for his morale, and natures like his need to be surrounded by the refinements of civilisation'.[10] But Chopin's apartment in the rue de la Chaussée d'Antin had been re-let, so he had nowhere to go back to. Grzymała and the unfortunate Fontana were therefore given the task of finding a new one. They were issued with endless instructions as to area, situation, floor, layout and general aspect. The brunt of this task fell on Fontana, who was still wrangling with publishers on Chopin's behalf, and with astonishing speed he found the perfect flat, at No.5 rue Tronchet, just behind the Madeleine. But his duties did not end there. A stream of letters flowed from Nohant, and this one, dated 25 September 1839, is typical:

My Dearest,

Thank you for your kind, friendly, very un-English, very Polish soul [Fontana's admiration for the English and their ways earned him continual jests about his 'Englishness']. *Choose a wallpaper like the dove-coloured one I used to have – only glossy or varnished – for both the rooms, and a not too wide dark green strip for the borders. Get something different for the hall, but make sure it's seemly. If you find something more beautiful; some newer, more fashionable paper which you like and know I would like, take that. I always prefer something smooth, clear and quiet to anything common or vulgar or* <u>grossier</u>. *That's why I prefer pearly colours, they're quiet and*

*not vulgar. Thank you for fixing about the servant's room, I
shall be needing that. As for the furniture, it would be
wonderful if you could take care of that too. Believe me, I
didn't dare to bother you with that problem, but since you're so
kind as to mention it, do collect it and move it in. I'll ask
Grzym to give you money for the moving; I'll write to him
myself. As for the bed and the desk, they ought to be given to
some cabinet-maker to be freshened up. Don't forget to take the
papers out of the desk first – lock them up somewhere. I don't
have to tell you how to do these things. Do whatever you want
and whatever you deem necessary. Whatever you do will be
fine. You have my fullest confidence. That's one thing. Now
something else; you must write to Wessel* [Chopin's London
publisher] *and tell him that I have six new manuscripts, for
each of which I want 300 francs (how many pounds is that?).
Write to him and get an answer. (If you think he won't give
that much, write to me first.) Write and tell me whether Probst
is in Paris. Also try to find me a servant – Perhaps some kind,
decent Pole. Tell Grzymała to look too. He'll have to look after
his own meals and don't offer him more than 80. I shall be in
Paris towards the end of October, not before, keep that to yourself.
The elastic mattress on my bed ought to be repaired, if it's not
too expensive – if it's expensive, leave it. Have the chairs and
things properly beaten and dusted. I don't know why I'm telling
you all this, you know very well what to do. Give my love to Jaś*
[Matuszyński]. *My dearest, I sometimes wonder in my heart –
Let the Lord grant him what is best, but he mustn't let himself
be taken in; although on the other hand . . . Yes, no, I don't
know – That's the greatest Truth on earth! And while it is so, as
it always will be, I shall love you for the kind soul you are, and
Jaś for another. Love to you both. Write. Soon.*

    Your ever longer-nosed

    Ch.[11]

The lack of any attempt at construction and the heavy crossings-out which litter the page make this more of a list of chores than a letter, and it is only one of many such. The letters to Grzymała, though also taking for granted a multitude of favours, presume a little less, and contain the assurance that 'if you need someone to help you or go running about for you, use Fontana. He'll do anything for me, and in business he's as exact as an Englishman.'[12] But Fontana, who was presumably paid for some of his secretarial work, and who depended on Chopin's recommendation for his pupils, seems to have thought nothing of this. Throughout his life Chopin managed to make slaves of his friends, and his behaviour towards them was often that of a spoilt child.

Fontana's prowess in finding a flat for Chopin earned him the task of seeking accommodation for George Sand, who intended to set up house in Paris along with her son Maurice – Solange was to go to boarding school. Again he was sent detailed instructions, including a sketch showing the desired layout of the rooms, and again he acquitted himself well. He found two small pavilions in a garden courtyard just off the rue Pigalle, in a newly built area in what was then the northern suburb of Paris. One of the pavilions was for George Sand, while the other could accommodate Maurice, his studio (he wished to take up painting) and the servants she would bring from Nohant.

Once the apartments had been found and the furniture moved, Fontana was sent scurrying around the tailors and hatters of the capital, as Chopin suddenly realised that, having been away for a whole year, most of his wardrobe would be out of fashion. It was only after this that the poor factotum was given his final instructions. 'And since you're so good at all these things,' Chopin wrote, 'arrange the apartment so that I should get no sombre thoughts in it, and no fits of coughing – and set it up so that I should be good – and don't forget to have them sweep out many episodes from my past. And, if you can manage it, I would like to find the next few years' work finished and waiting for me.'[13]

But when he did return, on 10 October 1839, the work loomed before him. News of his arrival had spread, and within a couple of days he was besieged by would-be pupils. Nor had Fontana been able to sweep out the past as thoroughly as Chopin would have wished.

George Sand and Chopin had told few people of their plans before leaving Paris for Majorca, but a good many knew anyway, and there was no particular attempt at keeping their journey secret. Charlotte Marliani could not resist showing around some of the letters she received from Majorca, so while the travellers spent months without any news from Paris, most of Paris was well informed of their movements. At the beginning of January, Berlioz was remarking in a letter to Liszt that 'Chopin is ill in the Balearic Islands', and a couple of months later he was writing to Chopin in Marseille to find out whether he was still alive, as by then rumour had it that he was dying.[14] The susceptible and fastidious Chopin, who might well have been anxious about all the publicity afforded to his relationship with France's most scandalous woman and about the consequences this might have on his relations with Parisian society, was remarkably un-worried. 'I am not surprised at the various tales; you must realise that I knew I should be exposing myself to them,' he wrote to Fontana, who faithfully reported everything. 'Anyway, it will all pass, tongues will rot, and nothing can touch our souls.'[15] He was right, for the gossip did not affect his standing in Paris or his peace of mind. What did was the vindictiveness of Marie d'Agoult, who had reappeared on the scene.

She had last seen George Sand at Nohant in the summer of 1837, a full year before the beginning of her liaison with Chopin, which she had done so much to encourage. The leave-taking between the two ladies had been edifyingly tearful, and vows of mutual esteem and love had been exchanged as the Countess set off for Italy with Liszt. The vows had been false on both sides.

George Sand was about to give Balzac all the material he needed for a novel which she could not afford to write herself: when his *Béatrix* came out in the spring of 1839, it was widely recognised as a portrait of the Liszt–Agoult affair. The Countess's defects were depicted with a venomous insight which many realised could not have been Balzac's. 'Now I've really managed to set the two females at each other's throats!' the delighted novelist exclaimed to Bernard Potocki at the opera one night a few weeks later.[16] In fact, he had only added fuel to a fire that was already smouldering.

While continuing to write sugary letters full of love and devotion to George Sand, Marie d'Agoult had begun to spread unflattering gossip about her. Somewhat unwisely, she vented her spite and dislike of George Sand in her letters to Charlotte Marliani, who lapped these up with delight, at the same time notifying George Sand that there were 'murky plots and foul betrayal' being stirred up against her.[17] Eager to lend a note of morality to the intrigue, she showed the letters to the abbé de Lamennais, who was horrified and suggested that George Sand break off all relations with the Countess and ignore her letters.

Marie d'Agoult's relationship with Liszt had in the meantime begun to founder, and in the summer of 1839 (while Chopin was at Nohant) they decided to part; he to go on a performing tour, she to return to Paris. In order to make her life there bearable, she would have to be on good terms with George Sand. She did not know that Charlotte Marliani had talked, but realised that something was wrong, since George Sand had not answered her last few letters. She decided to brazen it out, and therefore struck a righteous note in her next letter. 'I cannot really believe that you have anything to complain of in my behaviour,' she wrote. 'I have searched my conscience and can find no shadow of guilt on my side. Franz too is wondering how it is that your close connection with a man he feels he has the right to call his friend should have had the immediate result of breaking off all communication between us . . .'[18]

The Countess's truculence had a great deal to do with the fact that the Sand-Chopin ménage appeared to be flourishing while hers was not. It was she who had sacrificed everything to go and live with her pianist, but she had been disappointed in Liszt, who instead of sitting quietly in Olympus with her writing masterpieces, insisted on following the career of performing musician; in many respects George Sand's pianist would have suited her better.

George Sand felt inclined to ignore her peace-making approaches, but the Countess carried on her bluff when she came back to Paris in October, telling everyone that George Sand had wronged her and dropped her, and that this was not unconnected with Chopin's jealousy of Liszt as a pianist. George Sand realised that she would have to do something, for as she explained to Charlotte Marliani, Chopin's 'pride would prevent him from offering any explanation of his own behaviour, and if this were not demanded of him, which is possible (my silence being equivalent to an admission of guilt), he will have earned the bitterness of Liszt and the hatred of Madame d'Agoult'. She felt obliged to shield Chopin from the fallout of the Countess's wrath. 'Knowing her, she would provoke embarrassments and ructions which he can do without – he is so nervous, so discreet, so exquisite in all things.'[19]

Marie d'Agoult complained that she had been a victim of malevolent slanders, and wrote imploring letters to George Sand full of protestations of innocence. 'George, once again, for the last time!' she insisted. 'You are wandering in a labyrinth of gossip, where I shall not follow you. In the name of Heaven . . .'[20]

Her lofty tone faltered when she discovered that the source of the 'gossip' was her own letters, which Charlotte Marliani had by now handed over to George Sand. There was an icy moment on 13 November when the two women came face to face in the Marliani drawing room, but by now Marie d'Agoult was as eager to save her face as George Sand was to put an end to the whole business. A private interview was arranged, after which the two ladies publicly advertised their renewed friendship.

The Countess proceeded to take the war underground: she kept up a sustained flow of vituperative gossip about George Sand, and worked hard to drive a wedge between Chopin and Liszt. At the beginning of November, for instance, she informed Liszt that Chopin and Berlioz disapproved of his tour of Austria and thought him ridiculous (her own opinion was that he was behaving like a mountebank). A few days later, she wrote that Grzymała and Chopin were being 'rude' and ostracising her, a week or two later again that Chopin was behaving fatuously, 'like an oyster sprinkled with sugar'.[21] She informed Liszt that 'Chopin, whom you were naïve enough to regard as a friend', had not had the decency to call on her, even though the whole of Paris knew Liszt was ill and that only she had news of him. She went on to say that in view of all this there was only one option open to them: to collect their allies and declare open war on the Chopin-Sand coterie as soon as Liszt returned to Paris in the spring.

Luckily for everyone involved, Liszt had no intention of being placed in a foolish situation by his former mistress, and was seriously alarmed at the confrontation she was trying to bring about between him and Chopin. He therefore humoured her, assuring her that she was a far greater personality than George Sand, and made light of Chopin's behaviour. 'I wouldn't like you to take Chopin's rudeness too seriously,' he wrote soothingly. 'I should think that by now you have punished him enough for it. You know what a deplorable influence the Piffoëllic bedlam can have. One must not blame Chopin too much for his gaucherie. Sharper men than he (though he is very, and above all would like to be thought infinitely, sharp) have lost their bearings in it.'[22]

He managed to rein in the Countess, but could not stop her from gossiping and making trouble at every opportunity, for she was now desperate. Far from bringing Liszt any closer to her, as she had hoped, the whole episode put him off and had the effect of isolating her in Parisian society. And while she predicted that George Sand was about to jilt Chopin and 'take her lofty sentiments elsewhere', her efforts only served to bring the two closer together and to make them avoid her.[23]

'I never see Chopin at all,' Stephen Heller, a Hungarian pianist just arrived in Paris, wrote to Schumann in January 1840. 'He's up to his ears in the aristocratic swamp . . . he prefers exalted salons to lofty mountaintops.'[24] This was actually less true than ever during this season. Chopin was working hard at his lessons, giving up to eight a day, which sometimes exhausted him, but only physically. 'Feeble, pale, coughing much, he often took opium drops with sugar or drank gum-water, rubbed his fore-head with eau de cologne, and nevertheless taught with a patience, perseverance and zeal which were admirable,' as Friederike Müller, a new pupil, related.[25]

He also saw a good deal of the other musicians in Paris, and we know that he drove out to Passy to see Rossini, with whom he discussed the music of Bellini, whom they both admired. And that season, with the arrival in Paris of Moscheles, he was able to at last meet one of the musicians he had admired from his earliest years, and whose works he had been brought up on. Chopin's opinion had undergone some change, but he still regarded him highly. Moscheles, for his part, was a little perplexed by Chopin's music, and was keen to meet the man. He had been told by Mendelssohn, with whom he was in close touch, of Chopin's importance, but still had reservations. 'I am a declared admirer of his genius; he has given to pianists everything that is most novel, most enchanting,' he noted in his diary *à propos* of the second set of Études (op.25), but went on to say that, try as he might, he simply could not play them.[26] 'On the whole I find his music too sweet, not manly enough, and hardly the work of a profound musician,' he wrote to Mendelssohn, adding that there was much in Chopin that appeared 'unscholarlike' to him.[27]

The idea that music must be manly and scholarly might seem curious, but it was rooted in the German Romantic tradition, which endowed it with a degree of sanctity. There was a feeling in Germany, echoed to some extent in England, that the music emanating from Paris was both lightweight and somehow disreputable. Mendelssohn's opinion of Berlioz, for instance, was that 'his orchestration is such a frightful muddle, such an incongruous mess, that one ought to wash one's hands after handling one of his scores'.[28] Moscheles' and Mendelssohn's opinions of Liszt were not dissimilar. Mendelssohn described his manner as 'a perpetual fluctuation between scandal and apotheosis'; Moscheles considered him scruffy and inartistic; while Schumann felt that there was 'too much tinsel' about his playing.[29]

When he finally met Chopin, at the house of Auguste Léo in mid-October 1839, Moscheles must have had something of a shock: however much he might have matured musically, Chopin was still prone to childish pranks, and treated Moscheles to hilarious impersonations of Pixis and Liszt.[30] But when he heard Chopin play, he forgot his reservations. 'He played to me at my request and now for the first time I understand his music, and can also explain to myself the enthusiasm of the ladies,' Moscheles wrote in his diary. 'His *ad libitum* playing, which, with the interpreters of his music degenerates into disregard for time, is with him only the most charming originality of execution; the dilettante-like hard modulations which strike me disagreeably when I am playing his compositions no longer shock me, for he glides lightly over them in a fairy-like way with his delicate fingers; his *piano* is so softly breathed forth that he does not need any strong *forte* in order to produce the wished-for contrasts. It is for this reason that one does not miss the orchestra-like effects which the German school demands of the pianoforte-player, but allows oneself to be carried away, as by a singer who, little concerned by the accompaniment, entirely follows his feeling. In short, he is unique in the world of pianists.'[31]

The two composers saw much of each other during the next weeks, often playing together at soirées. As a result, it was together that they were asked to go and play to the royal family at Saint-Cloud on 29 October. They were fetched by the comte de Perthuis, the Director of the King's Music, who drove them out to the palace. The command performance is described by Moscheles with characteristic preciousness:

We passed through many state rooms into a salon carré *where the Royal Family were assembled* en petit comité. *At a round table sat the Queen, an elegant work-basket before her; beside her were Madame Adelaide, the Duchesse d'Orléans, and ladies-in-waiting. The noble ladies were as affable as though we had been old acquaintances. Chopin played first a number of Nocturnes and Studies, and was admired and petted like a favourite. After I had also played some old and new Studies, and had been honoured with similar applause, we seated ourselves together at the instrument – he again playing the bass, which he always insists on doing. The close attention of the little circle during my E flat major Sonata was interrupted only by the exclamations: 'Divine! Delicious!' After the Andante the Queen whispered to a lady-in-waiting: 'Would it be indiscreet to ask them to play it again?' This was naturally equivalent to a command to repeat it, so we played*

it again with increased abandon. In the finale we gave ourselves
up to musical delirium. Chopin's enthusiasm throughout the piece
must, I think, have affected the listeners, who now burst forth into
eulogies. Chopin again played alone with the same charm and
called forth the same sympathy as before.[32]

A few days later Chopin received a handsome piece of Sèvres
porcelain, while Moscheles was presented with an elegant
travelling case, which, Chopin is supposed to have quipped,
was a hint for him to go.

Chopin himself did not take part in any concerts that season,
and does not seem to have gone to many either. He went to
the Italian opera with Custine, and was present at Charles
Hallé's first public concert, in which Franchomme took part,
but more often than not he would drive round to the rue Pigalle
when his lessons were over and while away the evening with
George Sand. Her lodgings there are described by Balzac, in a
letter to his Polish mistress:

She lives at No.16 rue Pigalle, at the end of a garden, over the
carriage-house and stables of a house which looks onto the street.
She has a dining room furnished with carved oak, her little salon
is mushroom-coloured, and the sitting room in which she receives
is garnished with superb Chinese vases full of flowers. There is
always a jardinière full of flowers; the furnishings are green; there
is a dresser full of curiosities; paintings by Delacroix, her portrait
by Calamatta . . . the piano is magnificent, upright, square, of
rosewood. Chopin is always there . . . She only gets up at four
o'clock, and at four o'clock Chopin has finished giving his lessons.
One goes up to her room by a ladder staircase, steep and straight.
Her bedroom is brown, her bed consists of two mattresses on the
floor, Turkish style . . . There is a portrait of [Grzymała] in Polish
Castellan's costume in the dining room.[33]

Grzymała was one of the habitués of the rue Pigalle, along with Delacroix; Sand's friend the lawyer Emmanuel Arago; Marie Dorval, the actress with whom she was thought to have had sapphic relations; and Pauline Garcia-Viardot, the renowned nineteen-year-old singer whom George Sand had 'adopted' and around whose person she was constructing her new novel, *Consuelo*. The informal way of life at the rue Pigalle was congenial to Chopin, and he soon moved in himself. He would use his apartment in the rue Tronchet for lessons and for receiving visits, and occasionally entertained there in the evenings, but otherwise he was to be found at the rue Pigalle, where he usually slept. This had obvious advantages for both of them. When Chopin fell ill again in April with a sudden pain which attacked him in the middle of the night, George Sand was able to help. She did not like the idea of Matuszyński continuing to treat him, and called in a French doctor.

Matuszyński was himself slowly dying of tuberculosis and was convinced that Chopin had the disease, but George Sand felt he was wrong. The symptoms of this particular crisis involved no coughing or spitting blood, merely a cramp-like pain in the chest which restricted his breathing but did not otherwise affect him. The new doctor, Gaubert, prescribed a regime of soothing potions, morning and evening chest rubs, and the avoidance of all emotional agitation.[34]

But it was not easy keeping Chopin tranquil. The crisis prevented him from attending the concert on 20 April 1840 given by Liszt, who had turned up in a conciliatory mood. Chopin, whose reservations about Liszt had matured, wanted to keep up appearances, and was seriously upset at not being able to go. 'With my health one cannot do anything,' he told one of his pupils on this occasion. 'It is very annoying – I don't have the time to be ill!'[35]

The living arrangements suited George Sand as well: Chopin, 'the gentlest, the most modest, the most hidden of all men of

genius', was rarely in her way.[36] Moreover, his presence represented a certain security and support to her. 'Without his perfect
and delicate friendship I would often lose heart,' she wrote to
her half-brother Hippolyte, as the problems of staging her play
loomed before her.[37] Chopin also provided both the excuse and
the means for her to grow out of the affectation and licentious-
ness which had characterised her life during the 1830s. She had
for some time felt a need to settle down, but the lack of a suitable companion had condemned her efforts to failure. When
they came together she was still, with her philandering and her
fantastic clothes, an object of scandal in many quarters. After a
year or so with Chopin, she was rarely to be seen in anything
but the simplest grey or black dresses, and her behaviour had
grown more dignified. The restrained and scandal-free life she
led with him over the next few years silenced the gossips and
effaced her old reputation for nymphomania.

They continued to lead their own lives, often going out in-
dependently in the evenings, but in time they pooled their
friends, and Chopin soon found that people as respectable as
the Czartoryskis and as fastidious as Custine accepted George
Sand wholeheartedly. To begin with, however, this was of scant
importance to Chopin, who was happy to bask in the family
atmosphere of the rue Pigalle and to leave Parisian society to
itself. George Sand's play *Cosima* was staged at the end of the
season, which involved both of them (the only surviving note
between Chopin and Donizetti is one by the Italian begging
for a ticket). The play was a resounding flop, so George Sand
could not afford to open her house at Nohant for the summer
of 1840. Instead, she remained in Paris, only leaving for a week
in August in order to accompany Pauline Viardot on a concert
tour. Chopin felt even this short absence, and was clearly as
lost without her as her son Maurice, who wrote: 'Chopinet and
I spend the evenings staring at each other by the light of two
candle ends.'[38]

Chopin got on well with the seventeen-year-old Maurice, a somewhat effete and dim boy who was studying painting under Delacroix, but he preferred the twelve-year-old Solange, a difficult, turbulent girl who was not her mother's favourite and felt it, particularly now that she had been confined in a boarding school. Chopin often took her out at weekends and, along with Delacroix and Grzymała, spoilt her.

Chopin must have been a welcome addition to the household as far as the two children were concerned, for he was good company and was always prepared to amuse them by his acts and conjuring tricks, or by teaching them Polish tongue-twisters. They would make fun of his accent and his bad grammar, and would sign their names 'Solangska Sandska', or write notes in a pastiche of Polish, like 'Salutxi a Grrrzzziiimalla, quilski ne courski paska les filleski [*Saluts à Grzymała, qu'il ne courre pas les filles*].'[39] The atmosphere at the rue Pigalle is caught in a vignette drawn by George Sand in a letter written that September:

> *This morning we have acquired a delightful little puppy, no bigger than a fist, dark brown, with a white waistcoat, white stockings in front and white shoes on the hind legs. This gentleman followed Chopin in the street, and simply would not leave him. Then, o miracle! Chopin took the little dog in adoration and has spent the whole day looking after it, even though it did its 'something' in the drawing room and gave us all fleas. Chopin finds this charming, mainly because the dog is all over him and cannot stand Solange. Solange is fiercely jealous. At this moment the little thing is sleeping at my feet. It has been called Mops, which is, quite simply, the Polish for Pug.*[40]

The 1840–41 season held few attractions for Chopin, with the notable exception of Pauline Viardot's concert at the Conservatoire on 7 February 1841, an event he would never have missed. And he did not compose much himself. His output for the whole of 1840 consisted of three Waltzes, one Song and a Polonaise (F sharp minor, op.44), which compares poorly with that of other years. This was not the result of indolence or lack of inspiration.

This period was a breathing space during which he, as it were, collected his thoughts before embarking on the final and greatest stage of his work as a composer, and the group of intellectuals and artists that gathered round George Sand in the rue Pigalle probably played a part in this process. Although no great talker herself, she had a way of creating discussion around her. 'She's a good listener,' remarked Heine, while Liszt apparently felt that his ability to listen and absorb what people were saying made them more eloquent.[41] George Sand was interested in music and in the interrelationship between the arts, which were well represented by the various members of the group, and the talk dwelt compulsively on these subjects. As far as Chopin was concerned, the most interesting members of the group were Pauline Viardot and Eugène Delacroix.

Pauline Viardot was not yet twenty years old, and came from an exceptionally gifted family, which included the famous singer Maria Malibran, her elder sister. When Liszt had met her as a young girl he had wanted to make a pianist of her, while her gift for drawing suggested to others that she should have become a painter. She was intelligent and well educated, and this, according to some, enhanced her magnificent singing voice: she could give new depth to an operatic role or a song. Chopin had from his earliest years been fascinated by the human voice, in which he recognised the most perfect instrument of all, and in Pauline Viardot he found not only one of the greatest voices of the century, but also a musician of refinement and intelligence. He spent a great deal of time listening and talking to her, and helped her compose songs of her own. When he felt uninspired and bored, he would long for her company, as he claimed she could 'restore his musical faculty'.

Equally interesting as an influence on Chopin is Delacroix. Chopin had met him half a dozen years before and had occasionally run across him in Paris over the next years, although the painter was rarely seen in society. Delacroix was a friend and admirer of George Sand, and consequently Chopin began to see a great deal of him after the beginning of their liaison. Delacroix was immediately struck by Chopin's genius, but his admiration was not reciprocated. Chopin had little sympathy for the exuberance and daring of Delacroix's work, and it is likely that the reason the joint Chopin-Sand portrait was never finished was that he did not like it. The two men nevertheless became friends.

Like Chopin, Delacroix was reserved, discreet and fastidious – they were forever exchanging names of tailors and bootmakers, and Delacroix's collection of waistcoats was as legendary as Chopin's of gloves – and like Chopin he cultivated refinement of manners in himself and others. In his youth he had wanted to be a violinist, and throughout his life he remained fascinated by music, holding the same unfashionable views on it as Chopin, liking Haydn, Mozart and Bach better than Beethoven, and only acknowledging Bellini and Rossini amongst his contemporaries.

In 1840, Delacroix was forty-two years old and was embarking on a new stage in his career: he had recently been given a series of commissions for the large ceilings of public buildings, and this imposed on him a different approach to painting. He abandoned the spontaneity of his earlier Romantic style, studied the painters of the past more closely, grew more controlled in form and more intense in his use of colour, and sought a higher philosophical and aesthetic order and harmony. He also began to develop theories on the relationship between the artist and his instrument and that between the various forms of art. Like Heine, he saw Chopin as the quintessential artist, rather than just as a musician, and he was fascinated by the mixture of spontaneous creation and controlled purpose in Chopin's improvisations.

There is no clue as to what Chopin made of Delacroix's ideas. George Sand's accounts of conversations between them smack much more of her own idea of the two artists than of their actual opinions. What is certain is that the two did talk a great deal about art and music, and that this exchange ushered in a new phase of work for both of them. The year of 1840, which Delacroix spent in getting to grips with his developing ideas on form and expression, was almost fallow for Chopin. But the F sharp minor Polonaise (op.44), written towards the end of it, took him firmly into the last span of his creative life. It clearly belongs to Chopin's most mature period, during which he displayed many of the same tendencies as Delacroix: his music grew more dramatic and intense, and at the same time more controlled and subtle in form. The next few years were to see the birth of the great Polonaises, the Barcarolle and most of his greatest masterpieces.

TWELVE

The Church of Chopin

'A great, grrrreat Piece of news is that little Chip-Chip is going to give a grrrreat concert,' George Sand wrote to Pauline Viardot on 18 April 1841.[1] The next day, Marie d'Agoult wrote to a friend: 'A small malevolent coterie is trying to resuscitate Chopin, who is going to play at Pleyel's.'[2] The idea had indeed come from a group of friends, and Chopin had resisted it vigorously. He had only fallen in with it, according to George Sand, because he was certain that the various difficulties of arranging the event would eventually induce them to drop the plan, and he tried to cancel it when he realised that Pauline Viardot would be unable to take part. But things moved quicker than he expected, and in a couple of days everything had been prepared, while three-quarters of the tickets had been sold before the concert had even been announced in the press.

'He then awoke as from a dream,' writes George Sand, 'and there can be no funnier spectacle than the meticulous and irresolute Chip-Chip obliged not to change his mind any more. This Chopinesque nightmare will take place in Pleyel's Salons on the 26th. He doesn't want any posters, he doesn't want any programmes, he doesn't want anyone to talk about it. He is afraid of so many things that I have suggested he play without candles, without an audience on a mute piano.'[3] It was only by retiring to his room and playing Bach fugues that he was able to calm his nerves.[4]

On 26 April Delacroix came to collect George Sand and drove with her to the Salle Pleyel, where they found an audience of some three hundred people filling the hall, most of them friends or acquaintances. The scene is described by Liszt in his review of the concert:

At eight o'clock in the evening, the Salons of M. Pleyel were splendidly illuminated. At the foot of a staircase covered with carpets and perfumed with flowers, numerous carriages continuously deposited the most elegant women, the most famous artists, the wealthiest financiers, the most illustrious aristocrats, a whole elite of society, a whole aristocracy of birth, fortune, talent and beauty. A grand piano stood open on the podium, the places closest to it were universally coveted, ears were strained in advance, people recollected themselves, telling themselves that they must not miss a single chord, a single note, a single intention, a single idea of the one who would come and seat himself there. And they were right to be so avid, so attentive, so religiously moved, for the one they awaited, the one they were going to see, hear, admire, applaud, was not just an able virtuoso, a pianist expert in the art of making notes; he was not merely an artist of great renown, he was all of that, and much more than that – he was Chopin![5]

In this courtly atmosphere, Chopin was able to have things his own way in another sense. He played a selection of Mazurkas and Preludes, after which Madame Cinti-Damoreau sang a couple of pieces. He then played a duo with the violinist Heinrich Wilhelm Ernst, and finished with more of his own works. This was a far cry from the variegated programme, with a dozen or so heterogeneous artists taking part, which was still the accepted form. This was a recital: Chopin used a singer only in order to provide himself with a breathing space. The only precedent was a series of recitals Liszt had given in Rome the previous year, which he had called 'soliloquies' rather than concerts.

The reviews were unanimous in their praise. *Le Ménestrel* asserted that in Chopin 'heart and genius alone speak, and in these respects his talent has nothing to learn'.[6] *La France Musicale* acclaimed him as the creator of a school of piano-playing and of composition, and added that he 'should not and cannot be compared with anyone'.[7] The reviewers wrote of him as though he had already been transported to Parnassus.

'A complete silence of criticism had already established itself around his reputation, as though posterity had already arrived,' wrote Liszt in the *Gazette Musicale*, 'and in the brilliant audience which came running to hear the poet too long silent, there was no reservation, no hesitation; every mouth had only praise.'[8] This was not strictly speaking true: a particularly rude intrusion into the silence was to be made later that same year by the critic of the *Musical World* of London in a review of some newly published Mazurkas. 'Mr Frederick Chopin has, by some means or other which we cannot divine, obtained an enormous reputation, a reputation but too often refused to composers of ten times his genius,' he wrote. 'Mr Chopin is by no means a putter-down of commonplaces; but he is, what by many would be esteemed worse, a dealer in the most absurd and hyperbolical extravagances.' The critic went on to call him 'very crude and limited', termed his harmonies 'clumsy', his melodies 'sickly', and concluded by stating that 'The entire works of Chopin present a motley surface of ranting hyperbole and excruciating cacophony.'[9] Nor could he resist asking how George Sand could be 'content to wanton away her dreamlike existence with an artistic nonentity like Chopin'.

He was by no means the only one in England who found Chopin difficult to accept. One Victorian writer on the subject declared that the Nocturnes 'bewitch and unman'; another assured his readers that the Polonaise-Fantaisie 'on account of its pathological contents, stands outside the sphere of art'. An early biographer warned the public against the B flat minor

Sonata (the one which contains the famous Funeral March), stating that 'the music grows more and more passionate and in the concluding portion transcends the limits of propriety'.[10]

Chopin's music was utterly revolutionary and quite unlike anything being written at the time. Parisians, whether they were musicians or music-lovers, were better prepared to confront such modern works, for they lived in a world where the frontiers of novelty were continually being expanded. But people used to the more traditional musical fare of England or Germany found it deeply unsettling. Even Schumann, who admired Chopin greatly, was driven to question whether the B flat minor Sonata was actually music or not.[11]

That very year, while reviewing the two Nocturnes (op.37), Schumann exhorted Chopin to write a grand work such as a symphony in order to achieve greater effect than he was doing.[12] As Elsner had pointed out to Chopin years before, a piece for piano compared to a piece for orchestra was like an engraving compared to an oil painting.[13] What they were really saying was that they wanted him to work in more conventional ways.

Liszt, who understood him better, explains that Chopin was unable to achieve perfection in any form that he had not himself created, which is why, he argues, his Sonatas and Concertos are less successful than his Polonaises, Mazurkas and Ballades. 'If Chopin never tried his hand at symphonic music in any of its forms, it was because he did not wish to,' he writes. 'It was not out of some extreme modesty or misplaced disdain; it was the pure and simple consequence of the form which suited his sentiment best.'[14]

'But,' according to Liszt, 'that which for anyone else would have been a certain cause of total oblivion and obscurity, was exactly what assured him a reputation above the caprice of fashion, and what sheltered him from rivalry, jealousy and injustice.'[15] Even Schumann, who did not condone the direction in which Chopin now began to move, wrote, in 1840, that 'by now Chopin does not write anything which could as well come from another; he remains faithful to himself, and he has good reason for this'.[16]

As Debussy was later to point out, 'by the very nature of his genius, Chopin eludes all attempts at classification',[17] and that particular genius, one might almost say that particular and highly personal art form that Chopin had developed, elicited a strong response throughout Europe, and particularly in France, where the decline of the exuberant Romanticism of the 1830s had left something of a void.

The craftsmanship of Chopin, which had been outshone in the Paris of the 1830s by Meyerbeer, Rossini, Liszt and Berlioz, now appeared to many as the ultimate in artistry, and seemed to embody something more essential than the bombast of the previous decade. The result was that, as Liszt explains, 'in those days it was not so much the school of Chopin as the Church of Chopin'.[18] '[Liszt] is the Paganini of the pianoforte,' wrote Balzac, 'but Chopin is totally superior to him.'[19] In his novel *Ursule Mirouet*, Balzac described Chopin as not merely a musician but an artist with a heightened gift for expressing the lyricism in his soul.[20] It was no coincidence that Custine, in the note he sent Chopin after another concert, spoke of his playing not a piano, but 'the soul itself', or that Delacroix called his music 'nourishment for the soul'.[21]

Fifty years later, the archetype of the late Romantic musician, Anton Rubinstein, could not help wondering: 'Was it the piano that gave him the soul? Or was it Chopin who transferred his soul to the keyboard? I do not know; but his works could only have arisen from total absorption of one by the other . . . Chopin truly was the soul of the piano.'[22] Heine, whose position as a baptised Jew and an émigré from Germany made him sensitive on such points, discovered in Chopin a purer and therefore more universal artist than any other. 'Yes, one must admit that

Chopin has genius in the fullest sense of the word,' he mused; 'he is not only a virtuoso, he is also a poet; he can embody the poetry which lives within his soul; he is a tone-poet, and nothing can be compared to the pleasure he gives when he sits down at the piano and improvises. He is then neither a Pole, nor a Frenchman, nor a German, he reveals then a higher origin, one perceives then that he comes from the land of Mozart, Raphael and Goethe, his true fatherland is the dream-world of poetry . . .'[23] Only in the light of such judgements can one understand the religious enthusiasm with which Chopin's concert in the Salle Pleyel had been greeted. The public knew what they were coming for, and they got it; the press merely marked the event with appropriate solemnity.

There had been no comparable ceremony attendant on the event which took place on the day before at the Conservatoire – Liszt's concert to raise money for a monument to Beethoven, in which he had played and Berlioz had conducted a performance of the Pastoral Symphony. The very different trajectory of these two giants of the keyboard is telling. Liszt was growing more and more overtly political, making patriotic tours of Hungary and delivering speeches at public events. 'Liszt is bound to become a deputy – or maybe even a King in Abyssinia or the Congo,' Chopin quipped in a letter to Fontana, 'but as for the themes of his compositions, they will lie forgotten.'[24]

The moral victory implicit in Chopin's recital was accompanied by material satisfaction, for, as George Sand wrote to her half-brother, 'Chopin has put himself in the position of being able to loaf all summer, by giving a concert where, in a period of two hours, with a couple of flourishes of the hand, he put six thousand and several hundred francs in his pocket, amid applause, encores and the flutterings of the most beautiful women in Paris – The Rascal!'[25] These sentiments were echoed by Witwicki, who had also been present. 'You just try and recite your verse for a couple of hours and see if they give you six thousand francs!' he wrote to a fellow poet.[26]

There was now nothing to stop Chopin accompanying George Sand to Nohant, where he hoped to be able to get down to his much-neglected compositions. He had plenty of ideas and rough sketches, but in Paris he could never achieve the degree of concentration or find the time to turn these into finished works, a process which he was finding more and more strenuous, as one of his pupils describes:

> The other day I heard Chopin improvise at George Sand's. It is marvellous to hear him compose in this way; his inspiration is so immediate and complete that he plays without hesitation, as though it had to be thus. But when it comes to writing it down and recapturing the original thought in all its details, he spends days of nervous strain and almost frightening desperation. He alters and retouches the same phrases incessantly and walks up and down like a madman.[27]

Nohant provided the perfect conditions for this torment. Only ten days after his arrival there at the beginning of June, Chopin was able to send Fontana the first completed work, the Tarantella (op.43). This was followed over the next two months by a Prelude, two Nocturnes, and, most important, the A flat Ballade (op.47) and the Fantaisie in F minor (op.49). These 'cobwebs and manuscriptical flies' as he called his manuscripts, which did admittedly sometimes resemble the peregrinations of a spider through a series of ink drops, were dispatched to Fontana for copying with the apology that 'the weather is beautiful and my music horrible'.[28]

The weather was indeed fine that summer, and Chopin's health was good as a result. 'But as he is still at least ten years too young to be a really good boy,' wrote George Sand, 'he often gets bored in this happy state and thinks he is being idle since he is not crushed by work.'[29] It was not just boredom that made Chopin fear inactivity, but also a sort of nervous restlessness which manifested itself from the moment he arrived at Nohant, in the first place through a stream of finicky letters to Fontana asking him to procure quantities of things, most of which were declared to be unnecessary in the next letters. The following is an example:

My Dearest,

I enclose a hundred francs for various expenses, from which you can subtract what I owe you for the <u>Charivari</u> [a French satirical magazine], *pay the rent, pay the postman for my letters, the flower-woman, who wants six. At Houbigant Chardin of Faubourg St Honoré you can buy me some benjoin soap, two pairs of Swedish gloves (take an old one from somewhere for the size), a bottle of patchouli, and a bottle of Bouquet de Chantilly. In the Palais Royal, in the gallery on the same side as the theatres, almost in the centre, you will find a shop with galanteria (as we say in Poland); it has two windows filled with various caskets, jokes, gifts, gleaming, elegant and expensive. There you can ask if they don't have any ivory head-scratchers; you must know the kind; a white curled hand set on a black stick. I think I saw one like it there – ask them. Find one and send it to me, but don't spend more than 10, 15, 20 or 30. Get Pleyel to give you a copy of my Preludes, and get Schles. to give you all my Études. If my little bust by Dantan is available at Suss's, buy two and have them well wrapped, if not, then go to Dantan's, who lives in St Lazare, near Alkan (give him my love if you see him), and ask where you can get them, at the same time ask him about the bronze one he was supposed to cast for me. Somewhere in the upper reaches of my cupboard you'll find a Polish tin bottle covered in flannel for placing against the chest, also an inflatable new pillow which I bought for the journey. You can throw in Kastner [Théorie*

abrégée de Contrepoint et de la Fugue, by J. G. Kastner] and
send it all, well-packed (there's a packer opposite you), in a case
of reasonable size through Lafitte et Cayard, addressed like the
letters. Please hurry. Keep the rest of the money for other things
I shall want sent. Don't pay Schlesinger, and don't delay the
sending if he hasn't got Kastner in stock, but don't fail to send
Cherubini's <u>Traité</u>, *I think,* <u>de Contrepoint</u> *(I can't remember*
the title). If he won't give you the Cherubini without money,
pay him, as it may be that Cherubini paid for the printing
himself. I shall write to Troupenas in a couple of days through
you. I must finish now, as the post is going. Sorry about all
this, but you'll get this on Sunday; send everything on Monday.
    CH.[30]

Another cause for agitation was the Pleyel piano which had
been shipped to Nohant to coincide with his arrival, which
turned out to have a poor tone. Chopin pounded it petulantly
while trying to work on his music, and after a couple of weeks
insisted that Pleyel have it taken away and a new one sent down.
Next, he turned his attention to his servant, whom he fired and
sent away in July. But there was something else that was irritating him more profoundly. It was that Marie de Rozières, a
pupil whom he had introduced to George Sand as a piano
teacher for her daughter Solange, had somehow managed to
ingratiate herself with George Sand. This nettled Chopin, as
she had also recently become the mistress of the feckless Antoni
Wodziński, who was back in Paris. His sister Maria had recently
married Count Józef Skarbek, son of Chopin's godfather, a
circumstance which had caused a certain amount of awkward-
ness and embarrassment between the two families in Warsaw.
The last thing Chopin wanted was Marie de Rozières treading
on delicate ground. 'Between ourselves, she's an unbearable old
sow who has somehow managed to tunnel into my garden, and
is rooting around looking for truffles among the roses,' Chopin

wrote to Fontana. 'She is a person to avoid, for she only has to touch something to make an indiscretion. In a word, she's an old maid. We bachelors are far better.'[31]

During that spring Marie de Rozières committed some sort of indiscretion which infuriated him. She and Wodziński were to have come down to Nohant, but in view of Chopin's attitude George Sand wrote telling her not to come yet, and certainly not with Wodziński, whom she wrongly assumed to be the source of Chopin's irritation. When Chopin heard this, he became frantic. 'I thought he would go mad,' George Sand wrote. 'He wanted to leave, he told me I was making him out to be mad, jealous, ridiculous, that I was creating bad blood between him and his friends.'[32] The reason for these histrionics lay in the fact that, coming hard on the news of Maria Wodzińska's marriage, a sudden show of hostility towards Antoni would make Chopin look spiteful and foolish.

George Sand challenged Chopin on the subject, and a 'bitter discussion' ensued, but either he avoided giving an explanation or she failed to grasp his meaning.[33] The situation continued tense, as she wrote to Marie de Rozières:

> *You will ask me why he is piqued and why indisposed towards you? If I knew that I should know where the sickness lay, and would be able to cure it; but with his exasperating nature, one can never know anything. He went through the whole of the day before yesterday without uttering a syllable to anyone. Was he ill? Had someone annoyed him? Had I said something to upset him? I searched and searched. I know his sensitive spots as well as anyone can, but I was unable to discover anything, and I shall never know, any more than I know about a million other little things, which he may not even know himself.[34]*

Chopin's near-hysterical reactions to minor vexations are attributable in part to his illness, but his behaviour also suggests frustration. Those determined to pin down the date at which George Sand began to deny him her bed would do well to look at the spring of 1841; both his tense condition and their apparent alienation would appear to point in that direction. This is borne out by the tone of irony and impatience in which she now described his behaviour; there is something of the schoolmistress recounting the antics of a spoilt child in her letters on the subject.

Her feelings towards him altered perceptibly, and she began to humour him like a child rather than to challenge him like a lover. She failed to understand the cause of his neuroses, and saw them as symptoms of a 'malady', by which she meant a sickly mental attitude. This was a dangerous explanation, as it allowed her to put down every quirk and every fit of temper, whether it was understandable or not, to the 'malady'. She thereby absolved herself of any part in provoking his behaviour or inadvertently encouraging his tantrums.

Another element of discord which had entered their relationship was politics. While his patriotism had often placed him alongside those attacking the status quo, Chopin was no revolutionary. He was not insensible to the plight of the downtrodden and was friendly with many ardent radicals, but he was too focused on his work to get involved. And his personal tastes drew him towards the refinement, elegance and luxury that he found in the drawing rooms of the aristocracy. The conservative capitalist regime of Louis Philippe and the prosperity it generated provided the conditions in which Chopin could flourish artistically and live comfortably, so he was not inclined to subvert it. George Sand, on the other hand, was by nature a political animal, and she was growing increasingly radical, which led her to despise Chopin's outlook as shallow and reactionary.

The arrival of the new Pleyel at the beginning of August and a visit by Witwicki did much to restore Chopin's serenity.[35] The

Viardots also came to stay, which helped to ease the tension. Louis Viardot joined George Sand and her friend the philosopher Pierre Leroux in discussing their project for a new independent newspaper. Chopin and Pauline went for long walks or played billiards with George Sand's half-brother Hippolyte. Things went so much better that towards the end of September George Sand suggested that Chopin, who had been looking for a new apartment in Paris sunnier than the one in the rue Tronchet, give up the idea and come and live with her in the rue Pigalle. This seems to belie her later statements that she was desperately trying to loosen the bonds between them. Chopin liked the idea and agreed to take over a room in the pavilion occupied until now by Maurice, for which he paid her some rent. He would share her drawing room and give his lessons there.

Some of his pupils balked at the distance they now had to travel for their lessons, the rue Pigalle being a long way further out than the rue Tronchet. But Chopin politely explained that he gave better lessons in his own room at twenty francs, but that if they preferred to send their carriages and thirty francs, he was prepared to do his best at their houses. He could afford to play the *grand seigneur*, as people were queuing up for the privilege of taking lessons from him, and pianists from other countries travelled all the way to Paris to do so.

The most notable of these was the twelve-year-old Hungarian Karl Filtsch, who had arrived while Chopin was at Nohant and had taken a few lessons from Liszt while he waited for him. 'When that boy starts to travel, I shall shut up shop!' Liszt exclaimed after hearing him.[36] Chopin was equally impressed, calling him 'my little urchin who knows everything', and showed him off everywhere, introducing him with the words: 'That, ladies, is what is called talent!' The boy had a remarkable touch, and on one occasion Chopin burst into tears after hearing him play his music. 'No one in the world will ever play it like him . . . except myself,' he once declared after listening to Filtsch playing one of the Nocturnes of op.48, written that summer. His view of Filtsch's future was not even clouded by the appearance on the scene of that other twelve-year-old *wunderkind* Anton Rubinstein, to whose first concert in Paris he accompanied Liszt.[37]

Not long after his return to Paris, on 2 December 1841, Chopin was again asked to play to the royal family at the Tuileries and was rewarded with a sumptuous present. The previous year's success and the financial gains involved had whetted his appetite, and in the New Year he once more decided to give a concert of his own. The event took place on 21 February 1842. Once again the whole of Paris fought for the expensive tickets, and once again it was 'a charming soirée, a feast peopled with delicious smiles, delicate and pretty faces, small, shapely white hands; a magnificent occasion where simplicity was married to grace and elegance, and where good taste served as a pedestal to riches'.[38] Chopin played a Ballade, various Nocturnes, Preludes, Études, Mazurkas and an Impromptu, alternating with Pauline Viardot's singing of a song by Jozef Dessauer, some pieces by Handel, and a song of her own composition, in which he accompanied her. In the middle, Franchomme played one of his own pieces for the cello.

The reviews were ecstatic, going on for column after column of superlatives. 'The great Chopin's concert has been as beautiful, as brilliant, as lucrative as last year's (more than 5000 francs profit, a unique result in Paris, which merely proves how eager people are to hear the most perfect and the most exquisite of musicians),' George Sand wrote to Hippolyte Châtiron. 'Pauline was admirable . . . Chopin is relaxing by giving his lessons.'[39]

Such relaxation could not quickly repair the damage caused by the strain of the concert, however. 'He looks even worse than last year, there's only skin and bones left,' wrote a visiting compatriot who saw Chopin at the Marlianis' shortly after the event.[40]

A few days later Chopin went down with an attack of what George Sand called rheumatism, and was bedridden for the best part of two weeks. 'I have to lie in bed all day long,' he wrote to Grzymała, 'my mouth and tonsils are aching so much.'[41] Hardly had he recovered from this than, towards the end of April, Jan Matuszyński died of tuberculosis. He died in Chopin's arms, after 'a slow and cruel agony', which Chopin seemed to share. He showed himself 'strong, courageous and devoted, more so than one could expect from such a frail being, but afterwards he was broken'.[42] This is not surprising, as he saw such deaths as precursors of his own. As usual on such occasions, Chopin's general condition deteriorated, and George Sand took him down to Nohant at the first opportunity, on 6 May.

On his arrival there he was examined by Dr Papet, who found his chest and larynx sound, and diagnosed that the choking and the coughing resulted from the fact that both throat and larynx were awash with mucus. Such a diagnosis must have been reassuring. Chopin had got quite used to living with his condition; he accepted the chronic breathlessness and occasional neural aches as part of his everyday life, and it was easier to bear them if they did not portend something more serious. As soon as the crisis receded, he began to feel much better and started working again. Only three weeks after their arrival, George Sand wrote to Delacroix that 'Chopin has written two adorable Mazurkas which are worth more than forty novels and say more than the whole literature of this century.'[43] He was indeed at the apex of his art, and that year saw the birth of the Ballade in F minor (op.52), the Polonaise in A flat major (op.53) and the Scherzo in E major (op.54).

Everyone at Nohant was cheered by the news that Delacroix was coming down for a stay. 'My Chopinet is very happy and agitated as he awaits you,' George Sand wrote to him. 'He keeps wondering what we can do to amuse you, where we can go for walks, what we can give you to eat, what he can play you on his piano.'[44] Even Maurice, a surly character 'not generous with his affection', in his mother's own words, was happy, as he worshipped the painter.[45]

Delacroix was delighted with Nohant. 'The place is very agreeable and the hosts could not be more pleasing,' he wrote to a friend. 'When one is not gathered together for dinner, lunch, billiards or walks, one is left in one's room to read or laze around on a sofa. From time to time the window opening on to the garden admits gusts of music from Chopin, who is working in his room; it mingles with the songs of the nightingales and the scent of roses . . .'[46]

In the tranquillity of Nohant, Chopin paid more attention to Delacroix and his conversation, and began to feel respect for the artist as well as liking for the man. 'I have never-ending conversations with Chopin, whom I love and who is a man of rare distinction; he is the most real Artist I have ever met,' wrote Delacroix. 'He is one of the very small number whom one can both admire and esteem.'[47] It was during this stay at Nohant that Delacroix finally worked out his project for the ceiling of the library in the Palais du Luxembourg, a problem which had been worrying him ever since he had been given the commission. He now saw it clearly: Virgil presenting Dante to Homer, surrounded by the great poets of antiquity. The head of Dante was to be a portrait of Chopin.

Witwicki came for a few days towards the end of July, but Balzac, who had been expected, did not appear, to the great relief of Delacroix, for 'he is a chatterbox who would have broken the spell of nonchalance in which I am indulging with great pleasure'.[48]

The weeks passed too quickly for Chopin, and when Delacroix had gone he was once again a little bored. But his relations with George Sand remained ostensibly harmonious. When the subject of moving from the rue Pigalle came up that summer, there was no question of their not living together, and when they started looking for new accommodation, she wrote to Charlotte Marliani that 'Chopin could not decide on the apartment without me nor I without him.'[49]

For once the search was not being carried out by Fontana, nor indeed was any other part of Chopin's business, which had been transferred to Grzymała's shoulders. There are no extant letters from Chopin to his former factotum from this summer, and at some stage during the next year Fontana would leave Paris for America. What has survived is a letter from Fontana to his sister in Poland, written in Paris that May just as Chopin was setting off for Nohant, in which he tells her that he is at the end of his tether financially and psychologically. 'I always relied on one friend, who was to open up my career for me, but who has been consistently dishonest and false,' he wrote. 'I even left Paris for a time to get away from his influence, and that did me a lot of harm. I only started composing again after my return . . .'[50]

It is difficult to see how the friend who was going to open up Fontana's musical career could have been anyone but Chopin, and this is seemingly corroborated by the fact that Fontana was in dire poverty at a time when the proverbially generous Chopin had just pocketed thousands of francs from his concert. How far Chopin could have helped a musical mediocrity like Fontana is debatable, particularly as Fontana suffered from stage-fright to such a degree that he would fall ill before and after taking part in a concert. He was an awkward, bitter man who easily took offence, and he resented the efforts Chopin made on behalf of his admittedly equally mediocre pupil Adolf Gutmann.[51] How Chopin repaid Fontana for his copying, his secretarial work and his devotion is not known, but at least he allowed him to live free at the rue Tronchet apartment until he gave it up in the autumn of 1841. It does appear that the unfortunate Fontana had let himself be used without getting much out of it, and however one chooses to look at it, Chopin's treatment of him does not redound to his credit.

It was Charlotte Marliani who searched for new accommodation this time, and at the end of July Chopin and George Sand travelled up to Paris to see what she had found. Having decided which apartment to take, they returned to Nohant for the rest of the summer. The extreme heat of that August overwhelmed Chopin, and he could not compose. George Sand too suffered from the heat and had persistent migraines. 'It is then that one has to see Chopin exercising his function of zealous, ingenious, devoted nurse,' wrote Marie de Rozières, who had come down to look after Solange and recover from having been jilted by Antoni Wodziński. 'He calls her his angel,' she added, 'but the angel has very large wings which sometimes hit you.'⁵²

The Viardots came to Nohant for a couple of weeks, after which the whole party returned to Paris in the last days of September, and Chopin and George Sand settled into their new home.

This was situated in the Square d'Orléans, a large private courtyard off the street. George Sand had taken a medium-sized apartment on the first floor of No.9, which consisted of a large drawing room with a billiard table, a smaller salon with a piano, and accommodation for herself and Maurice, who had rented a studio in one of the other houses on the square. Across the gravelled courtyard, at No.5, Chopin had taken two rooms on the ground floor, with a view onto the courtyard on one side and gardens at the back. The Marlianis had an elegant apartment in one of the other houses in the square, and it was there that they all usually met for dinner, George Sand lending her cook and Chopin contributing financially. The square was nicknamed '*La petite Athènes*', as it was favoured by artists and writers. When Chopin moved in, other apartments were occupied by Kalkbrenner and his family, the pianist Zimmermann, and his friend the young composer Alkan.

For Chopin it was an ideal arrangement. The rent was low, since he only needed two rooms and a little attic for his new servant, Jan, whom Witwicki had found for him. In these two rooms he was as independent of George Sand and her family as he could wish, while at the same time being close to her and other friends, whom he could call on whenever the need arose.

It was a busy winter: he was working harder than usual at his lessons, which now did not usually end before six o'clock. He was also going out a good deal more than in the last few years. There were receptions at the Czartoryskis' and at the Rothschilds', where he and Karl Filtsch played his E minor Concerto on two pianos before five hundred guests. A good deal less brilliant was the unfortunate Fontana's matinee concert on 17 March 1843, to which Chopin took Thalberg, for, as one witness put it, the event 'did not rise above mediocrity at any point'.[53]

Chopin fell ill in February, and this time a new doctor was called in. He was the homeopathic specialist Jean Jacques Molin, and he brought a radical change into Chopin's treatment. Whether Molin thought that his patient had tuberculosis or not is not known, but he prescribed the gentlest regime, designed mainly to ease his respiration. 'Every second day [Chopin] spends five minutes sniffing a little bottle of something,' a Polish friend noted in his diary. 'The result of this is that he breathes more freely, he can walk up stairs without becoming exhausted, and he no longer coughs. He has developed a rash from ear to ear which, according to some, augurs well.'[54]

In mid-May, Chopin and George Sand went down to Nohant, this time taking the newly built railway as far as Blois, and spent the next two months entirely alone, except for Pauline Viardot's baby daughter, whom George Sand had taken in while her mother went on tour to Vienna. There was an element of sadness and resignation in their relationship, George Sand working hard on her writing, Chopin trying to work but spending most of the days playing with the child instead. 'She says petit Chopin in a way that would disarm all the Chopins on earth, and Chopin loves her and spends his days kissing her little hands,' George Sand reported to Pauline Viardot.[55]

It is tempting to think that it was now that he first had the idea of writing the Berceuse (op.57), a work full of intense, though restrained, feeling. It illustrates more clearly than most of the pieces written at this time how far Chopin had developed in the last few years. It is brimming over with sentiment and tenderness, and yet there is no trace of sentimentality in it, for the expression is reduced to the indispensable, contained in a form both simple and sophisticated. Along with a few Mazurkas, the Berceuse constitutes Chopin's entire output for that year.

Physically, he was feeling well and made the most of the good weather. 'Chopin and I go on long excursions, he on a donkey and I on my own legs,' George Sand related. 'The donkey is a fine creature. It will only walk with its nose in my pocket, which is full of crusts of bread. The day before yesterday we were pursued by an enterprising ass who wanted to make an attempt on her virtue. She defended herself like a real Lucretia, with hefty kicks. Chopin shouted and laughed, while I attempted to fend off the Sextius with my umbrella.'[56]

In July they were joined by Delacroix, who again spent whole days with Chopin 'strolling along the avenues, talking of music, and the evenings on a sofa listening to it, when God descends upon his divine fingers'.[57] When Delacroix left, Chopin went up to Paris to collect Solange for the holidays, and they were soon followed down to Nohant by the Viardots. They would explore the countryside on long excursions, Chopin on his donkey, sleeping on straw in stables, and he thrived on the exercise. But as soon as the guests had left he began to find the atmosphere of Nohant stifling and to long for Paris and the comfort of his own friends. When he realised that George Sand was planning to stay on in the country until the winter, he decided to go back to Paris on his own at the end of October.

THIRTEEN

The End of the Affair

When Chopin left Nohant at the end of October 1843, he was followed by a torrent of letters from George Sand to various friends in Paris, urging them to look after him. Grzymała was begged to see him and take him out in the evenings, Marie de Rozières was told to keep an eye on his health and mood, Maurice was to report on his everyday condition, and Charlotte Marliani also received her instructions:

> *Here is my little Chopin, I entrust him to you, look after him in spite of himself. He doesn't look after himself when I am not there, and his servant is good but stupid. I am not worried about his dinners, for he will be invited on all sides, and it is no bad thing for him to have to wake up a little at that time of day. But in the morning, in the rush of his lessons, I am afraid that he will forget to swallow a cup of chocolate or bouillon which I usually force down his throat when I am there . . . Nothing could be easier than for his Pole to make him a little broth or a cutlet, but he will not order it and may even forbid it. You must therefore lecture and threaten . . .*[1]

Her apprehensions were not misplaced, for Chopin did fall ill halfway through November, during a cold damp spell. 'He is all right during the daytime, but at night he coughs, chokes and spits,' Maurice informed his mother. Dr Molin confined

Chopin to his room for a couple of days and gave him some homeopathic potions.[2] His appetite remained good, and after a few days he felt quite well again.

But George Sand was not convinced. 'I know very well that he suffers without me, I know that he would be happy to see me,' she wrote to Grzymała, 'but I also know that he would be saddened and almost humiliated in the delicacy of his heart if he saw me abandon my important work in favour of being his sick-nurse, as he puts it, the poor child! although I am his sick-nurse so willingly.' Her concern for him was by no means selfless. 'I miss him as much as he misses me, I need to look after him as much as he needs my care,' she continued. 'I miss his face, his voice, his piano, his slight sadness, and I even miss the heartrending sound of his cough. Poor Angel! I shall never abandon him, you can be sure of that; my life is consecrated to him for ever.'[3]

It is difficult to reconcile these sentiments with those expressed only a couple of days later in a letter to her friend Ferdinand François. 'Chopin's love for me is of an exclusive and jealous character,' she wrote. 'It is a little fantastic and sickly, like him, the poor angel. If he were strong enough to bear the suffering it creates in him, I should combat it with mockery and I should laugh it off. But it hurts him so much that I find myself forced at the age of forty to put up with the ridicule of having a jealous lover at my side.'[4]

George Sand had always shown protective and motherly instincts towards her friends. In the early 1830s she had steered Liszt through a psychological crisis, and within days of meeting Grzymała she was mending his shirts for him. A couple of years later she took up the young Pauline Garcia, engineered her marriage to Louis Viardot, and organised her career. She invariably referred to Pauline as her 'daughter', and bestowed similar epithets on other favourites, such as the young revolutionary Louis Blanc. By the mid-1840s these tendencies had grown into a real need to play the mother, and by the end of the decade into something of an obsession.

She had looked after and pampered Chopin from the start. She had often referred to him as her 'little one' or her 'child', but it was only now that she began to call him her 'son' – a word that can hardly be seen as a term of endearment. Having cast him as one of her children, she tried to laugh off his continuing love for her, and branded it as 'sickly'.

'No soul could be nobler, more delicate, more disinterested; no friendship more faithful and loyal, no wit more brilliant in its gaiety, no intelligence more complete and more serious in its own domain,' she writes of Chopin in her autobiography, 'but on the other hand, alas! no temper was more unequal, no imagination more umbrageous and more delirious, no suscep-tibility more difficult not to irritate, no demand of the heart more impossible to satisfy. And none of this was his fault. It was the fault of his malady . . .'[5]

It does not seem to have occurred to her that her treatment of him might have been at fault, and instead of examining her own behaviour or reassessing the state of the relationship, she merely indulged her instincts more and more. 'The net result of my total devotion is to render his life at best bearable!' as she explained to Charlotte Marliani. 'But that is something at least, and I shall not grow tired of it because he deserves it and because all devotion carries its own reward. It has almost become a necessity for me to assist and nurse him.'[6] Her devo-tion was double-edged, for while it made Chopin increasingly dependent on her, it also made him more insecure, as it became more obvious that she acted less out of love than kindness. Her refusal to acknowledge his love made him jealous and sus-picious, and his neurotic tendencies flourished in this climate.

Nowhere can this be seen as well as in the pages of the meticu-lously kept diary of Zofia Rozengardt, the nineteen-year-old daughter of a Warsaw restaurateur who had come to Paris to take lessons from him. The diary is that of an exalted girl who, having nurtured visions of garrets and dedication to art, was put out to find Chopin so worldly, and who took things very personally. It is nevertheless a priceless document, for it provides an outside view at the moment of crisis in his emotional life.

Miss Rozengardt took lessons from Chopin at irregular intervals throughout November, December and January, and his mood was different every time she saw him. One day he would be cold and distant, another charming, another angry and frightening. On 2 January 1844 she arrived at the wrong time, owing to a mix-up by his servant, which threw Chopin into a rage. He shouted and stamped his feet 'like a spoilt child', and she was sorely tempted to 'administer a sound rap across those divine fingers'.[7] Having vented his rage for a while, he started the lesson and she sat down at the piano, but then it turned out that she had not brought the score of the Nocturne she was studying, meaning to play it from memory. He was furious and upbraided her at length, telling her she did not know how to take lessons and that he had no time for others to waste. When he had calmed down again, she started playing the Nocturne, but it was not to Chopin's liking, and he walked up and down the room nervously. His manner was so peremptory and hostile that she finally burst into tears, at which point he melted and became charming. At the end of the lesson, he gave her the score of one of his works. 'What shall I write on it for you?' he asked, to which she replied: 'Write that I am a very poor pupil and that you scold me too much.' He picked up a pencil and wrote: 'To Miss Zofia Rozengardt, because she is a great baby, F. Chopin.' When she saw this, she thought to herself: 'The scoundrel, he knows the world – he knows how to make it up when he has hurt someone!'[8]

'Strange, incomprehensible man!' she wrote of him in a letter home. 'You cannot imagine a person who can be colder and more indifferent to everything around him. There is a strange mixture in his character: vain and proud, loving luxury and yet disinterested and incapable of sacrificing the smallest part of his own will or caprice for all the luxury in the world. He is polite to excess, and yet there is so much irony, so much spite hidden inside it! Woe to the person who allows himself to be taken in. He has an extraordinarily keen eye, he will catch the smallest absurdity and mock it wonderfully. He is heavily endowed with wit and common sense, but then he often has wild, unpleasant moments when he is evil and angry, when he breaks chairs and stamps his feet. He can be as petulant as a spoilt child, bullying his pupils and being very cold with his friends. Those are usually days of suffering, physical exhaustion or quarrels with Madame Sand . . .'[9]

All such portraits are perforce subjective, and this one brings together the most negative aspects of the composer's character and behaviour, but all of these are corroborated by other accounts. Two separate sources tell of an occasion on which Meyerbeer dropped in on Chopin during a lesson and pointed out that one of the pieces being played was in a different time to that printed in the score. Chopin icily replied that he was mistaken, but Meyerbeer insisted he was right. Chopin played the piece through, beating time as he went, but Meyerbeer was adamant. Chopin grew angry, and after another attempt at convincing his visitor, left the room slamming the door. One of Chopin's pupils said that he always felt he had to treat him like a lady he was eager to please. But most reminiscences dwell only on his charm, good manners, kindness and consideration. And when he was not prey to some violent mood, he was still the most painstaking and inspiring teacher.[10]

Although he complained to Zofia Rozengardt that he was more easily tired than in previous years and was permanently short of breath, Chopin never let up in his teaching work. He also went out often. The Czartoryskis, who had just moved into the magnificent Hôtel Lambert on the Île Saint-Louis, entertained on a grand scale. There were musical soirées like that given by the baron de Rothschild in December, and there was the opera, where Donizetti was in vogue that season. Liszt turned up towards the end of the season and gave the usual couple of concerts to which Chopin had to go in order to maintain the appearance of friendship, and in March there was the concert of his own pupil Gutmann to be attended and supported.

In February Chopin had caught the influenza which brought down half of Paris, but to him the slight deterioration in his condition was less noticeable and less aggravating than to healthy people, like George Sand, whom he helped to nurse when she too caught it. Nor did it stop him from having himself driven on a freezing day to the cemetery of Père Lachaise for the burial of Camille Pleyel's mother.

On 25 May 1844 he went, with George Sand, Victor Hugo and Lamartine, to a performance at the Théâtre de l'Odéon of Sophocles' *Antigone* set to music by Mendelssohn; on their return home he received news from Warsaw that his father had died. He shut himself up in his room and refused to speak to anyone, neither George Sand, nor Franchomme nor Dr Molin, whom she had called over to help her break in on his grief. It was not so much a question of the loss he had sustained, for he had not seen his father for some nine years, and had in any case not been particularly close to him either temperamentally or intellectually, but it was another link with home and family that had broken, and another death to be taken personally. Although he soon came out of his isolation (a severe toothache forced him to admit Dr Molin), he would not stop brooding, and wrote off to one of his brothers-in-law begging for a detailed description of the last hours of his father's life.

George Sand looked after him admirably, wrote to his mother, and tried to reason with him, but soon realised that the best cure would be activity. She took him down to Nohant, where she dragooned him into long walks and rides through the countryside, and managed at length to break down his melancholy through sheer exhaustion. But while her care and attention made him more dependent on her, he began to long with ever greater intensity for some kind of ideal of his lost family and home.

Exiles generally pine more ardently for their own country the longer they live in an adopted one, in spite of or partly because of the fact that the memory of their original home becomes more disembodied, unreal and confused. This was true of Chopin, and news like that of his father's death tended to alienate him from his actual surroundings by bringing to mind the lost and increasingly idealised environment.

In these circumstances, nothing could be more welcome than the news that Chopin's favourite sister, Ludwika, was coming to Paris for the summer with her husband. George Sand hastened to write to her explaining Chopin's state of health, for she feared the shock Ludwika would experience on seeing how much her brother had changed in fifteen years. She assured her that although there had been illness, there had been no marked deterioration in the last six years (since they had been together), and that Chopin was now set on a steady course and would 'last as long as any other, given a regular way of life and some care'.[11]

On 15 July Chopin travelled up to Paris to meet Ludwika and her husband, Józef Kalasanty Jędrzejewicz, a professor of law and now a judge in Warsaw, a practical and dull man of forty-one. They stayed in George Sand's apartment in the Square d'Orléans, and Chopin spent the next ten days with them, showing them the sights and taking them to the opera. On 25 July he went back to Nohant, whither they were to follow him in a couple of days, after they had finished their sightseeing. But Kalasanty, who was interested in technology and viewed his stay in Paris as a golden opportunity to see things of which he could only dream in Warsaw, was not eager to go down to

Nohant, and made Chopin wait another two weeks before bringing down his wife.

'We've gone mad with happiness,' Chopin wrote to Marie de Rozières when, on 9 August, the Jędrzejewiczes did eventually arrive at Nohant.[12] George Sand had feared that Ludwika would turn out to be a more provincial version of Chopin, whom she regarded as backward and bigoted in everything except music, but to her delight she found in her 'a woman totally superior to her age and her country, and with an angelic character'. She spent most of her free time with them, going for walks or sitting around talking, and later remembered that summer as 'one of the happiest periods in our life'.[13]

On 28 August the Jędrzejewiczes left Nohant, accompanied by Chopin and Maurice, who were to bring Pauline Viardot back on their return journey. Chopin spent a couple of days with them in Paris, took them to the opera again, and on their last evening played for them with Franchomme. It was with a heavy heart that he saw them leave for Warsaw, and his mood was not improved when, instead of returning with him, Maurice followed Pauline Viardot down to her country house, where he proceeded to have an affair with her.

On 4 September Chopin was back at Nohant, where the mood of happiness persisted throughout the rest of the stay. 'Without irony and without exaggeration, Chopin is all that is purest and best on earth,' George Sand wrote to Pauline Viardot, for, once harmony had been re-established the old affection returned.[14]

They both worked hard, she at her writing, he on the B minor Sonata (op.58) and on teaching a Beethoven Sonata to the sixteen-year-old Solange, who had now finished at her boarding school. Apart from a flying visit to Paris towards the end of September, he spent the next three months at Nohant. He was working on 'quite a little baggage of new compositions, saying, as usual that he cannot seem to write anything that isn't detestable and miserable', George Sand informed Delacroix, adding that 'the funniest thing is that he says this in perfectly good faith!'[15]

Once again he returned to Paris ahead of George Sand, on 28 November, but he kept his return quiet so as to have a few days of peace before would-be pupils started laying siege to his apartment. He called on old friends like Franchomme and Thomas Albrecht, and was delighted to find Grzymała recovered from a fall and 'dancing like a twenty-year-old'. This was in marked contrast to his own health, which began to make him feel 'mummifically old' and helpless, for he now often had to be carried up stairs or in and out of his carriage by his devoted Jan.[16] It was a bitterly cold December and he found himself sitting in front of the Franchommes' fire with three layers of flannel underclothes, nevertheless feeling 'yellow, wilted and frozen', while their baby son, 'pink, fresh, warm and barefoot', played at his feet.[17]

He clung to the discipline imposed by having to give lessons, and this kept him going. Lindsay Sloper, an English musician who had begun taking lessons from him, recorded that when he came for them, at eight o'clock in the morning, he would invariably find Chopin perfectly dressed and ready to start, even though he was sometimes so weak that he had to conduct the whole lesson reclining on a sofa and sniffing his bottles. Music, whether he was listening to it or playing it, always eased his suffering. Charles Hallé accompanied Franchomme to Chopin's rooms one day, and they found him 'hardly able to move, bent like a half-opened penknife and evidently in great pain'. They begged him to postpone the performance he had promised them, 'but he would not hear of it; soon he sat down at the piano, and as he warmed to his work, his body gradually resumed its normal position, the spirit having mastered the flesh'.[18]

Among the new pupils Chopin acquired during this winter,

two were to play an important part in his life. One was Jane Stirling, an energetic and earnest Scottish lady, an undistinguished pianist but an ardent admirer of his music. The other was Princess Marcelina Czartoryska. She was born Princess Radziwiłł and had married Prince Adam Czartoryski's nephew Aleksander, an amateur musician of note who lived in Vienna. Princess Marcelina had studied under Czerny, and was, according to Berlioz, 'a musician of wide knowledge and exemplary taste, and a distinguished pianist'.[19] She was to become one of Chopin's best pupils, and by general consensus the most faithful to his style. She was also a striking young woman of twenty-three, and although not beautiful in the conventional sense, she was, according to Delacroix, the sort of woman with whom one could fall hopelessly in love. Chopin appreciated the *grande dame* in her as well as the fine musician, and a deep affinity quickly developed between them.

This was all the more welcome to him, for not only was the harsh winter preventing him from recovering his strength, but his relations with George Sand were growing more difficult during the first months of 1845. She was beginning to face with trepidation the prospect of being lumbered for the rest of her days with somebody who was turning into a physical and, in her view, emotional invalid – she was still convinced that it was not his health but his 'malady' that lay at the root of his condition. She consoled herself as best she could by having a short affair with Louis Blanc, and at the same time heaped more devotion on Chopin, who for his part sought consolation in music and in his friends.

The lack of warmth Chopin sometimes met with at George Sand's apartment in the Square d'Orléans was made up for by that he found at the Hôtel Lambert, which had grown into a sort of Polish court in exile. The various members of the Czartoryski family and some of their relations had apartments in different parts of the great building. There was also an

Astolphe de Custine,
watercolour by
the comtesse de
Menou, 1846.

Above: Wojciech Grzymała,
lithograph by Bazin.

Right: Julian Fontana,
photograph taken in the 1850s.

Left: Maria Wodzińska, an unfinished self-portrait.

Right: Chopin, watercolour by Maria Wodzińska, Marienbad, 1836.

George Sand, from a
painting by Luigi Calamatta.

Marie d'Agoult,
after Henri Lehmann.

George Sand's house at Nohant.

Right: Chopin in the early 1840s, copy of a portrait by Ary Scheffer.

Below: Chopin, drawing by Franz Xaver Winterhalter, 1847.

Left: Ignaz Moscheles, contemporary lithograph.

Above: Pauline Garcia-Viardot, self-portrait.

Left: Auguste Franchomme.

Adam Mickiewicz, sketch by
Eugène Delacroix, c.1832.

Stefan Witwicki.

Bohdan Zaleski, lithograph by
James Hopwood, 1840.

Right: Eugène Delacroix, self-portrait.

Below: Chopin, caricature by Pauline Viardot, 1844.

Chopin 1844

Pauline Viardot fecit

N° 314

Left: Marcelina Czartoryska, lithograph by Auguste Sandoz, 1850.

Below: Maria Kalergis, drawing by Cyprian Norwid, c.1849.

Above: Chopin, photograph taken during the last months of his life.

Right: Jane Stirling.

institute for Polish young ladies run by the Princess in an adjoining house. The Hôtel Lambert served as a rallying point for Grzymała and many other friends. During the spring of 1845 Chopin celebrated Easter there, and he often went there for soirées and musical evenings, at some of which he played.[20]

He was not, however, to be tempted to play outside the homes of friends, except for one occasion in April, when the dying republican Godefroi Cavaignac expressed a wish to hear music before his end. Louis Blanc, to whom the request was made, immediately went to beg Chopin for the favour, which Chopin readily granted, knowing and liking the young man and apparently ignorant of the affair he was having with George Sand. He played for hours to the dying man, who listened with tears running down his face.[21]

That season Chopin kept away from most of the concerts. He had to go to Gutmann's in March, and in April Stamaty begged him to come to the debut at the Salle Pleyel of his own pupil, the thirteen-year-old American pianist Louis Moreau Gottschalk. This turned out to be a pleasant surprise. The boy was exceptionally gifted, and his *pièce de résistance* that day was Chopin's E minor Concerto, which he played beautifully. Chopin went to his dressing room after the concert to congratulate him, and is supposed to have said: 'Give me your hand, child – I tell you, you will become the king of pianists.'[22] But apart from these, Chopin only went to two concerts during the first months of that year. Their nature is eloquent: Mozart's Requiem and Haydn's *Creation*. No less telling is the fact that Chopin chose Delacroix to accompany him to both.

However independent their behaviour may have seemed during the winter and spring of 1845, there was still no hint of Chopin and George Sand parting, and on 12 June they drove down to Nohant together in Chopin's new *calèche*. Not only were they going to spend the summer together as usual, but George Sand had made up her mind to scrape together as much money as possible in order to go to Italy or the South of France with him for the winter.

Chopin sat around 'cooking in the sun' with Pauline Viardot, who had accompanied them, but after three weeks she left for Paris, and Chopin relapsed into listlessness.[23] 'I am not made for the country,' he wrote in one of several letters to Ludwika. The notoriously lazy letter-writer, who preferred to drive across Paris rather than pen a note of three lines, who often kept his parents waiting up to six months for a letter from him, now spent hours writing long, rambling epistles to his sister. They spread over several days, and clearly reveal that they were written in order to kill time:

> *I'm not playing much, as my piano has got out of tune, and I'm writing even less. I feel strange here this year; I often look into the room next door* [where Ludwika and her husband had stayed in the previous year], *but there's nobody there. It is sometimes taken over by some guest who comes down for a couple of days – And I don't drink my chocolate in the morning – and I've moved the piano to a different place; by the wall, where the sofa and the little table used to be, where Ludwika used to sit and embroider my slippers while the lady of the house worked at something else. In the middle of the room stands my desk, on which I write, to the left are some of my musical papers, M. Thiers and poetry; on the right, Cherubini; in front of me the repeater you sent me, in its case (4 o'clock). Roses and carnations, pens, and a little piece of sealing wax Kalasanty left behind. I have always one foot in your world – the other in the room next door, where the lady of the house is working – but I am not at all with myself at the moment, only, as usual, in some strange space . . .*[24]

During the first month at Nohant he had managed to write three new Mazurkas (op.59), but by the beginning of July he was incapable of putting his mind to anything. He spent whole hours pacing his room or staring idly out of the window, or else he would play the piano for a moment with Solange. She was the only person who seemed to have time to go for drives with him, and they would set off aimlessly, accompanied by the huge dog Jacques, whose head stuck out of one side of the cabriolet, while his rump and tail hung out on the other. Chopin would then come back to his room and sit down once more to his letter to Ludwika, adding the latest gossip about Victor Hugo's amorous adventures, jumbled up with snippets gleaned from the papers about the opening of the telegraph between Washington and Baltimore and Liszt's antics at the unveiling of the Beethoven memorial.[25]

Chopin's mood had much to do with the tensions that were building up at Nohant. While George Sand kept to her room and her work most of the time, Maurice now began, imperceptibly at first, to assume the role of master of the house. He had been a rather shy boy, but encouraged by his mother's doting admiration, he had grown in self-assurance. 'Maurice paints, teases, twirls his moustaches, sniggers, swaggers, wears his boots outside his trousers, and smells of the stable,' George Sand proudly wrote to Marie de Rozières that summer.[26] He also began to question, at first only by his manner, the composer's position and rights in the Sand household.

Solange, who was illegitimate, had never been George Sand's favourite, and had been packed off to boarding school as a child. Later attempts to make up for this early neglect by spoiling her had been predictably counter-productive. 'It was not dresses and a horse that I needed, but love,' Solange would later write.[27] What little she did get came from Chopin, who had from the start taken a liking to her and stood in for her absent father. Now that Chopin himself began to feel that he was being excluded from George Sand's affection in favour of Maurice, he and Solange were naturally thrown together. She was as bored as he was at Nohant. 'Solange gets dressed, then undresses, climbs onto her horse and then gets off it, scratches, yawns, opens a book and then closes it, combs her hair . . .' George Sand wrote to Marie de Rozières.[28]

What often happens in this kind of situation occurred here too, for while Maurice grew more aggressive and protective of his mother, and she began to treat Chopin with a certain tolerance that suggested a weakening of his position, Solange began to court him, and, since he was not her father, did not fail to use all the appeal that a nubile seventeen-year-old girl can hold for a depressed, insecure and prematurely ageing man of thirty-five.

Already having one daughter who felt unloved and wronged, George Sand proceeded to do the worst thing she could have done: she 'adopted' another. This was Augustine Brault, the twenty-one-year-old daughter of a cousin of hers, a wretched and loutish character unable to pay for his daughter's education and unwilling to look after her. Augustine was pretty and intelligent, and George Sand thought the world of her. She had helped the Braults on the girl's behalf before, and now decided to take her into her own family, knowing Maurice to be extremely partial to her, and ignoring Solange's dislike of her.

Maurice and Augustine soon became inseparable. George Sand looked on benignly as they flirted, and thought them both charming, while Solange lowered in sullen resentment, supported only by Chopin, who did not take to Augustine either. But while Nohant divided into two camps over the girl, the only rumblings of war that summer took place over Chopin's servant.

Jan was not popular in the kitchen, as he vented his antipathy towards the cook in the crude but direct French he had picked up: the more mentionable examples were 'ugly like pig' and 'mouth like arsehole'.[29] He was not popular with George Sand either, and Chopin had for some time been thinking of getting rid of him. But he was loath to do so, for he had got used to him, and needed to have someone around with whom he could speak Polish. But Jan soon fell foul of Maurice, and that settled the matter.

Outwardly, relations between Chopin and George Sand remained unchanged, and when, in September, he had to go to Paris briefly to settle some business, they wrote to each other every day, as was usual when they were apart. Hardly any of her letters to him survive, but one of those that do dates from this trip, and ends with the words: 'Love me, my dearest angel, my dearest happiness, I love you.'[30]

Chopin returned to Nohant at the end of the month, and spent the whole of October and November there. His health was quite good, but he was, according to George Sand, 'worrying, like all sickly people, and burying himself in advance all the time, with a certain relish'. This view was echoed by Dr Papet, who again made a full examination and found no signs of illness, but thought him 'inclined to hypochondria and destined to be perpetually alarmed until he reaches the age of forty and his nerves lose some of their excessive sensitivity'.[31] One cannot help wondering at Papet's opinions. By now the thirty-five-year-old composer looked moribund to most people, and there was clearly something other than 'excessive sensitivity' at the bottom of his condition. But Papet's invocation of the magic age of forty found favour with George Sand, who soldiered on in the belief that all the neuroses would vanish when this was reached.

It is true that Chopin's condition was aggravated by anxiety, particularly on account of his work. 'Oh, how time does fly!' he wrote to Ludwika. 'I don't know why, but I just do not seem to be able to do anything good, and it's not that I'm being lazy; I don't spend my time wandering about like I did with you, but stay in my room for whole days and evenings. I must finish some manuscripts before I leave here, because I cannot compose anything during the winter.'[32] His anxiety was understandable, for although in terms of quality he was at his peak (he had just started work on the Barcarolle, which some consider to be his greatest achievement), there was a marked falling-off in the facility with which he could work, and therefore in the quantity produced.

The last and greatest stage of his output had begun in 1841, when he had produced a dozen important works, including some of his best. The next two years saw a progressive drop in the quantity being produced, with half a dozen substantial pieces in 1842 and the same number of shorter ones in 1843, while in the whole year of 1844 he could only finish one work, the B minor Sonata (op.58). In the following year, he wrote three Mazurkas and started on the Barcarolle. He was putting more and more thought into these later works, self-critically reviewing them many times before allowing them to go to the printer. Their composition represented weeks of agonised reworking and frustration. His powers of concentration were failing and his inspiration was beset by anguish, both emotional and intellectual.

On the other hand, he was being more adventurous in his composition. The Barcarolle, most of which he wrote after his return to Paris at the end of November, was a new depar-ture, both in form and content. Another was the Sonata for Piano and Cello which he had been thinking of for some time. The last time he had written anything for an instrument other than the piano had been over ten years before, and then he had let Franchomme write most of the cello part. But, having spent many hours over the last years playing pieces with him, he had developed a familiarity with the instrument. At the same time he was embarking on 'something else which I don't know what I'll call', as he described it to Ludwika.[33] He would call it the Polonaise-Fantaisie (op.61), and it was to be the final and logical step in Chopin's development of the Polonaises of the late 1830s and early 1840s, so evocative of past grandeur and so declamatory in their rebelliousness, into the pure musical fantasy couched in the language of the Polonaise.

His attempts at working in Paris were thwarted by the constant flow of visitors to his rooms. Liszt was back, Meyerbeer was on a visit from Berlin, August Klengel, a musician Chopin had known in Dresden, had also come. Christmas was lugubrious in Paris that year, with half of society brought low by an influenza epidemic, and the first months of 1846 were hardly more lively. Apart from a grand ball at the Hôtel Lambert, to which he went with George Sand, Solange and Delacroix, Chopin did not go out much, for he felt fragile and tired easily. While the epidemic carried off many far healthier people than him, including his favourite pupil, Karl Filtsch, who had died in Venice aged fifteen after an exhausting year giving concerts around Europe, the influenza barely affected Chopin. 'I've outlived so many people who were younger and stronger than me that I'm beginning to think I'm eternal,' he wrote to Ludwika.[34] His evenings were most often spent with Delacroix, Grzymała, the poet Zaleski and Franchomme, with whom he kept trying out pieces of the sonata he was writing. In April he went to stay with Franchomme's family near Tours, but was back towards the end of the month in order to prepare for his journey to Nohant. Before leaving Paris he held a musical evening at his own apartment, to which he invited the Czartoryskis, Princess Sapieha, Delacroix, Louis Blanc and the Viardots. It was a typically Chopinesque evening: the rooms were filled with flowers and beautifully lit, ices and delicacies were served, and he played for hours.

On 27 May Chopin arrived at Nohant, whither George Sand had preceded him a couple of weeks before. He came with presents for her and an ingenious new ice-making machine so they could have cold drinks when the heatwave started. Concessions had been made on both sides. Chopin had acquired a French servant who was quiet and polite; George Sand had invited a friend of Chopin's sister, Laura Czosnowska, whom she did not particularly like. But the spirit of conciliation was at odds with what was really taking place at Nohant that summer.

For the last couple of months George Sand had been engaged in writing a new novel, *Lucrezia Floriani*. It tells the story of a famous actress who, disillusioned with love and fame, retires to the seclusion of a lakeside villa hidden away in the depths of the countryside, where she avoids all contact with the world and devotes herself to the upbringing of her illegitimate children. Chance brings two travellers into her wilderness: one an erstwhile friend and admirer, the other a delicate, virginal and melancholy prince. The prince falls ill and cannot be moved in the morning, and by the time Lucrezia has nursed him back to life, they are in love. There follows a period of bliss, but gradually the prince's restless mind, his jealousy and his 'malady' begin to torment him and drive her mad. One day she simply 'dies' of sorrow and exasperation.

Lucrezia is sagacious, understanding, strong yet supremely feminine, unaffected and noble. She is eminently practical as well as being spiritually on a higher plane. Her guiding principle in life has been love, and she has been misunderstood and reviled for this. Disappointed in her various lovers, she has abjured sexual love and has concentrated all her affections on her children, to whom she intends to devote the rest of her life. Although some stress is laid on the fact that Lucrezia is still highly attractive, she does not want to have any more affairs with men, and the fact that the prince is an intruder into her retreat, albeit an unintentional and passive one, is represented as a violence done to her. The novel clearly depicts her as a victim.

The prince is a disembodied creature exuding refinement and nervousness, an exquisite work of art hopelessly unsuited to normal life. As a character he is insipid and unconvincing, little more than a stage prop used to create the conditions for the author's descriptions of Lucrezia's emotional martyrdom. But there are occasional passages describing particular traits in his character which have a ring of truth about them.

The book is unmistakably about George Sand and Chopin (the prince has a Polish name, Karol, and his travelling companion is the spitting image of Grzymała). This was clear to most readers in Paris as soon as the first instalments began to appear in the press in June, and even in faraway St Petersburg, the novelist Ivan Turgenev was in no doubt as to whom it referred.[35] Most people were profoundly shocked, for while George Sand was known to enjoy carrying out vicious autopsies on her dismissed lovers, this was the only instance of her going in for vivisection. There was an abundance of intimate detail, and the book was a public humiliation of Chopin. Delacroix, Heine and even Liszt were appalled.

'One should never put those one loves or those one hates into a novel,' George Sand later wrote, and although she rarely put anything else into her own, one must assume that she did so subconsciously.[36] In the introduction to a later edition of *Lucrezia Floriani*, she wrote that in literature it is not possible to portray a character, only 'a sentiment'. 'One therefore has to create the characters to suit the sentiment one wishes to describe, and not the sentiment to the characters.'[37] By 'sentiment' it seems she meant the reactions of a character to a situation, for that is indeed what the book is about. George Sand wrote so much, so quickly and so subjectively, and the line separating personal experience from fantasy in her novels is so thin, that it is possible she was not aware of the fact that she was describing her own relationship with Chopin. She certainly denied it vehemently when accused. This enhances the value of the book as a document, for it provides an insight into how she saw the relationship at this stage.

The central theme of the novel is the gradual transformation of Prince Karol's gentle character by his 'malady', which in turn kills Lucrezia. The traits of this character are well drawn, if a little one-sidedly, as the following passage illustrates:

> *As he was polite and reserved in the extreme, nobody could even suspect what was going on inside him. The more exasperated he was, the cooler he grew, and one could only judge the degree of his fury by his icy contempt. It was then that he was truly unbearable, as he wanted to reason and to subject real life, of which he had never understood a thing, to principles he could not define. Then he would find wit, a false and brilliant wit, in order to torture those he loved. He would become supercilious, stiff, precious and aloof. He seemed to nibble playfully, yet inflicting wounds which penetrated to the depths of one's soul. Or else, if he lacked the courage to contradict and mock, he would wrap himself in disdainful silence, in a distressing sulk.*[38]

The various neuroses which one can recognise as Chopin's are presented by George Sand as symptoms of some spiritual evil, and not as the result of any human emotional tangle. Prince Karol is also shown to be invariably wrong, whether on matters of principle or on practical ones. When he stands by his judgements or opinions, he is merely being 'sickly'. This combination of physical, emotional and spiritual ineptitude not only makes the character of Prince Karol hard to believe; it also demonstrates that George Sand was making no effort to understand Chopin as a person.

Lucrezia's reactions to Prince Karol's neuroses reveal the main reason for the disintegration of the Chopin-Sand ménage. Lucrezia feels smothered by the situation, and her continual allusions to being 'murdered with pinpricks' are echoed in George Sand's contemporary correspondence with reference to Chopin. The same is true of the almost pathological way in which Lucrezia uses her children as a pretext for all her actions, labouring the idea that they have a sacred priority in her life to which everything else must be sacrificed. George Sand was suddenly becoming very conscious of her duty towards her own children, whom she had hitherto not only neglected but ruthlessly subordinated to her own priorities.

Although the message of the book is full of menace for Chopin, it is unlikely that it was written as a warning. If it was, it failed to get through. As was her wont with new works, George Sand read out instalments before Chopin and her house guests that summer, and while the others listened in horror, Chopin failed to spot the obvious. 'I was in agony during the reading,' recalled Delacroix, 'the victim and the executioner amazed me equally. Madame Sand seemed to be completely at ease, and Chopin did not stop making admiring comments about the story.'[39] It seems more likely that the plot of the book crystallised by itself, without any intentional direction from George Sand, under the influence of her growing paranoia. Lucrezia's identification of a conflict between children and lover mirrored a similar one emerging in George Sand's own consciousness, which demanded discussion.

Whatever the intention behind it, the book shows how she viewed her relationship with Chopin. She was convinced that he was in some way stifling and tormenting her. In this she was not alone, as many of her friends felt that she was being trapped, and even Mickiewicz believed that Chopin was her 'moral vampire', and that he would kill her in the end.[40] What is also clear from a reading of the book is that she had come to see her children as her main responsibility, and that she was going to make use of them in order to escape from the perceived trap.

The first step in this was a hardly perceptible transference to Maurice of the rights which Chopin, as the man in the family, had come to consider as his. Soon after his arrival that spring, Chopin was dismayed to find that the old gardener, who had been at Nohant for twenty years, had been sacked, and two more old retainers were dismissed during the course of the summer. Chopin saw this as Maurice's doing, and showed his disapproval. Halfway through June he had a difference of opinion with Maurice on a domestic matter, and was mortified when George Sand took her son's side. 'I lost my temper, which gave me the courage to tell him a few home truths, and to threaten to get sick of him,' she wrote to Marie de Rozières, adding that 'since then, he has been sensible, and you know how sweet, excellent, admirable he is when he is not mad'.[41]

Augustine Brault and Maurice had begun having an affair. Solange was bored. She was jealous of Augustine, who seemed to be attracting more attention than her, and she therefore began to actively flirt with Chopin, whose frustrated feelings for George Sand were gradually transferred to her. In these circumstances, the arrival of Grzymała and Laura Czosnowska, a coquettish thirty-six-year-old friend of Ludwika's from Warsaw, did little to ease the tension. Everybody liked Grzymała, but neither George Sand nor Augustine nor Maurice could stand Laura. Snide comments were made and there was sniggering behind her back, which Chopin noticed and attributed to Augustine's influence. Solange agreed with him, and provided the sympathy he was not getting from the rest of the family.

That summer there was a terrible heatwave which enervated everyone, most of all Chopin. 'Chopin is amazed to find himself sweating,' George Sand reported to Marie de Rozières. 'He's quite upset by it and claims that, however much he washes, he still stinks! We laugh to the point of tears to see such an ethereal creature refusing to sweat like everyone else, but don't ever mention it – he would be furious. If the world or even just you were to know that he sweats, he could not go on living. He only reeks of Eau de Cologne, but we keep telling him he stinks like Pierre Bonnin the carpenter, and he goes scuttling back to his room, as though he were being pursued by his own smell.'[42] After the heat came swarms of little bugs which bit everyone, gradually working their way up the legs. Soon everyone was sitting around scratching unashamedly, particularly Delacroix, who had come down for the last two weeks of August.

His visit brought relief to Chopin, and they spent some delightful moments together, talking of Mozart's operas and Beethoven's sonatas, some of which Chopin played to his friend. Chopin was so glad to be with Delacroix that he now, for the first time, uttered a phrase of recognition of his talent, calling him, in a letter to Franchomme, 'an artist worthy of the highest admiration'. He entered into Delacroix's metaphysical speculations about colour and contour in painting and their relationship to rhythm and tone in music, and 'painted' pictures on the piano at his dictation.[43]

Chopin was desolate to see him go, and wished he could go back to Paris with him, but his habitual inertia kept him at Nohant. As he and George Sand saw Delacroix aboard the mail coach at Châteauroux on 30 August, carrying Chopin's entire work for the summer, three Mazurkas (op.63), they met her friend Emmanuel Arago and a young friend of Maurice's off the incoming coach. As they drove back to Nohant, Chopin felt more isolated than ever.

But he put on as brave a face as possible. When the English poet Matthew Arnold dropped in to visit George Sand, he found Chopin very much in evidence, and he could be counted on whenever the house party needed entertaining. A typical evening was recorded by another visitor, who describes how Chopin started with a take-off of a Bellini opera, which produced general mirth, 'such was the finesse of the observation and the witty mockery of Bellini's musical style and habits'. He then played a 'prayer for Poles in distress', followed by an Étude and a funeral march, after which he roused everyone with a lusty rendition of a *bourrée*, a local peasant dance of which he had made some transcriptions. He finished off the evening with another joke, an imitation of a defective musical box. 'If we had not been in the same room we could not have believed that it was a piano tinkling under his fingers,' the visitor wrote.[44]

At other times, Chopin would invent musical mimes: he would use the piano to mimic an argument between two people, or a drunk walking down the street. As he did so, younger members of the household would pick up his cue and mime or dance comic scenes and ballets. 'He would lead them as he wanted, and would, according to his whim, make them pass from the pleasant to the severe, from the burlesque to the solemn, from the graceful to the passionate,' George Sand wrote. 'Costumes were improvised in order to play the successive roles, and as soon as the artist saw them appear, he would vary his theme and his accent wonderfully to suit their character.'[45]

In spite of this, Chopin could not help feeling left out much of the time, and when in September the whole house party went away on excursions, he remained at Nohant, writing letters to Ludwika and trying to work, with only one of the dogs for company. The work did not come easily, however, and he complained to Franchomme that 'I do everything I can in order to work but it's no good. If this goes on, my new compositions will not resemble the chirruping of warblers or even the sound of smashing china.'[46] He was probably referring to the Sonata for Piano and Cello, which had already taken him longer than any other work, and was still not finished. He had managed to complete the Polonaise-Fantaisie, a couple of Nocturnes and the Three Mazurkas, but he was not quite satisfied. 'When you write something it seems good – otherwise one would never write anything,' he explained. 'Later on, reflection comes, and one either accepts or rejects. Time is the best censor and patience the best teacher.'[47] But he felt time was running out; he could no longer concentrate and was beginning to feel that he was drying up.

As he watched the way of life he had grown used to gradually falling apart, Chopin was haunted by the old fear of being alone. 'Now I don't have a single one of my school friends left alive in Paris,' he complained to Ludwika.[48] In his entire extant correspondence, the subject of dreams crops up only three or four times; yet two of the dreams, related almost twenty years apart, centre round the theme of dying away from home, family and friends. In the last couple of years of his life, the image of dying in a poorhouse is conjured up several times in his letters. He had never been an independent or self-sufficient person, and eight years of George Sand's tenderness had made it impossible for him to envisage life on his own.

There was little he could do, except wait, as the plan of spending the winter in a warmer place had been shelved at the insistence of Maurice, who had decided that the whole family, including his mother, should remain at Nohant. The only ray of hope for Chopin was that Solange had met a young man who wanted to marry her, and that Maurice seemed to be thinking of espousing Augustine, a match that George Sand was encouraging. Chopin thought that when the children were married off and settled, the mother would return to him, and so, thinking it best to be out of the way, he left for Paris alone on 11 November. George Sand was taken in by his apparent serenity, and felt that he was finally going to 'round the cape' and settle down to a quiet middle age.

While they were both deceiving themselves, Parisian society had already jumped to various conclusions. Coming not long after the publication of *Lucrezia Floriani*, Chopin's return to Paris alone set tongues wagging. 'Is the break between Chopin and Madame Sand definite? And for what reasons?' Liszt quizzed Marie d'Agoult from the depths of Ukraine.[49] Although there had been no dramatic break, he was not wrong to make such surmises, for the affair had come to an end.

FOURTEEN

An Ugly Fracas

Chopin's relief at finding himself back in his Parisian world is evident. Those of his letters to George Sand that survive make him sound a little distant, although full of good wishes and tenderness. He felt well, in spite of the bad weather, and the treatment he had just started to receive from a Swedish masseur was doing him good – it seems likely that apart from anything else, he suffered from poor circulation. He did not lack attention and care, as Charlotte Marliani was still living in the Square d'Orléans, and he could drop in for dinner whenever he felt too lazy to go out. Marie de Rozières was in almost daily attendance, as were Grzymała and Franchomme, while friends such as Delacroix and Delfina Potocka, now back in Paris, did their best to distract him.

He resumed his lessons and tried to write, but, as he complained to Ludwika, 'I write a little and cross out a lot.' He was still wrestling with the Sonata for Piano and Cello. 'I'm sometimes happy with it, sometimes not,' he wrote. 'I throw it into a corner and then take it up again.'[1] In November, he wrote a *Veni Creator* for the wedding of his friend Bohdan Zaleski to his former pupil Zofia Rozengardt. This now lost piece, presumably for choir and organ, is the only religious work Chopin is known to have composed, and an astonishing new departure for him at this stage in his life.

He now clung more than ever to his ties with Poland, even

seeing a good deal of his fellow musician Józef Nowakowski, who had come from Warsaw, though the man had gone a little senile: Chopin 'often knocked at his soul, but there was nobody there'.[2] Grzymała's soul, however, could be depended on, and Delfina Potocka was as affectionate as ever, while the Hôtel Lambert in itself represented a small kingdom of Poland. On 24 December, Prince Adam's name day, Chopin went to a reception there, during which the venerable Soliva conducted a choir of girls from the Princess's institution, which must have brought back poignant memories. It was there too that Chopin saw in the New Year of 1847, wearing every overcoat he could find, and probably wishing that he could have been in Italy with George Sand instead of in snowbound Paris.

George Sand arrived in Paris on 7 February, accompanied by Solange and Augustine, in order to settle the legal aspects of her daughter's marriage to the young Fernand de Preaulx. She was busy with these matters and behind in her work, so Chopin did not see much of her. But she was naturally present, along with Grzymała, Delacroix and her friend Emmanuel Arago, when on 17 February Chopin and Franchomme played through the final version of the Sonata, and three days later she accompanied Chopin and Delacroix to Franchomme's concert at the Conservatoire.

A few days before, at the Marlianis', she had been introduced to a sculptor by the name of Auguste Clésinger. She took Solange to visit his studio, and was impressed by his work. He showered mother and daughter with compliments, presents and flowers, and begged to be allowed to carve busts of them both. This involved further visits, during which he overwhelmed them with his artistic temperament. Before the end of February Solange told Preaulx that she had to reconsider her decision to marry him.

'She's changed her mind,' Chopin wrote to Ludwika. 'I regret it and I'm sorry for the boy, who is decent and loving, but

I suppose it's better it happened before than after the wedding.'[3] Clésinger was a feckless drunkard and a gambler, but George Sand was overwhelmed by his exuberance and saw in him a sort of Delacroix in marble. Delacroix himself summed up the sculptor's talents as 'daguerrotype in sculpture', and disliked his manner.[4] The Marlianis disapproved of him, and the man who had introduced him to George Sand wrote to her warning that he was not to be trusted. Chopin thought him odious. He wondered at all the admiration heaped on him by George Sand and Solange, but assumed that the infatuation would pass.

On 1 April Delacroix took George Sand and Chopin to see the finished ceiling of the library in the Palais du Luxembourg, in which Chopin could recognise himself in the figure of Dante. A few days later George Sand left Paris with Solange, and Chopin was to join them at Nohant at the beginning of June with Delacroix. But he felt little enthusiasm. 'I honestly don't feel like it, as, apart from the lady of the house, the son and the daughter, the other people will be new faces I shall have to get used to, and I can't be bothered any more,' he wrote home. 'Of all those Ludwika saw there, not a single one is left. Five new servants.'[5] He was in half a mind to try to meet up with some of his family or with Tytus in Germany instead.

To George Sand he wrote: 'Be happy, well disposed, look after yourself and write a few words when you have the time.'[6] He was making an effort to distract himself, as his suddenly rather more detailed letters to Ludwika reveal. On 13 April he gave several lessons and went to a soirée at Auguste Léo's; on the fourteenth he gave five lessons and then went to Ary Scheffer's studio to pose for a portrait; he did the same on the following day, and on his way home dropped in on Delacroix for a chat. When he got home, he did not feel like dressing for dinner, 'so I spent the evening playing to myself . . . I played it away with melodies from the banks of the Vistula.'[7] The following day he gave seven lessons, after which he went to a vaudeville with Alkan, who lived next door. Next morning he received a letter from George Sand announcing that she would be coming up to Paris for a few days at the end of the month, so he gave orders for her rooms to be prepared. He gave four lessons and spent the evening at the comte de Perthuis's soirée.

Instead of arriving in Paris, George Sand sent Chopin a letter in which she announced that Solange was to be married to Clésinger. She professed herself happy with her prospective son-in-law, whom she described as 'bold, well-read, active and ambitious'. 'I suppose she thinks those are virtues!' Chopin wrote to Ludwika.[8] 'All her friends – Marliani, Arago, Delacroix and Myself – have had the worst reports concerning the person; that he's in debt; that he's a brute who beats his mistress, whom he has abandoned in pregnancy now that he's getting married, etc., etc.; that he drinks (we all knew that, but of course it's put down to genius) . . . I don't give them a year after their first child – and the mother will have to pay the debts.'[9] But he kept his opinion to himself, for he was ostentatiously not being encouraged to give it.

'I think Chopin, standing outside all this, must feel upset at being kept in ignorance of the persons and factors involved, and from not being able to advise,' George Sand wrote to Grzymała. 'But his advice in the real business of life cannot possibly be considered. He has never looked straight at realities, never understood human nature on any point; his soul is pure poetry and music and he cannot tolerate anything that is different from himself. Moreover, his interference in the affairs of my family would mean total loss of all my dignity and love both from and towards my children.'[10]

George Sand was now doing all she could to hurry along her seventeen-year-old daughter's marriage to the thirty-three-year-old sculptor. 'It is impossible not to like him,' she assured Delacroix. As Chopin wrote to his sister: 'Madame Sand is a dear, but she hasn't a ha'pence worth of common sense.' 'A pity really,' he added meditatively, 'or perhaps not at all, looking at it from the point of view that Madame Sand always acts in remarkable ways, and that everything always works out well for her – even things that look impossible at first sight.'[11]

On 2 May the painter Franz Winterhalter came to Chopin's rooms to make a pencil portrait, but found him suffering from an attack of something like asthma, which lasted four days. Chopin begged Gutmann and Marie de Rozières, who were looking after him, to keep his illness secret from George Sand so as not to worry her needlessly, but Princess Czartoryska mentioned it in a letter to Nohant. George Sand was 'sick with worry' and would have come up to Paris but for the fact that she could not leave her daughter unchaperoned with her fiancé in the country. Even though Chopin wrote telling her he was well and happy, she remained anxious, more for her own sake than for his. 'For the last seven years I have been living with the certainty that I shall not see him age at my side, but one never gets used to these horrible certainties, and one goes on suffering,' she wrote to her publisher. 'He has done me so much harm with his sickness that for a long time I hoped to die before him.'[12] On the same day she wrote to Grzymała, saying that:

> It is all very difficult and delicate, and I can see no way of helping a sick mind which is irritated by the very efforts one makes to cure it. For a long time now the disease which gnaws at the body and soul of this poor creature has been killing me, and I see him fading away, without ever having been able to do him any good, since it is this anxious, jealous and touching affection he bears for me which is the main cause of his misery. For the last seven years I have lived like a virgin with him and with other men. I have made myself old without any effort or sacrifice, for I was weary of passion and disillusioned beyond hope. If there is a woman on this earth who should inspire him with confidence it is me. He has never understood that. I know that

people accuse me, some of having killed him by the violence
of my passion, others of having exasperated him with my
temperance. I think you know the real state of affairs! He
complains that I have killed him by denying him, while I was
certain that I would kill him if I acted otherwise. Look at my
position in this fatal friendship, in which I have made myself his
slave in every situation I could without actually showing a
wrongful and impossible preference for him over my children,
and in which the dignity I have had to maintain before my
children and my friends has been so delicate and difficult to
preserve! On that score I have achieved miracles of patience of
which I did not believe myself capable, I who am not endowed
with the nature of a saint like the Princess [Czartoryska]*! I have*
achieved martyrdom, but the heavens are implacable towards
me, as though I had great crimes to expiate; for in the middle of
all these efforts and all these sacrifices, the man I love with an
absolutely chaste and maternal love is dying, the victim of the
ridiculous love he bears me![13]

There is a curious discrepancy between her view of the situation, and particularly of her supposed enslavement to Chopin's needs, and his apparently relaxed equanimity. On 15 May, in answer to her letter containing the details of Solange's impending wedding, he wrote thanking her and sending his best wishes to Solange. He signed off: 'God support you always in your purpose and your deeds. Be happy and serene. Your completely devoted Ch.'[14]

Solange was married quietly to Clésinger a few days later, while Chopin went off to Ville d'Avray near Paris to spend a week with Thomas Albrecht. When he returned, he found that the young couple were back in Paris, so he called on them and gave Solange a bouquet of roses and carnations. 'Sol was polite to me, as always, he was also as polite as he could be, I was my usual self – but I felt sad inside,' he wrote to Ludwika.[15] He rarely saw the Clésingers after that. George Sand herself arrived in Paris on 1 June to arrange the marriage between Augustine Brault and the young painter Théodore Rousseau, but he did not see much of her either. Two weeks later she returned to Nohant, looking forward to a long, restful summer, and to the arrival of Chopin and Delacroix, who were to come down together.

She had apparently recovered her serenity of mind. 'I am neither as crazy, nor as good, nor as great [as Lucrezia], for if I were united to Prince Karol, I must admit that I would not let myself be killed, but would politely dump him there and then,' she wrote to a friend who naïvely wondered whether *Lucrezia Floriani* was about her and Chopin. 'However, I am feeling very well, and would never dream of separating from a friend who has become invaluable to me through eight years of mutual devotion.'[16]

Chopin was in good spirits, in spite of the news of Witwicki's death in Italy, which reached him in June. He was beginning to get used to the way in which death seemed to be encroaching, and merely acquiesced with sadness, as he had done when he had heard of Antoni Wodziński's demise a couple of months earlier. He must have realised that others thought he too would be dying soon, for he was now posing for the fourth portrait of himself specially commissioned by a friend – in this case Auguste Léo – during the last two months. By the beginning of July he had stopped most of his lessons and was busy copying and correcting the Cello and Piano Sonata for the printers, feeling that it was, at long last, ready. He had decided he would go to Nohant after all, since Delacroix was prepared to go with him, and he aimed to set off halfway through July.

Meanwhile, the Clésingers, who had gone down to stay at Nohant, began to make trouble. The sculptor had married mainly for what he believed to be George Sand's riches and, having been given very little, began to suspect everyone, particularly Maurice and Augustine, of plotting against him. Solange seconded him ably, and did all she could to spite the rest of the family. Clésinger eventually had a row with Maurice, threatened to kill him with a hammer, hit George Sand who interposed herself, and nearly had his head blown off by Maurice, who had fetched his gun.

George Sand threw the Clésingers out of the house, saying she never wanted to see either of them again, whereupon they moved into the neighbouring town of La Châtre and began spreading the foulest slanders against all the inhabitants of Nohant. To Chopin, Solange wrote:

> *My dear Chopin! I am ill and the journey by the Blois mail coach would tire me out. Will you lend me your carriage for my return journey to Paris? Please answer immediately. I await your answer at La Châtre, where life is difficult for me. I have left Nohant forever, after the most horrible scenes by my mother. Wait for me, I beg you, before leaving Paris. I need to see you urgently. I was positively refused your carriage, so if you wish me to use it, send me a note with your permission, which I can send on to Nohant. Goodbye, until soon, I hope. Solange.*[17]

Chopin received this on 13 July, and immediately wrote a letter to George Sand, which has not survived but which seems to have enquired about what had happened and clearly expressed some sympathy for Solange. It also stated that she could use his carriage if she wished. Next day he wrote Solange a laconic note, telling her the carriage was at her disposal. George Sand had already written to Marie de Rozières and Delacroix, describing the events at Nohant in detail and enjoining them to keep as much from Chopin as possible. 'Don't tell him how far things went, we shall try to hide as much as possible from him.'[18] Her reply to Chopin is lost, but some of its contents can be deduced with certainty. She described the scene at Nohant only in the vaguest terms, but went on at some length about Chopin himself and his place in her life. She announced to him that Clésinger was a bounder, and even seems to have reproached Chopin for not having warned her. Finally, she ordered him to keep his doors closed to Solange when she turned up in Paris, and not to mention her name at all when he and Delacroix came down to Nohant the following week.[19]

Chopin immediately told Delacroix of the letter, and a few days later, on 20 July, showed it to him. 'One has to admit that it [the letter] is horrible,' the painter noted in his diary. 'Cruel passions and long-pent-up impatience erupt in it, and by a contrast which would be amusing if it did not touch on such a tragic subject, the author from time to time takes over from the woman, and launches into tirades which look as though they were borrowed from a novel or a philosophical homily.'[20] Chopin did not answer the letter for some ten days.

Meanwhile the Clésingers had turned up in Paris. Solange wasted no time in calling on Chopin and telling him about the events at Nohant, and her version was by now becoming increasingly lurid. Whether he believed it or not, it was the only account he had been given, since George Sand was determined to keep him out of her family affairs. She had been expecting Chopin and Delacroix daily, but time passed and there was no sign of either. She grew anxious about Chopin's health, thinking that perhaps he had had another attack, and considered rushing to Paris to see him. Then, two weeks after she had written, she received his reply:

I have nothing to say to you about M. Cl[ésinger]. I had not heard the name of M. Cl until the day you decided to give him your daughter. As for her, she cannot be indifferent to me. You will remember that I interceded with you on behalf of your children, without preference, whenever the opportunity presented itself, in the certitude that you were destined to love

*them always – for those are the only affections that do not
change. Misfortune can cloud them but never alter their nature.
The misfortune must be very great at this moment if it forbids
your heart to hear the name of your daughter, at the beginning
of her mature life, at the moment when her physical condition
requires more than ever the care of a mother.*

*   In the face of such a serious matter, which concerns your
most sacred affections, I shall not go into the matters
concerning myself. Time will act. I shall wait always the same.
Your wholly devoted, Ch.*[21]

This letter could not have reached George Sand at a worse
moment. Exhausted by work, which she had stepped up in
order to cover the expenses of Solange's wedding, she had
endured terrifying scenes at Nohant, and watched the marriage
she had arranged turn into a fiasco. Her efforts to marry off
Augustine had also come to nothing, the young painter having
heard rumours spread by Solange and backed out. Maurice was
not only useless as a support, he was going through a personal
crisis and needed his mother's help. To Marie de Rozières she
wrote that were it not for him, she would end her own life.[22]
She was longing for the arrival of a calm Chopin and an affable
Delacroix, and when she perceived treason in that quarter too,
she overreacted.

Chopin's reply found her in the middle of a letter to her
friend the republican lawyer Emmanuel Arago, which turned
into one of the longest ever written, as she began setting down
her reactions and venting her thoughts on paper. The astonishing seventy-one-page document is of immense value in
revealing her state of mind.[23]

What stung her to the quick in Chopin's letter was its cool,
collected and slightly pompous tone. And its contents could
not fail to exasperate her: he pointed out that the match with
Clésinger was her doing, at the same time turning against her

her own hobby-horse of the sanctity of maternal instincts. From the 'impractical' Chopin who 'has never understood a thing about human life', she found such observations downright insulting, and indeed disloyal. 'If I had committed faults, even crimes, Chopin should not have believed them, should not have seen them,' she later complained to Louis Viardot. 'There is a certain degree of respect and gratitude past which we no longer have the right to examine the behaviour of those beings who have become sacred for us.'[24]

In her search for an explanation of his perfidy, she hit on the 'revelation' that Chopin had been in love not with her but with Solange all along: the two had always got on well, and during the last couple of years they had enjoyed an intimacy which excluded her and Maurice. Chopin's attack of asthma the day after he heard of Solange's engagement to Clésinger was proof of his jealousy (the fact that there had been no similar fit after her engagement to de Preaulx, a union which he had warmly encouraged, was conveniently forgotten). Chopin's dislike of Augustine Brault, too, was seen as emanating from Solange's influence (although his dislike predated Solange's). Now George Sand saw clearly that Chopin's jealousy of other men who approached her, which had irritated her so much over the years, was in fact not jealousy over her, but Solange. Clear as daylight too was the fact that Chopin's feelings for her had in fact been not love but hatred all along.

There had indeed been something between Chopin and Solange, and Arago, on whom Solange had tried her charms as well, had witnessed it. 'For several years, he has been fascinated by her and accepted from her with pleasure behaviour that would have exasperated him coming from another,' wrote Arago in his reply to George Sand's interminable letter. 'I could see, did see, and saw often that he had for her a deep feeling which at first resembled paternal affection, and which changed, probably under her influence, when she turned from a child into a young girl and from a young girl into a woman.'[25] There was, however, a great difference between the bored and ageing Chopin's no doubt somewhat prurient appreciation of the golden-haired Solange's coquetry, and the lurid sexual passion suggested by George Sand (who could not resist making crude observations on his possible sexual performance with her daughter).

The crux of the matter was that George Sand was deeply wounded by what she saw as Chopin's desertion, and mortified that a man she had taken for granted and considered an importunate lover could show such independence. Her answer to his letter, dated 28 July, was no less icy and pompous than his own had been:

I had ordered post-horses for yesterday and was about to leave by cabriolet in this awful weather, although very ill myself; I was proposing to spend a day in Paris in order to find out how you were. Your silence had worried me on the score of your health. Meanwhile you were reflecting calmly, and your answer is very composed. That is fine, my friend, do what your heart dictates, and take its instinct for the language of your conscience. I understand perfectly.

As for my daughter, her illness is no more worrying than last year's [There are in fact two letters from George Sand to other people from the same period expressing deep concern over her daughter's health], *and neither my zeal nor my care, nor my entreaties have ever been able to dissuade her from defying her constitution and behaving like someone who wishes to make herself ill. She can hardly be saying that she needs the love of a mother whom she slanders and loathes, whose most sacred actions and whose house she sullies with her hideous insinuations. You are happy to listen to all that and perhaps to believe it. I shall not enter into a battle of that nature, it repels me. I prefer to see you go over to the enemy rather than to defend myself against an enemy born from my womb and nourished with my milk.*

*Look after her, since it is to her that you think you should
devote yourself. I shall not hold it against you, but you will
understand that I am cast in the role of outraged mother, and
that nothing from now on can make me abandon the authority
and the dignity of this role. It is enough to be fooled and made
a victim. I forgive you and will not address any reproaches to
you, since your confession is sincere. It surprised me a little, but
since you feel more at ease and freer now, I shall not suffer
from this extraordinary volte-face.*

*Goodbye, my friend, may you be rapidly cured of your
malady, as I believe you will (I have my reasons for that), and
I shall thank God for this strange dénouement to nine years of
exclusive friendship – Give me news of yourself sometimes. It is
pointless to ever come back on the rest.* [26]

Chopin was dumbfounded by this letter, with its talk of his
'going over to the enemy' and of his 'confession'. He was
informed that he was being forgiven, though it was not at all
evident why forgiveness should be called for. But the greatest
shock was that this was a final and irrevocable dismissal. It was
the last letter that passed between them.

Chopin thought that George Sand had gone a little mad,
and that the attack of hysteria would subside. He saw his own
behaviour as being perfectly correct throughout, as his letters
home make clear. Sooner or later George Sand would surely
recognise this and their friendship would resume. Pauline
Viardot, who had been told of the events by George Sand, went
to see Chopin, and although she had always been primarily a
friend of George Sand, felt obliged to take Chopin's part in a
letter she wrote to Nohant. 'There is in your good letter one
passage that I cannot allow to pass over in silence,' she wrote.
'It is that in which you state that Chopin is a member of a
Solange faction, representing her as a victim and denigrating
you. This is absolutely false, I swear to you, at least as far as he

is concerned. On the contrary, this dear and excellent friend is afflicted by one thought only: the harm that this whole un-fortunate business has done you and is still doing you. I have not found the slightest change in him – he is as kind, as devoted as ever – adoring you as always, rejoicing only in your joy, afflicted only by your sufferings.' Her husband's postscript was even more specific: 'I may sum up what Chopin said as follows: Solange's marriage is a great misfortune for herself, her family and her friends. Daughter and mother were both deceived and realised their mistake too late. But since they both shared in the mistake, why should only one bear the blame? The daughter wanted, insisted on, an ill-assorted match; but had the mother, who consented, no share in the fault? With her great gifts and experience, could she not have enlightened a girl who was led more by mortification than love? . . . one should not be piti-less towards a mistake to which one has contributed. I, pitying both from the bottom of my heart, try to console the only one I am allowed to see.' He added that Chopin spoke of her 'without reproach or bitterness, only with deep sorrow'.[27]

This rubbing in of her own rash behaviour, of the way she had let herself be taken in by Clésinger in the face of so many warnings, only wounded George Sand's pride deeper. She almost included the Viardots in 'the enemy camp', which was already impressively crowded: Delacroix, who had written to say that he was not coming down to Nohant after all, the 'silly goose' Marie de Rozières, the 'weak and frivolous' Grzymała, the Marlianis, and even the 'saintly' Princess Anna Czartoryska were all ruthlessly relegated to it.[28]

With time, George Sand did come to realise that Chopin had not been disloyal or motivated by lust for Solange, but by then she had moved on to the view that the break with him had been a good thing. She dredged up every piece of unfavourable evidence concerning his behaviour over the past nine years and convinced herself that she had been imprisoned by him and his 'coterie', who had made her responsible for his health and happiness. As she concluded, in her letter to Arago, she would now at last be able to 'Work, Run, Sleep!'[29] To Marie de Rozières, who suggested a reconciliation, she replied that she had 'no cause to regret the loss of his affection'.[30]

In her later writings on the subject, she depicted Chopin as a hopeless neurotic with whom she had had a chaste relationship, based only on her admiration for the artist and her feeling of maternal duty towards a lost and unhappy soul. With the help of her son she destroyed all the letters between herself and the composer on which she could lay her hands. This was in marked contrast to Chopin's behaviour: he kept her letters amongst his most valued possessions, and carried the first note he had received from her with him everywhere until his death.

George Sand's behaviour ensured that the affair and its dénouement were widely discussed. While some believed her version, many more saw Chopin as a victim and her as a sort of man-eating harpy. Before ten years were out, Liszt, in the first biography of Chopin to appear, summed up the relationship as 'a prison in which he found himself being garrotted by bonds saturated with venom; their corrosive suppuration could not touch his genius, but they consumed his life and took him off too soon from the earth, from his motherland, from Art!'[31]

Chopin did not realise what was going on in George Sand's head. He was sure that there would soon be a reconciliation between mother and daughter, and pressed Solange to bring it about, not realising quite how badly she had behaved. He lent her money and tried to help Clésinger get work, for his debts had now overtaken him. To Chopin's great relief, the couple left Paris to go and stay with Solange's father. Neither Grzymała nor Delacroix, Marie de Rozières nor the Marlianis had any news from Nohant. But Chopin remained confident that all would be well in the end. 'Madame Sand cannot but find a good memory of me in her soul when one day she looks back,' he wrote to Ludwika.[32]

It was not a happy time for him. He stayed a few days with Thomas Albrecht at Ville d'Avray and a weekend at the Rothschild mansion at Ferrières, but otherwise spent the summer and autumn in Paris. Grzymała had crashed financially, the Marlianis were getting divorced, and Delacroix was in a doleful mood. Other friends tried to keep Chopin busy, and the void left in his life by the absence of George Sand was filled by a gaggle of women eager to mother him. The Czartoryski ladies were joined by Delfina Potocka, Marie de Rozières, his pupil Elise Gavard, Princess Obreskoff, mother of another pupil, and by Jane Stirling, who vied with the others in her zeal. She was a generous and motherly Scottish spinster, six years older than Chopin. She was not one of his favourite pupils, and his joy was all the greater when he acquired a new one whose talent and personality were more to his taste. This was the six-foot beauty Countess Maria Kalergis.

Born in Warsaw to a Russian father and a Polish mother, she had married a Russian diplomat of Greek extraction, whom she soon deserted. Her father, Count Nesselrode, was the Chief of Police in Warsaw, and her uncle was Chancellor of the Russian Empire. Countess Maria enjoyed embarrassing them by her unorthodox behaviour and manifestations of pro-Polish feeling. She was only twenty-five years old, but had already managed to have affairs with Liszt, Musset, the future Napoleon III and Théophile Gautier, who wrote a poem for her entitled 'Symphonie en Blanc Majeur' (she always dressed in white). Heine, who disliked her, retaliated with another poem called 'L'Éléphant Blanc' and described her as a 'Pantheon in which so many great men lie buried'.[33] She was a talented pianist and just the sort of person Chopin enjoyed teaching, and she helped to distract him as he sat in a state of limbo, waiting to see what would happen next.

Nothing did happen. George Sand made no overtures, even though some measure of reconciliation had taken place with her daughter. By December she had taken on a young lover, who was duly installed in Chopin's old room at Nohant. 'I am like an old cobweb, and the walls are beginning to fall away,' Chopin moaned to one Polish friend.[34] Mendelssohn's death in November reinforced the feeling that something was coming to an end, for they had been almost the same age. As usual, it provoked a bout of self-pity in Chopin. When the subject was raised over dinner with Jane Stirling's sister Katherine Erskine, he said that 'there was something almost enviable in his fate, dying in the midst of his family surrounded by love – and with his wife beside him'.[35]

The cold winter and the influenza epidemic intensified the lugubrious mood of that season. 'I have my own habitual splutterings to think about, so I don't fear the *grippe*,' Chopin wrote to his family. 'I occasionally sniff at my homeopathic bottles, I give a lot of lessons at home, and somehow I'm managing not too badly.'[36] He was even capable on occasion of recovering a childlike enthusiasm, and one young English girl recorded his 'making rabbits on the wall' and performing other tricks one evening in December.[37] But to Solange he wrote: 'This horrible year must end,' a sentiment echoed in a note from Princess Czartoryska, which ended: 'What sadness everywhere!'[38]

FIFTEEN

London and Scotland

The year 1848 began in France under the clouds of a political storm that had been brewing for some time, and there was a widespread feeling that it would not end without civil unrest. The conservative prime minister François Guizot sought to forestall this by banning political meetings organised by a growing liberal opposition, but this only served to channel it down the road to revolution.

The possibility of this breaking out was probably not far from the thoughts of Thomas Albrecht, Camille Pleyel, Auguste Léo and the comte de Perthuis when they called on Chopin one day towards the end of January and suggested he give a concert. He raised every conceivable objection, but they dismissed these and promised to take all the arrangements on themselves. It seems likely that they were prompted not only by the desire to hear him, but also by the concern that as his health deteriorated he would have to cut down on giving lessons and his income would dwindle as a result, and that he would need a cash reserve with which to face the difficult times that might lie ahead.

A brief announcement appeared in the press to the effect that the public might expect a concert by Chopin in the near future, and Pleyel's offices were instantly flooded with letters and callers applying to reserve tickets. By the time a date had been fixed, some two weeks before the night itself, all three hundred tickets had been sold, and there was a waiting list of six hundred people trying to obtain seats for a possible second concert. Pleyel was keen that he should take advantage of this, but Chopin had no intention of complying, declaring that one concert was 'quite enough of a bore'.[1] 'I am amazed by this enthusiasm,' he wrote to Ludwika, 'and now I shall have to play if only out of gratitude, although I feel that I play worse than ever.'[2]

At the beginning of February he was ill for a few days, but he came to life once more as the event approached. A few days before the date set, 16 February, he held a small rehearsal at Delfina Potocka's before the Czartoryskis, Maria Kalergis, Delfina's sister the princesse de Beauvau and the Zaleskis. The event itself was to be hardly less courtly. There were no posters, no programmes, and the tickets were stiff cartons printed like invitations: Monsieur Frédéric Chopin requested the presence of whoever it was at a musical evening at Monsieur Pleyel's salons. Pleyel filled the hall with flowers, while Jane Stirling saw to its being warm enough, yet not too stuffy. 'I shall be completely at home and see only familiar faces,' Chopin assured Ludwika, and on the night he was surrounded by friends: on the dais itself sat Grzymała, Custine, the Czartoryskis, Delacroix and Zaleski. All this has given rise to the impression that it was not a public concert at all, and that the whole audience had been carefully selected by Chopin.[3] This was not the case. It was simply that his friends, who knew of the impending event sooner, put their names down first, while he reserved some seats for others among them who applied late.

Chopin played a Mozart Trio with Franchomme and the violinist Delphin Alard, and the last three movements of his Sonata for Piano and Cello with Franchomme. The rest of the evening he filled on his own, playing the Berceuse, the Barcarolle and the D flat major Waltz (op.64). Despite his fears, his increasing frailty did not impair the quality of his playing.

He had been weakening so gradually over the years that he had had time to substitute technique for force. Already in 1842 one of his pupils had commented that 'his pianissimo is so delicate that he can produce the greatest effects of crescendo without requiring the strength of the muscular virtuosi of the modern school'.[4] An English pianist who was present at the concert was astonished to find the emaciated Chopin capable of playing with force.[5]

The audience were in raptures. The *Revue et Gazette Musicale* stated that one would need Shakespeare's pen to describe Chopin's playing, and the other papers echoed its paean of praise. *Le Ménestrel* called him 'the sylph of the piano, the ineffable artist, attached to this mortal world by the merest touch of a finger and nourished by dreams from on high', and compared his playing to 'the sighing of a flower, the whisper of clouds, or the murmur of stars'.[6] Perhaps the most fitting comments on the concert and on Chopin's position in general were made by Custine, who sent him a little note afterwards. 'You have gained in suffering and poetry; the melancholy of your compositions penetrates still deeper into the heart; one feels alone with you in the midst of a crowd; it is no longer a piano, but a soul, and what a soul!' he wrote. 'Preserve yourself for the sake of your friends; it is a consolation to be able to hear you sometimes; in the hard times that threaten, only art as you feel it will be able to unite men divided by the realities of life; people love each other, people understand each other in Chopin. You have turned a public into a circle of friends; you are equal to your own genius; that says it all.'[7]

Chopin must have been persuaded to change his mind about giving a second concert, as Pleyel announced one for 10 March. But on 22 February revolution broke out in Paris, and with the barricades up in the streets there could be no question of such an event taking place. Chopin was feeling ill, and lay in bed listening to the fighting that engulfed the capital for two days, at the end of which King Louis Philippe and his family fled and made for the coast, whence they took ship for England. As soon as the fighting had subsided, Chopin tried to resume his normal life, but it was difficult getting about, since the cobbles had been torn up and some of the barricades were not cleared away for weeks, and most of his pupils, while not directly affected by the events, were not inclined to come for their lessons.

The court that had patronised Chopin was gone, and friends like the comte de Perthuis with it, but on the whole there was little for his pupils and friends to fear, particularly as most of them were either foreigners or musicians, and Poles were more popular in Paris than ever. Nevertheless, outbreaks of street violence were a hazard, and it was impossible to tell what course events would take. There were disturbances over the border in Germany, and much talk of Europe-wide revolution. The climate of instability frightened Chopin as well as threatening his livelihood, and the prospect of spending another summer in Paris was not one to which he looked forward. He again considered the possibility of meeting some of his family in Germany, but most of that, too, was in a state of political ferment. Jane Stirling on the other hand hotly advocated the idea of his visiting England and taking in the London season.

There certainly seemed to be nothing left to keep him in Paris. In the first days of March he had a letter from Solange, announcing that she had had a baby. The news delighted Chopin, who felt the event might provide a bridge for recon-ciliation between mother and daughter. A vague hope lingered in his mind that George Sand might get over the 'kind of madness' which he saw as the explanation for her behaviour, and relent in her attitude towards him as well, though he was not optimistic on that score.[8]

The fall of the July Monarchy, which she had despised, brought George Sand to Paris, as several of her friends were in the provisional government, and she herself wanted to play an active part. Chopin did not know this, for she had long before given up her apartment at the Square d'Orléans, and now took rooms elsewhere. On 4 March he went to dinner, as he still often did, at Charlotte Marliani's. As he was leaving with the French traveller Edmond Combes, he came face to face with George Sand, who was just on her way in. They greeted each other politely, and then Chopin asked whether she had heard from her daughter recently.

'More than a week ago,' she replied. 'You did not get a letter yesterday, or the day before?' asked Chopin. 'No.' 'In that case I must inform you that you are a grandmother; Solange has a daughter, and I am happy to be the one to tell you of it.' With these words, he went on down the stairs, but reaching the bottom, realised that he had not mentioned Solange's condition. As he could not climb the stairs himself, he begged Combes to run up and tell her that Solange was well. George Sand came down the stairs with Combes and eagerly asked for details, after which she enquired after his own health. He said it was good, and, bowing, called to the concierge to open the door.[9] 'I pressed his trembling and icy hand, I wanted to speak to him; he fled,' she later reminisced. 'It was my turn to say that he no longer loved me. I spared him that suffering...'[10] Combes walked Chopin home, and noted that he was very sad and depressed.[11] He was never to see her again.

Revolution in France had produced aftershocks across Germany, starting a chain reaction of unrest and revolution – in Berlin, Prague, Vienna, Budapest, Milan, Venice and Madrid. Inevitably, Poland was affected too, and the Prussian-occupied part, the Duchy of Posen, briefly achieved a measure of autonomy. Many of the Parisian exiles, including Prince Adam Czartoryski, set off for the Duchy in the expectation that it would become a springboard for the liberation of the whole country. Some of the poorer ones borrowed money from Chopin for the journey, but to Fontana, who had written from America saying he wanted to go and fight for Poland, Chopin replied advising him to await further developments. He found it difficult to share the sanguine hopes of some of his compatriots.

His own instincts were conservative, and he was appalled at the prospect of more violence. At the same time he could not repress a surge of patriotic feeling. 'It won't come without horrors,' he is alleged to have written to Fontana, 'but at the end of it all, there must be a great, a magnificent Poland; a true Poland.'[12] The idea must have seemed vaguely comforting as he sat in Paris watching his own world collapse around him. 'My public career is over,' he said to another who was setting out for Poland. 'In your village you have a little church; you can give me a little bread for the rest of my life, and I shall play hymns to Our Lady on the organ.'[13]

Watching others spring into action made him feel more redundant than ever – even Princess Belgiojoso had left her Paris salon and was rallying patriots on the streets of Milan. And Chopin was anxious; in the helpless condition to which his illness had reduced him, upheaval of any kind was a frightening prospect. The only place in Europe that seemed immune to disturbance was England. In the end he gave in to Jane Stirling's blandishments, and decided to join her in London.

He left on 19 April and arrived in London the following day, which happened to be Maundy Thursday. He found the city 'quiet and dreary', but the coal smoke made an immediate impression on his lungs.[14] Jane Stirling and her sister, Mrs Erskine, had provided him with an apartment in Bentinck Street off Cavendish Square, and had done everything to make him comfortable, including providing his favourite drinking chocolate and notepaper with his monogram on it. But the rooms were expensive and did not suit him, so he mobilised Major Szulczewski, the London agent of the Czartoryskis, to look for more suitable ones.

Over the Easter weekend he drove down to Kingston-upon-Thames to see the exiled French royal family and their entourage. Otherwise he kept to himself during the first ten days, as he did not feel well and could not face starting his calls. At the end of April he moved into new rooms in Dover Street, off Piccadilly. 'At last I have a room – fine and large – in which I shall be able to breathe and play – and today the sun has visited it for the first time,' he wrote to Franchomme on 1 May.[15] His Pleyel piano was unpacked, and since Érard and Broadwood both insisted on lending him instruments, he had three in his large drawing room; but, as he wrote to Gutmann, 'What use are they, since I have no time to play them?'[16]

He had begun paying calls on acquaintances and on those to whom he had been given letters of introduction. He visited the Chevalier d'Orsay at Kensington Gore; went to Cheyne Row to see Thomas Carlyle, dined with Ralph Waldo Emerson, met Charles Dickens and Lady Byron, 'with whom, apparently, I have great affinity – we talk like a goose to a pig, she in English, I in French'. 'I'm not surprised she bored Byron,' he added.[17] At the opera, he was impressed by the figure of the young Queen, more so still by 'Wellington in the box below the Queen's, like an old monarchist watchdog sitting in a kennel beneath his crowned lady'.[18]

One thing that Chopin had not expected to find in London was the swarm of musicians, which included Berlioz, Thalberg and Pauline Viardot, who had also fled the uncertainties of the Continent. An unexpected pleasure was the possibility of meeting the acclaimed Swedish soprano Jenny Lind, who had also taken refuge in England. He found her voice astonishing and the character of her singing fascinating. 'Yesterday I went to dinner at Jenny Lind's, who then sang Swedish things for me until midnight,' he wrote to Grzymała on 13 May. 'They have a very special spirit, just as our music has. We have something Slavonic, they something Scandinavian, and they are completely different, but we're closer to each other than an Italian is to a Spaniard.'[19]

But the surfeit of musicians did have practical and financial implications. 'Will the British capital be able to maintain so many exiles?' wondered an alarmed Berlioz.[20] Chopin, who badly needed to make his mark with a wider public, started off with what might have been an extremely unwise move. He was paid the compliment of being asked to play one of his concertos with the Philharmonic Society, an honour recently denied to Charles Hallé and Kalkbrenner. He refused this offer, explaining to Grzymała that 'their orchestra is like their roast beef or their turtle soup – strong, pungent and nothing more'.[21] What actually put him off was the fact that there was no possibility of a rehearsal with the orchestra before the public performance, and he was growing fussier than ever about getting things right. Another consideration was that he would not be able to muster the requisite strength. With solo works he could lower the volume, thereby making it possible to produce powerful crescendos at the appropriate moments, but if he lowered the volume of the piano part when playing with an orchestra, it would be completely drowned out. It was for this reason that he had not played one of his concertos with a full orchestra for well over a dozen years.

Chopin was determined to make his mark in his own way. 'When I have played before the Queen, I shall have to give a matinée musicale in a private house for a limited number of listeners!' he explained to Gutmann.[22] One point that he had overlooked was that the director of the Philharmonic Society was the man responsible for arranging concerts at court, and he was not pleased when Chopin turned down his offer of a concert. Chopin did get an opportunity to play before Victoria, though not at court. It was on the occasion of the christening of the Duchess of Sutherland's baby, to whom the Queen stood godmother, at Stafford House (now Lancaster House) on 15 May.

The party consisted of some eighty people, including the Queen and her Consort, the future William I of Prussia, the Duke of Wellington, and 'everything that is most Garter', as Chopin put it in a letter to Grzymała.[23]

He played a few short pieces of his own, and then some Mozart for two pianos with the English pianist Julius Benedict. The Parisian singers Mario, Lablache and Tamburini also performed, but Chopin felt he had made an impression on the Queen, who 'addressed a few gracious words' to him afterwards. He seems to have been taken in by the regal good manners, because the entry in her diary for that evening reads: 'There was some pretty music, good Lablache and Tamburini singing, and some pianists playing.'[24]

Chopin earned a respectable sum of money from playing at soirées at the Marquess of Douglas's, the Duchess of Somerset's, the Duchess of Cambridge's, Lady Gainsborough's and the homes of 'many other Ladies, whose names go in one ear and come out the other'.[25] 'They don't talk while I play, and apparently they all speak well of my music, but it is above all the hopelessness of my local colleagues, who are in the habit of being pushed around, which is the reason why they consider me a sort of amateur,' he reported to Grzymała. 'I shall soon become a grand seigneur, because I have clean shoes and don't carry about cards saying: "Will give lessons at home, available for evening parties, etc."'[26]

The English were apparently less squeamish of talking about money than their French counterparts. On one occasion, Lady Rothschild approached Chopin and, on hearing how much he asked for playing, said that, to be sure, he played 'very prettily', but that the price was wanting in 'moderation'.[27] Another lady, whose daughter took two lessons a week at half a guinea each from another pianist, wanted her daughter to take some from Chopin, but on hearing that he charged a whole guinea a lesson, decided that one per week would do just as well in his case.[28]

Expensive as he was for the English market, Chopin did not lack pupils. 'They all look at their hands and play the wrong notes with feeling,' he quipped.[29] By the middle of the season he was giving up to five lessons a day, and since there was no shortage of demand for him to play at soirées, he was doing well financially. In a letter to Grzymała, he claimed that he would be able to save a considerable sum if the season lasted long enough. But the season was short and hectic, and he did not have the energy to fall in with its pace. He complained that he could not get up before eight in the morning, and that much of his time and energy was being taken up by Jane Stirling and her sister, who insisted on dragging him from one acquaintance to another.

On 23 June he gave the first of his public concerts, at the house of Adelaide Sartoris in Eaton Place. The daughter of the celebrated actor Charles Kemble, she had made a name for herself as an actress and singer, and had met Chopin when she was singing in Paris. She had fallen under the spell of his playing, and was one of his warmest advocates in England. The audience was restricted to 150 people. Among them was the novelist Thackeray, who had come to hear the 'very pretty music' – some way from Balzac's vision of 'a soul expressing itself in lyricism'.[30] As far as Chopin was concerned, the main attraction of the event was the financial gain, which at 150 guineas was considerable. Two weeks later, on 7 July, he followed it up with a matinee concert at the house of Lord Falmouth, an amateur violinist of eccentric ways. 'In the street you'd give him threepence, but his house is full of servants – dressed better than him,' Chopin wrote.[31]

While Broadwood was arranging the concert, Pauline Viardot heard of it and offered to take part. She sang her own arrangements of his Mazurkas, which were her *pièce de résistance*, much in demand wherever she appeared. Chopin himself played mostly short pieces, with the exception of the B flat minor

Scherzo. The audience was again small but the takings large, and this time he felt that he was getting through to his listeners.

This is corroborated by the reactions of Jane Welsh Carlyle, whose eyes were opened by the first concert, to which she went with her husband. 'I never heard the piano played before – could not have believed the capabilities that be in it,' she recorded.[32] She went to the matinee alone, as Thomas Carlyle was visiting Stonehenge with Emerson. 'I never liked any music so well,' she wrote to Jane Stirling, 'because <u>it feels</u> to me not so much a sample of the man's <u>art</u> offered "<u>on approbation</u>" (the effect of most music for me) but a portion of his soul and life <u>given away</u> by him – <u>spent</u> on those who have ears to hear and hearts to understand. I cannot fancy but that every piece he composes must leave him with many fewer days to live.'[33]

The matinee was extensively reviewed in the press, and while Chopin's old enemy Davison (who had written the vituperative review of some Mazurkas in 1841) reviewed his playing unfavourably in 'The Teims', as Chopin insisted on spelling it, most of the notices were favourable.

The *Daily News*, for instance, praised his 'original genius as a composer and his transcendental power as a performer'. 'His music is as strongly marked with individual character as that of any master who has ever lived,' it went on. 'It is highly finished, new in its harmonies, full of contrapuntal skill and ingenious contrivance; and yet we have never heard music which has so much the air of unpremeditated effusion. The performer seems to abandon himself to the impulses of his fancy and feeling, to indulge in a reverie, and to pour out unconsciously as it were, the thoughts and emotions that pass through his mind.'[34]

All this led Chopin to consider the possibility of staying on and even settling in England. There were several arguments against this. 'These English are so different from the French, whom I have grown to accept as my own people,' he explained to his family. 'They are so pound-conscious in everything, liking the arts above all because they represent luxury; they are kind people, but so weird . . .'[35] More to the point was what Chopin saw as their attitude to music. To Grzymała he explained that the English middle classes only wanted things fantastic or mechanically exciting; he was always being asked to play the little Waltzes with their pearly passages, and then being told that 'it sounds just like water'. The aristocracy, though discerning and cultivated, were brought up to treat music as background noise: there was music at every social function, whether it was a flower show or a dinner, and the local musicians allowed themselves to be treated as servants. London was full of 'Czechs and Savoyards', according to Chopin, and they would play whatever was expected of them, without demanding anything in exchange except their fee.

'If you say you're an artist, the Englishman will think you're a painter, a sculptor or an architect,' he wrote to Grzymała; 'no musician will be called an artist in word or print, because in their view it is not an art but a profession.'[36] He nevertheless thought he might be able to break the mould. When he stopped playing after someone had started talking at the Duchess of Kent's soirée in July, it was the Duchess herself (she was Queen Victoria's mother) who called for silence and then begged him to resume.[37] 'If I could still spend my days calling on this one and that one, if I had not been spitting blood for the last few days, if I were younger, if I did not have my head full of attachments, as I have, then I would perhaps start life all over again,' he wrote to Grzymała.[38] To his family, he put it more practically: 'If London were not quite so black, the people not quite so heavy, and if there were no smell of coal and no fog, I would probably start learning English.'[39] The climate was the crucial factor. 'Often in the morning I think I'm going to cough up my very soul,' he wrote at the beginning of June, and although Mrs Grote, the eccentric wife of a Whig MP who had introduced him to Jenny Lind and helped him in various ways, thought that 'the climate rather suits him, because it is cool and fresh this season', he was almost perpetually ill.[40]

As usual with Chopin, dejection followed in the wake of physical collapse. He was often in 'a fit of spleen', and felt lonely in London, brooding ceaselessly over the events which had washed him up there with nobody close to talk to. Major Szulczewski provided a comforting presence, as did Chopin's former pupil Tellefsen, now working in London, and Broadwood, 'the most wonderful and genuine friend'.[41]

Broadwood was full of delicate attentions. When he heard Chopin had slept badly, he had good pillows and a mattress sent round to his lodgings; when, later, he was arranging Chopin's journey to Scotland, he booked the seat opposite, so the composer could stretch out his legs. But this could not make up for the absence of friends like Grzymała, Franchomme or Delacroix. As Chopin himself observed, '20 years in Poland, 17 in Paris – it's not surprising I don't feel happy here.'[42] Just as in Vienna seventeen years before, he was surrounded by kindness and goodwill, but felt sorry for himself. 'I no longer know how to be sad or happy about anything any more,' he wrote, '– I have exhausted all my feelings completely – I'm just vegetating and waiting for it all to end soon.'[43]

A minor, but for Chopin powerful, irritant was the fact that the Italian servant he had taken on after his arrival was inefficient, lazy and dishonest. By now he often needed to be carried up stairs and helped with many functions, some of them intimate, and he therefore required a servant with whom he could have a rapport. This one was unsympathetic and threw Chopin's money around, which, combined with the composer's own profligacy and the expense of life in London during the season, meant that his sizeable earnings were whittled down to some two hundred guineas after all the bills had been paid.

By the end of the season he was exhausted and at a loose end. Most of the revolutionary movements of the spring had been put down, and the radicals in France had been suppressed during the bloody June Days. But the political situation on the Continent remained highly charged, and the threat of further upheaval lingered. The resulting insecurity Chopin felt, and the hysteria attendant on his state of health, drove him to agonise over his future, and even to express extreme views on occasion. When the pianist Ignacy Krzyżanowski, who had settled in London and visited him regularly, questioned the Pope's need to preserve his temporal power, which was under attack from Italian revolutionaries, Chopin exploded. He rounded on his friend, telling him he was a fool who should not presume to talk about things he knew nothing of, and all but threw him out.[44]

For the time being, England seemed the safest place for him. He had accepted a booking to give a concert in Manchester at the end of August, but had no idea of how he would fill up his time before and after that. He had invitations to stay in the country, but could not muster enough enthusiasm to take them up. It was only at the persuasion of Jane Stirling that he left London at all.

In the first days of August he went to Edinburgh, where he spent a day sightseeing, and thence to Calder House in Midlothian, to stay with her brother-in-law, Lord Torphichen. 'The park here is beautiful, the host very excellent – and I am as well as I can be,' Chopin wrote to Franchomme, but this was not very well: after a week or so he was again coughing badly and spitting blood. Had he been able to rest at Calder for some time, his health might have improved, but after a couple of weeks he was on the move again.[45]

He arrived in Manchester towards the end of August, and was put up at Crumpsall House, just outside the city. This was the mansion of Salis Schwabe, a German Jew who had settled in England thirty years before and amassed great wealth. The widely travelled and cultivated Schwabe had a brother in Paris, whom Chopin knew. (Coincidentally, another Mancunian, and one of those responsible for attracting Hallé to the city, was Hermann Leo, the brother of Chopin's friend Auguste Léo.)

Chopin was astonished to find that 'in this smoky place there is the most charming music room imaginable', although he found himself face to face with one of the largest audiences he had ever played to, twelve hundred people.[46] The pianist Osborne, who had returned to settle in England a few years before, was accompanying one of the singers taking part in the concert, which took place on 28 August, and Chopin begged him not to listen to his own playing. 'You, my dear Osborne, who have heard me so often in Paris, will you not remain with those impressions?' he pleaded. 'I know that my playing will be lost in such a large room, and my compositions will be ineffective. Your presence will be painful to both you and me.'[47]

As the critic of the *Manchester Guardian* noted, Chopin ascended the platform with 'an almost painful air of feebleness in his appearance and gait, but once he was seated at the piano, this vanished'.[48] Osborne felt that Chopin's prediction had been right, for 'his playing was too delicate to create enthusiasm, and I felt truly sorry for him'.[49] Charles Hallé, who was also present, felt that Chopin had been 'little understood', and this was borne out by one of the critics, who found him inferior to Thalberg and Herz.[50] But Chopin himself was delighted with the event and with the money he had earned, and did not dwell on whether he had been understood or not.

A couple of days after the concert Chopin left for Edinburgh, where instead of staying at a hotel he put up with Dr Łyszczyński, a Pole who had settled in the city in 1831. 'I don't know what I shall do next – I shall choke and I shall cough, that is certain, and I shall love you as much as ever,' he wrote to Thomas Albrecht.[51] His indecision was once again resolved by the appearance of Jane Stirling, who took him off to stay with one of her sisters, Mrs Houston of Johnstone Castle.

There was a large house party at the castle, but this did little to cheer Chopin, who found himself stuck indoors all day with the old and infirm, while the younger guests were out shooting grouse. 'The conversation is invariably genealogical,' he complained to Grzymała.[52]

In the first week of September, while he was out for a drive, the horses bolted and the carriage smashed into a tree. Chopin emerged unscathed but profoundly shaken. He realised how helpless he would have been had he been seriously injured, for while he loved attention and needed it, he resented being made to feel like an invalid. 'I'm angry and sad, and people irritate me with their exaggerated care,' he wrote. 'I cannot rest and I cannot work. I feel alone, alone, alone, although I am surrounded by people.'[53]

He had not written a single piece for over six months, and could not get into the mood for it. 'Not one musical thought,' he complained to Franchomme. 'I am out of my rut, I feel like a donkey at a masked ball, or a violin bow trying to play a double bass.'[54] For someone whose whole existence had been devoted to the creation of music, this was worse than any physical suffering. 'We are like two old harpsichords on which time and circumstance have played out their wretched trills,' he wrote to Fontana, '– the belly is excellent, only the strings have snapped and some of the pegs have fallen out. The trouble is that we were built by some famous old craftsman, some Stradivarius *sui generis*, who is no longer around to repair us. We cannot give out new sounds under poor hands, and we stifle inside us everything that, for lack of a good craftsman, nobody will ever manage to draw out of us. I'm hardly breathing, *je suis tout prêt à crever* . . . I don't know why I suddenly find myself thinking of poor dead Jasio and Antek, and Witwicki, and Sobański! Those with whom I was in the closest harmony have died; even Ennike, our best tuner, has drowned himself. So I can never again have a piano tuned just as I want it. Moos has died, so nobody will ever make me a comfortable pair of boots again. If another four or five go to St Peter's gates, then my whole life would really become more comfortable in the other world . . .'[55]

Another concert had been organised for Chopin in Glasgow on 27 September, but instead of resting beforehand at nearby Johnstone Castle, he travelled all the way to Strachur to stay with Lady Murray, a former pupil. And he had not been there long before he was off again. The reason was that he had received a letter from Princess Marcelina Czartoryska, who had arrived in Edinburgh with her husband. 'I breathed again in their Polish spirit,' he wrote to Grzymała, 'and it gave me enough strength to play in Glasgow.'[56]

The Glasgow concert was held under the patronage of the Duchess of Argyll and most of the local aristocracy, and was well attended as a result. Chopin played a selection of Études, Nocturnes, Mazurkas, and the ever-popular Waltzes of op.64. The longest works he played were a Ballade and the Berceuse. By now he tended to avoid longer pieces or those, like the Polonaises, which required greater strength. The audience were delighted, and all the reviews were very favourable. A Glaswegian amateur musician who was there gives some idea of the event:

I had frequently seen Thalberg sitting with serene countenance banging out some air with clear articulation and power, in the midst of perpetual coruscations the most magnificent fioriture. Liszt too I had often beheld, tossing his fair hair excitedly, and tearing the wild soul of music from the ecstatic keys. But the manner of Chopin was different. No man has composed pianoforte music of more technical difficulty. Yet with what consummate sweetness and ease did he unravel the wonderful varieties and complexities of sound! It was a drawing room entertainment, more piano than forte, though not without occasional episodes of both strength and grandeur. He took the audience as it were into his

confidence, and whispered to them of zephyrs and moonlight rather
than of cataracts and thunder. Of the whirl of liquid notes he
wove garlands of pearls. The movements and combinations were
calculated to excite and bewilder.[57]

After the concert the Czartoryskis accompanied Chopin back
to Johnstone Castle for dinner, during which he seemed happier
than he had been for a long time. But when they left he relapsed
into his former languor. He had invitations to stay at Inverary
Castle and other great houses, but could not muster the enthusiasm to go, and had it not been for Jane Stirling's insistence,
he would have gone nowhere at all. She took him off to Keir
House to stay with another member of her family. 'Everywhere
received with the most cordial kindness and boundless hospitality, I find excellent pianos, beautiful pictures and choice
libraries; there are also shoots, dogs, dinners that never end
and cellars, of which I take less advantage,' he wrote to Gutmann
from Calder, where he arrived once more in mid-October.[58]
But even the comfort and the easy-going atmosphere of these
house parties were exhausting.

'The whole morning, until about two o'clock, I am now
completely useless – later, when I've got dressed, everything
makes me uncomfortable, and I sit there panting until dinner
time – after which one has to sit for two hours with the men
at the table and look at them speaking and listen to them
drinking,' he wrote to Grzymała. 'Bored to tears (thinking of
other things, in spite of their attentions and the attempts at
conversation in French at the table), I then go to the drawing
room, where I need all my strength of mind to come to life a
little – because then they usually want to hear me play – after
that my kind Daniel [his new Irish servant] carries me up the
stairs to my bedroom, undresses me, puts me to bed, lights a
candle, and leaves me to pant and dream until morning, when
it all starts over again. As soon as I get a little more used to

some place, I have to move to somewhere else, because my Scottish ladies won't leave me in peace, and keep coming to fetch me in order to drive me round their family.'[59]

At the beginning of October he returned to Edinburgh once again to give a recital that had been arranged by Jane Stirling. He again stayed with Dr Łyszczyński, being put up in a tiny nursery and spending most of the day sitting with his feet almost in the fire, shivering. The unfortunate Mrs Łyszczyńska found him an awkward guest, for ever complaining that his laundry was not white enough and his boots not clean enough, but he did occasionally atone for everything by sitting down at their little piano.[60] On 4 October he managed to pull himself together enough to give his recital in the Hopetoun Rooms, where he played alone for two hours. The reviews were satisfactory, but Chopin cared more for the fee he had earned. Instead of resting from the exertion, he went to stay with Lady Bellhaven at Wishaw, then to Calder once again, and finally spent a few days at Hamilton Palace before returning to Edinburgh and the care of Dr Łyszczyński.

He was by now desperate to leave Scotland, and not just on account of the cold weather. Mrs Erskine had decided to convert him to the Church of Scotland, and drove him mad with Bible readings, while her sister Jane Stirling revealed more mundane intentions. Chopin was used to being pampered by women, and had therefore allowed her to insinuate herself into his life, not realising that she was in love with him. When it became obvious that she was, he told her firmly that he had no intention of going beyond friendship, but this does not seem to have put her off. 'My Scottish ladies are kind, but such bores, God help me!' he wrote. 'Every day I get letters from them, I don't reply to a single one, and the moment I go anywhere they come running along after me if they possibly can.' Jane Stirling had to drag her sister about with her as a chaperone, but even so tongues wagged and rumours reached Paris, whence an alarmed

Grzymała wrote to enquire the truth. Chopin answered that he was 'closer to the grave than the nuptial bed'.[61]

The ridiculous notion that he might begin a new life with someone else only served to highlight his real condition. He was convinced that he was spent, that his life was over, and that his body only needed time to expire. 'Where has my art gone?' he wrote to Grzymała. 'And where did I lose my heart? I can hardly remember how they sing back in Poland. This world seems to be leaving me behind; I'm losing myself; I have no strength left . . .' The physical suffering and the artistic barrenness of his life during this period made him long for release. 'Why does God not kill me straight away, only bit by bit,' he complained, and in his despair he could not prevent his thoughts from drifting back to George Sand. 'I have never cursed anyone, but life is so unbearable now that I am beginning to think that I might feel better if I could curse Lucrezia. But she must be suffering too . . .' [62]

At the end of October he returned to London, where he promptly fell ill. For the next three weeks he did not leave the rooms Szulczewski had found him in St James's Place. He sat in front of the fire in his overcoat, because he had to keep the windows wide open so he could breathe in the small room. Princess Marcelina, who was installed in his old rooms in Dover Street two hundred yards away, took charge. She called in Dr Mallan, the leading homeopath in London, and the Royal Physician, Sir James Clark, who was an authority on tuberculosis and had treated Keats in Italy. There was little they could do except suggest that he leave London as soon as he was strong enough.

But before he did, and despite Dr Mallan's entreaties, Chopin felt he had to fulfil a debt of honour and play in public one last time. The occasion was the 'Annual Grand Dress and Fancy Ball and Concert in aid of the Funds of the Literary Association of the Friends of Poland', held at the Guildhall on 16 November.

He insisted on lending his support not only because Princess Marcelina was involved in organising the event, but also because the Polish cause, for long highly popular in Britain, particularly in Whig circles, had recently come under attack from City interests and socialists: another fund-raising ball, held shortly after his arrival in May, had nearly been cancelled in the face of a fierce campaign led by *The Times* and the *Morning Post*, which were now out to sabotage this one. Chopin wanted to do his bit for the cause.

The evening began with a concert; Chopin played and his former pupil Lindsay Sloper conducted a small orchestra. This was followed by the ball, for which he did not stay. The event was deemed a great success, but Chopin's playing was somewhat wasted. 'The concert went off very well,' Princess Marcelina reported to her uncle the next day. 'Chopin played like an angel, much too well for the inhabitants of the City, whose artistic education is a little problematic.'[63] Chopin was delighted, and his appearance caused the predictable sensation amongst the Poles present, but on his return home he could not sleep, and he felt weak for the next few days.

The second half of November brought fog and cold weather, and Chopin began to panic at the prospect of spending the winter in England. His desire to leave was reinforced by the arrival in London of Jane Stirling and her pious sister. 'One day longer here and I won't just die – I'll go mad,' he wrote to Grzymała. 'My Scottish ladies are such bores that God preserve me – they've latched on so tight that I cannot get away. Only Princess Marcelina is keeping me alive, and her family, and good Szulczewski.' He asked Grzymała to prepare his rooms in the Square d'Orléans, and to place a bouquet of violets, his favourite flowers, in the drawing room. 'At least I can have a breath of poetry when I return, as I pass through on the way to my bedroom, where I shall probably lie down for a very long time.'[64]

On 23 November, Chopin and his travelling companion

Leonard Niedźwiedzki (another Czartoryski agent) were driven to the station by Broadwood, who brought last-minute gifts, settled Chopin into the compartment he had booked, and recommended him to the conductor of the train. Princess Marcelina, her husband and her son also came to see them off. As the train pulled out, Chopin suddenly had a seizure: a cramp on the right side below his ribs. As the terrified Niedźwiedzki looked on helplessly, Chopin unbuttoned his coat, waistcoat and trousers and started massaging himself, explaining that this often happened. The cramp passed, and they continued their journey uneventfully as far as Folkestone, where they had a lunch of soup, roast beef and wine. This was subsequently 'taken away' by the sea during the crossing, Chopin being copiously sick into a bowl held by Niedźwiedzki. After a bad night at Boulogne, the two travellers took a train to Paris.[65] No sooner had his cab rolled into the Square d'Orléans than Grzymała, Franchomme and Marie de Rozières appeared to greet him. He was home at last.

SIXTEEN

The Jealousy of Heaven

Chopin's relief at getting back to Paris was not accompanied by any improvement in his health. Dr Molin, who had the secret of alleviating his sufferings, had died, and he was replaced by a succession of doctors in whom Chopin had little faith. 'They poke about but do not bring me any relief,' he wrote to Solange in January 1849. 'They all agree on the need for a good climate, calm and rest. I shall have the rest one day without their help.'[1] They annoyed him with their diets and by ordering him to drink no coffee, only cocoa, which he claimed made him sleepy and 'stupid'. Nevertheless, he felt confident that he would revive, and wrote to Solange that 'the spring sun will be my best doctor'.[2]

Much had changed in Paris while he had been away. The radical republicans who had toppled Louis Philippe had themselves been pushed aside, and two weeks after Chopin's return Louis Napoleon Bonaparte would be elected President of the Republic in a huge swing of public opinion in favour of law and order. While revolution and war continued to rage in parts of Germany, Italy and Hungary, France settled down to a new regime.

The only friend left in the Square d'Orléans was Alkan; the Marlianis had left Paris, many of Chopin's aristocratic French friends were still lying low, and even Grzymała was kept away by a combination of financial and political problems. Most of

Chopin's French pupils had left, and he was now limiting his lessons to those who were advanced and therefore less demanding, and who were prepared to put up with last-minute cancellations on account of his health. These included Princess Soutzo, Maria Kalergis, Delfina Potocka, the baronne de Rothschild and, from March, Princess Marcelina.

Although he could go out only rarely that winter, Chopin did not suffer too much from the loneliness he dreaded. A small group of friends, including Franchommme, Legouvé, Princess Obreskoff (Princess Soutzo's mother), Baron Stockhausen, Thomas Albrecht, Charles Gavard and Marie de Rozières, conspired to keep it at bay. Delacroix too used to call on 'my poor great dying man', as he referred to him. He would often come to the informal evenings at the Square d'Orléans, where Delfina Potocka and Maria Kalergis sang and Chopin played. Otherwise he would drop in late in the day when he knew Chopin would have finished giving lessons, and the two would talk for hours about life, art and George Sand. Sometimes he accompanied Chopin on the drives he began to take with the arrival of spring. On a typical afternoon, at the beginning of April, the two friends climbed into a cabriolet and set off along the Champs-Élysées, chatting about art and music. Delacroix questioned Chopin at length on the theory of music, and asked him to explain what constituted logic in musical thought. 'He enlightened me on the meaning of harmony and counterpoint,' the painter noted in his diary, 'explaining that the fugue is what one might call the pure logic of music, and that therefore to be a master of the fugue is to be familiar with the elements of all reason and all development in music.'[3] They went on to talk of Mozart, Chopin giving reasons why he considered him superior to Beethoven, and after stopping at the Étoile for a drink they trundled back to the Square d'Orléans.

On other days, Delacroix would find Chopin 'hardly breathing' and unable to move. 'His health is declining gradually, with passable days when he can drive out and others when he has fits of coughing that choke him and he spits blood,' Pauline Viardot reported to George Sand. 'He no longer goes out in the evenings, but he still manages to give some lessons, and on his better days he can be quite merry.'[4] He did in fact go out occasionally, and in mid-April he dragged himself to the first night of Meyerbeer's *Le Prophète*. He had been looking forward to hearing Pauline Viardot in the leading role and to seeing the elaborate sets, the rising of an electrical sun and a fire contrived with gas on stage, all much publicised. But the music horrified him, and the vaunted production failed to fill him with the same enthusiasm as had that of the same composer's *Robert le Diable* in his first days in Paris almost eighteen years before.

On better days he also tried to compose, but the effort involved was daunting, and he found it difficult to concentrate. The fruits of these labours, the Mazurkas no.2 of op.67 and no.4 of op.68, bear the mark of this. Probably at the instigation of Delacroix, Chopin also began to put his ideas on music down on paper, but this was an even greater challenge. He nevertheless produced some notes for a theoretical method for the piano. His own rather irregular instruction as well as his undisciplined literary style must have made it difficult for him to formulate thoughts on the subject, and the notes remained just that.

One thing that all the doctors treating him agreed on was that it would be madness for him to remain in Paris during the summer months, when the heat and the dust would make it difficult for him to breathe. Other considerations were that a cholera epidemic was spreading, and that the forthcoming elections were expected to be accompanied by violence. As a result, it was decided that Chopin should move out of the city, and his friends duly found him an apartment in Chaillot, a quiet place more or less where the Trocadéro now stands. The apartment was expensive, but half the rent was secretly paid by Princess Obreskoff, and Chopin wondered at the cheapness of it. He moved towards the end of May, and his spirits rose. He liked the spacious main room and the magnificent 'Roman view' afforded by the five windows of the apartment, which took in the Tuileries and the Chamber of Deputies, Notre Dame, the Pantheon, Saint-Sulpice and the Invalides. The fresh air and the fact that he had stopped taking medicine altogether improved his appetite, and after a few weeks he felt much better, although he still could not work.

June passed pleasantly enough, and he was not as isolated as he had feared. Cholera, which had just carried away Kalkbrenner and the singer Angelica Catalani, who had given Chopin a gold watch in Warsaw thirty years before, was chasing everyone from the capital. Delfina Potocka moved to Versailles, while Princess Obreskoff retired to Saint-Germain, and they visited him frequently. In the case of the 'Scottish ladies', who had reappeared on the scene, it was clearly too frequently. 'They will drive me into my grave,' Chopin could not help complaining to Grzymała.[5] Delacroix had left Paris for the summer, wondering sadly whether he would ever see Chopin again. But Franchomme and Gutmann often visited him at Chaillot, as did various members of the Czartoryski family, who supplied him with one of their nannies as a night nurse, and early in June he had a pleasant surprise when Jenny Lind came to see him. Although she was only in Paris for a few days, she came back for a small musical evening he arranged, during which she and Delfina Potocka took turns to sing.

In the last week of June he started haemorrhaging dramatically and his legs began to swell up. The night nurse alerted Princess Sapieha, who called in Dr Jean Baptiste Cruveillher, the greatest authority on tuberculosis in France, who had treated Talleyrand and Chateaubriand. The symptoms of persistent diarrhoea and swelling of the legs were consistent with the final stages of tuberculosis, and from the drugs Cruveillher prescribed, Chopin deduced that he had diagnosed as much (it is worth noting that these symptoms are also common in the terminal stage of cystic fibrosis). He must have realised that the end was near, for while he made brave noises about going to Poland the following spring, he began to make desperate appeals for Ludwika to come to Paris. 'I am very weak, and no doctor can help me as much as you can,' he wrote, telling her to bring her needle and thimble, for there would be much sitting at his bedside.[6] For some two months both Princess Marcelina and Delfina Potocka had been using their influence and connections to obtain a passport for Ludwika, so there must have been a secret plan afoot earlier to bring her to Paris.[7] Her husband, Kalasanty, would take much persuading, and Ludwika had to borrow the necessary funds.

The month of July passed slowly and wretchedly; Chopin was lonely and bored, and had given up all attempts at keeping himself occupied with work. He still gave a few lessons, but could only play the piano with the greatest difficulty. A niece of Prince Adam's and former pupil of his, Eliza Brzozowska, moved into the apartment above his with her husband and children, which meant that she could play to him to dispel his boredom. It also meant that the Prince and his mother-in-law, Princess Sapieha, called more often, supplementing the faithful Franchomme and Charles Gavard, who would sometimes read to him in the afternoons. He occasionally went for a drive in the Bois de Boulogne, and once even drove as far as Passy to take tea with the Zaleskis.

At the end of July his life was disturbed once more by the antics of his 'Scottish ladies'. One day he had apparently complained to Franchomme that he had little money left, and Franchomme mentioned the fact to Jane Stirling, whom he knew to be wealthy and devoted to Chopin. Hearing this, she made a great show of surprise and announced that she had sent him the staggering sum of 25,000 francs as recently as

March. Quizzed on this point, Chopin stated that he had never received any such sum, and would have sent it back if he had. Jane Stirling then got hold of the man who had allegedly delivered the packet to Chopin's concierge, and sent him to see a renowned clairvoyant by the name of Alexis, who promised to solve the mystery, but said he needed something belonging to the concierge to help him think. Chopin was induced to persuade Madame Étienne to come all the way from the Square d'Orléans, and to invent a stratagem to get her to give him a lock of her hair. This was duly delivered to Alexis, who then announced that the packet had been handed to Madame Étienne and placed by her behind the clock on her mantelpiece in a moment of distraction. There it was found, to the astonishment of the concierge, who could remember no such packet being delivered, and would certainly not have treated a sum of money of this order with such nonchalance.

Chopin trusted Madame Étienne implicitly, and was convinced that the farce had been arranged by Jane Stirling out of a desire to cover up some self-imputed neglect of his needs. 'There's a good heart behind it, but also a lot of ostentation,' he wrote to Grzymała. The whole business worried and irritated him so much that he could not sleep at night and his efforts to get to the bottom of it induced migraine. He refused the gift, but eventually accepted 15,000 francs as a loan.[8]

By early August he was feeling very weak, and was beginning to despair of Ludwika. 'I pant and cough and feel sleepy; I don't do anything, I don't want to do anything,' he wrote to Grzymała, who only visited him fleetingly in Chaillot, since the police were trying to round up and deport members of the Polish Democratic Club, of which he was one.[9]

On 9 August, Ludwika arrived with her husband Kalasanty and their daughter. Chopin was happy as could be; at last he had someone to talk to, and not just during the day, for he suffered from insomnia and grew anxious on his own. 'He liked to talk at night,' Ludwika later wrote, 'to tell me his sorrows and to pour into my loving and understanding heart all his most personal thoughts.'[10] Kalasanty soon got tired of sight-seeing and returned to Warsaw, but Ludwika was determined to see her brother through his illness, still deluding herself that he might survive it.

Chopin himself alternated between anticipation of death and denial of the severity of his condition. States of euphoria have been noted as a symptom of the terminal stage of tuberculosis. He now pathetically nourished the delusion that he might go and meet Tytus, who was travelling across Germany. He also wanted to take up Delfina Potocka's invitation to spend the winter at her villa in Nice, whither she had gone herself. But on 30 August Cruveillher, who had been in attendance every couple of days, called in two other eminent doctors and held a consultation. They declared that travel was out of the question, and that if he was to survive the winter at all he must be found a warm and sunny apartment in central Paris.

While his friends set to work looking for the right place, rumours began to spread that Chopin was dying. Even George Sand wrote to Ludwika asking for news. But the tone of the letter was ill-judged and jarring in its assumption of motherly rights. 'One can be deserted and forgotten by one's children without ceasing to love them,' she wrote, which was not only pompous, but also insulting, since it was for voicing a very similar sentiment that Chopin had been expelled from her life two years before.[11] The letter went unanswered.

The Polish poet Cyprian Kamil Norwid was among those who, alarmed by the rumours of Chopin's rapid decline, came to pay their last respects. 'I found him lying on his bed fully dressed, his swollen legs encased in stockings and pumps,' recorded Norwid. 'He had, as always, something in even the most casual of his movements that was accomplished, monu-mental . . . something the Athenian aristocracy might have made into a rite at the height of the Hellenic civilisation . . . In a voice interrupted by coughing and choking, he began to berate me for not having called on him recently. Then he teased me in the most childlike way for my mystical tendencies, to which, as it evidently gave him pleasure, I readily lent myself. After that I talked with his sister. There were more fits of coughing. Finally the moment came to leave him in peace, so I started taking my leave. Pressing my hand, he brushed the hair back from his forehead and said: "I'm leaving this . . . " and was interrupted by coughing. Hearing this, and feeling that it was good for him to be contradicted, I assumed the usual false tone, and, embracing him, said, as one does to a healthy man: "Every year you say you're leaving this world, and yet, thank God you're still alive!" But Chopin, finishing the sentence interrupted by his coughing, said "I'm leaving this apartment and moving to another in the Place Vendôme."[12]

The apartment which had been found for him consisted of five rooms on the *entresol* of No.12 place Vendôme, the house in which Thomas Albrecht had his office. The rooms were warm and sunny, as the windows faced south onto a small courtyard, rather than onto the square. The rooms in the Square d'Orléans were re-let and the furniture and effects brought to the place Vendôme, where, along with the things from Chaillot, including the mahogany grand piano still on loan from Pleyel, they filled the five rooms.[13] Chopin moved in at the end of September, and although he was once or twice well enough to wander about the apartment, he never left it. He soon took to his bed, and by 12 October Dr Cruveillher was so certain of impending death that he suggested the Last Sacrament be administered.

Chopin's spiritual preparedness for death had been worrying many of his Polish friends for some time, as he had not practised his faith for years. Princess Sapieha, Norwid, Zaleski and others tried, without success, to make him address the matter and make his peace with God. But he would simply ask them to pray for him and listened with devotion when they did so at his bedside.[14]

At this point, Chopin's old acquaintance Aleksander Jełowicki, who had since taken Holy Orders, turned up in Paris and made a more determined onslaught. He came on 12 October and begged Chopin to make a full confession and accept the Last Sacrament, but Chopin replied that while he would gladly confess his faults to him as a man whom he respected, he found it impossible to believe in the act as a Sacrament. This has the ring of truth. 'I have never known a more atheistic poet, or a more poetic atheist,' George Sand would write to a friend shortly after Chopin's death. 'He <u>thought he believed</u> in some kind of divinity and a fantastical afterlife, but at bottom it was no more than inspired vagueness and an abeyance of reflection.'[15]

Jełowicki returned the next day, and claims he found Chopin in an altered mood. In his probably embellished account, Jełowicki relates that the dying man made his confession and received the Last Sacrament, after which he gave the sacristan an enormous sum of money instead of the usual token gift. When Jełowicki protested at this, Chopin is supposed to have answered: 'It is not too much, because what I have received is priceless!' adding: 'Without you, my friend, I would have died like a pig.'[16]

Death was closing in fast, and his friends knew it. Aside from Ludwika, who had moved into the apartment with him, he was attended by Solange, who had come up to Paris specially; Princess Marcelina, who had taken rooms in the same square; and one or two others, including Thomas Albrecht and Gutmann. They looked after Chopin and kept him company, talking to him, reading to him and praying with him.

While his condition continued to deteriorate, he hung on with astonishing determination and refused to let himself go to pieces. Although he was choking much of the time, he was entirely lucid and admitted to his bedside many of the friends and pupils who came to say farewell. He took his leave of them bravely, thanking some, encouraging others. Dozens of others simply called in at the apartment as a mark of respect, which gave the gossips their cue.

'He had in his ante room I know not how many princesses, countesses, marchionesses, and even a few bourgeoises, who, on their knees, awaited the hour of his last agony,' wrote Jules Janin fancifully.[17] Pauline Viardot, who was not one of them, wrote to George Sand, with a note of sourness, that 'all the grandes dames of Paris felt obliged to come and faint in his room'.[18] George Sand developed the theme with unquestioned authoritativeness in a letter to Étienne Arago. 'My poor sick friend died in the arms of priests and pious women,' she wrote, adding that they made him kiss relics while he thought only of the music to be played at the funeral.[19]

Chopin did indeed attend to such details, and gave careful instructions about his affairs. He asked that all unfinished musical manuscripts in his portfolio be destroyed, and that only complete pieces be published. He bequeathed his notes on the proposed piano method to Alkan as a mark of respect for his revolutionary piano technique. He even remembered to leave Madame Étienne, the concierge at the Square d'Orléans, the princely sum of a thousand francs. He begged that his body be cut open (out of a widely shared horror of being buried alive) and his heart sent to Warsaw, and asked for Mozart's Requiem to be sung at his funeral. A lifetime's self-discipline in the face of tormenting pain permitted him to hide the true extent of his suffering in front of others, but it would become evident when they left. 'The evenings spent with him were enough to break the hardest heart,' recalled Solange. 'His gasping breaths were hardly more than pitiful stifled cries, horrifying sobs.'[20]

On 15 October, Delfina Potocka arrived from Nice, a gesture of loyalty that must have moved Chopin. He begged her to sing for him one last time, and, the piano being duly rolled up to the bedroom door, she obliged. Throughout his last illness he craved music, particularly that of the human voice, and he seemed to draw strength from it. The following day he kept asking for music, even though he was in agony. The piano was again wheeled up to the doorway, and Princess Marcelina and Franchomme played him some Mozart. He then asked to hear his own Sonata for Piano and Cello, but after a few bars of this he began to suffocate, and they stopped.

By this time it had become obvious that the end was close. Most of the callers had gone, leaving only intimate friends. 'The whole evening of the 16th was spent reciting litanies; we gave the responses, but Chopin remained silent,' relates Charles Gavard. 'Only by his strained breathing could one tell that he was still alive. That evening two doctors examined him. One of them, Dr Cruveillher, took a candle and, holding it before Chopin's face, which had become quite dark with suffocation, remarked to us that his senses had ceased to act. But when he asked Chopin whether he was suffering, we quite distinctly heard the answer: "No longer!"'[21]

As the night wore on, more people went home, leaving only Ludwika, Princess Marcelina, Gutmann, Solange and Thomas Albrecht.[22] The end came at about two o'clock on the morning of 17 October. Ludwika had fallen asleep, but Chopin lay awake and Solange sat beside him, holding his hand. 'Don't stay here, this will be ugly. You must not see it,' he suddenly said to her. He appeared to have a seizure, and the terrified Solange called Gutmann, who took Chopin in his arms. 'We wanted to give him a drink, but death prevented us,' wrote Solange. 'He passed away with his gaze fixed on me, he was hideous, I could see the tarnishing eyes in the darkness. Oh, the soul had died too!'[23]

The following morning, Clésinger turned up to make a death-mask, having already started work on a project for the gravestone. The mask was so painfully eloquent of the agonised death throes of the composer that he put it aside and produced a doctored version. The painter Teofil Kwiatkowski spent the whole day drawing Chopin's face, also endowing it with an ideal beauty and an expression of youthful serenity. Dr Cruveillher carried out an autopsy, which revealed that Chopin's heart had been in very poor condition and may have been the immediate cause of death. The heart itself was removed and preserved separately, to be sent to Warsaw in accordance with the dead man's wishes. The body was taken to the crypt of the Madeleine, and the apartment was sealed up by the French authorities.

Ludwika had removed Chopin's private papers for fear of potential prying on the part of the Russian Consul, and set about sorting them out. She found all George Sand's letters to him neatly wrapped in a little casket which contained all his money and treasured possessions. There was more money than anyone had expected, and she was able to settle most of the outstanding debts immediately, as well as his various legacies.[24]

The funeral proved far from easy to arrange. As Mozart's Requiem was to be performed, special dispensation had to be obtained from the Archbishop of Paris to permit women to sing in the Madeleine. Since it was bound to be well attended, invitation cards had to be issued in order to control numbers. The ceremony eventually took place almost two weeks after Chopin's death, on 30 October 1849. By then, he was already being immortalised.

The composer's death had been proclaimed to the world in lengthy obituaries, from the pens of eminent musicians such as Hector Berlioz and poets such as Théophile Gautier. They mostly underlined what, for want of a better word, might be termed his 'political' importance. And it is not difficult to see why.

The language Chopin's music speaks is perhaps the most intimate in the whole canon of Western music. It transcends everything we know about the man and draws the listener into a world of the spirit which is the very essence of the Romantic artistic experience. And taken as a whole, his life itself epitomises the notion of the Romantic artist – of the ethereal exile from heaven, half man half angel, who comes into this life to inspire mankind, but does not belong here and suffers the torments of a creature out of its natural element.

Few of the obituaries were as moving as that by the poet Norwid. 'He knew how to divine the greatest mysteries of art with astonishing ease – he could gather the flowers of the field without disturbing the dew or the lightest pollen,' he wrote. 'And he knew how to fashion them into stars, meteors, as it were comets, lighting up the sky of Europe, through the ideal of art. In the crystal of his own harmony he gathered the tears of the Polish people strewn over the fields, and placed them as the diamond of beauty in the diadem of humanity.'[25]

The reference to the Polish people is significant: Chopin was the quintessential national composer. Not in the same sense that a Dvořák, a Bartok, a Tchaikovsky or a Rimsky-Korsakov were. Far from embellishing folklore and historical imagery, Chopin created a musical idiom that transcended music, an idiom that in many ways actually helped to mould and condition the nation itself. That is why he is so central to the national narrative: along with the poets and artists, he helped compose it.

Ultimately, however, Chopin's reputation must rest on the artistic value of his musical *oeuvre*, and this stands out in a number of respects. It is often said that there are three composers who never wrote a bad piece of music – Bach, Chopin and Debussy. This is verifiably so in Chopin's case, as even his earliest works are characterised by a satisfying completeness that results from his working and reworking of a piece until it made perfect musical sense. Pretty tunes aside, Chopin's works are not easy listening: they are highly intelligent harmonic exercises exploring depth and range of sound, and they are all characterised by complete intellectual and artistic integrity.

'Composition, to speak frankly, has come to an end,' wrote the virtuoso pianist Anton Rubinstein in 1890. 'Its parting knell was rung when the last incomparable notes of Chopin died away.'[26] His is not an isolated view, and it was not inspired by nostalgia for a lost form or a defunct fashion. On the contrary, what people like him valued in Chopin was the ability to use his profound knowledge and understanding of the classical canon of past ages to stretch the boundaries of music and break new ground.

The slight Polish pianist who worshipped Bach and thought Beethoven sometimes vulgar was, in effect, a real revolutionary. 'That sweet evening star that shone only for a moment,' as Saint-Saëns described Chopin, 'revolutionised the art form and opened the way for all modern music.'[27] He profoundly influenced not only the likes of Debussy, Scriabin and Rachmaninov, but also composers as different as Brahms, Wagner, Tchaikovsky and Prokofiev. And that is why, although his works speak to all, Chopin is the ultimate musician's musician. Those who study or play his works endlessly discover new things in them and find themselves being led along by the composer's ordered musical intelligence.

Similarly, while his music is deeply rooted in Polish tradition and folklore, it is universal, and Chopin has a greater following in places as distant as Japan, China, India and Africa than most classical composers.

Yet behind these works of genius, tantalisingly elusive, hovers the spirit of the man himself. 'The story of a life is as secret as life itself,' commented the novelist Elias Canetti. 'A life that can be explained is no life at all.'[28] Although Chopin could be extremely down-to-earth and sometimes startlingly matter-of-fact in his approach to life, and although one can have a sense of getting close to understanding him as one reads his delightful letters, there is a part of him that remains utterly out of reach, and almost other-worldly. Delacroix, who missed both the man and the artist perhaps more than anyone else, and who to his dying day kept in his bedroom a little drawing of Chopin, felt this very strongly as he considered 'the incomparable genius for whom heaven was jealous of the earth, and of whom I think so often, no longer being able to see him in this world, nor to hear his divine harmonies'.[29] In those words he summed up so much of what his generation felt about art, and why Chopin was so emblematic of the Romantic vision.

'The soul of an angel, cast down upon earth in a tortured body in order to accomplish some mysterious redemption,' was how Solange remembered him. 'Is it because his life was a thirty-nine-year agony that his music is so lofty, so sweet, so sublime?' she wondered.[30]

List of Chopin's Works

Date	Title	Opus No.	Dedicated to	First published
1817	Polonaise G minor		Countess Viktoria Skarbek	Privately 1817
	Polonaise B flat major			Posthumous
	Military March			Lost
1818	Two Polonaises		[Empress Maria Feodorovna]	Lost
1820	Mazurka D major			Posthumous
1821	Polonaise A flat major		[Adalbert Żywny]	Posthumous
1822	Polonaise G sharp minor		[Madame Du Pont]	Posthumous
1824	Variations for Flute and Piano on Rossini's *Cenerentola*			Posthumous
	Waltz C major			Lost
	Mazurka B flat major			Warsaw 1826
	Variations E major on German air: *Schweizerbube*		[Katarzyna Sowińska]	Posthumous
1825	Rondo in C minor	1	Madame Linde	Brzezina 1825
	Mazurka A minor	17/4	Madame Lina Freppa	Schlesinger 1834
	Mazurka G major			Warsaw 1826
	Waltz C major			Lost
1826	Polonaise in B flat minor on Rossini's *Gazza Ladra*		[Wilhelm Kolberg]	Posthumous
	Songs to words by Adam Mickiewicz		[Emilia Elsner]	Lost
	Variations D major for four hands			Posthumous
1827	Rondeau à la Mazur	5	Countess Alexandrine de Moriolles	Warsaw 1828
	Andante Dolente B flat minor			Lost
	Ecossaise B flat major			Lost
	Waltz A flat major			Lost
	Variations F major for four hands		[Tytus Woyciechowski]	Lost
	Polonaise D minor	71/1		Posthumous
	Funeral March C minor	72/2		Posthumous
	Nocturne E minor?	72/1		Posthumous
	Waltz A flat major		[Emilia Elsner]	Posthumous
	Waltz E flat major		[Emilia Elsner]	Posthumous

Date	Title	Opus No.	Dedicated to	First published
	Mazurka A minor	68/2		Posthumous
	Sonata C minor Variations	4	[Józef Elsner]	Posthumous
	for Piano and Orchestra on *La ci darem la mano* from Mozart's *Don Giovanni*	2	Tytus Woyciechowski	Haslinger 1830
1828	Trio for Piano, Violin and Cello in G minor	8	Prince Antoni Radziwiłł	Schlesinger 1833
	Fantasia on Polish Airs for Piano and Orchestra	13	Johann Peter Pixis	Schlesinger 1834
	Krakowiak Rondo for Piano and Orchestra	14	Princess Anna Czartoryska, *née* Sapieha	Schlesinger 1834
	Mazurka D major			Posthumous
	Polonaise B flat major	71/2		Posthumous
	Polonaise F minor	71/3		Posthumous
	Rondo C major for Two Pianos	73		Posthumous
	Waltz D minor			Lost
	Waltz E sharp			Lost
1829	Waltz A flat major			Lost
	Three Nocturnes	9	Madame Marie Pleyel, *née* Moke	Schlesinger 1833
	Polonaise for Cello and Piano	3	Joseph Merk	Mechetti 1831
	Concerto in F minor for Piano and Orchestra	21	Countess Delfina Potocka	Schlesinger 1836
	Études in F major, F minor, A flat major, E flat major	10/8, 9, 10, 11	Franz Liszt	Schlesinger 1833
	Mazurka C major	68/1		Posthumous
	Waltz B minor	69/2	[Wilhelm Kolberg]	Posthumous
	Waltz D flat major	70/3		Posthumous
	Polonaise G flat major			Posthumous
	Mazurka G major		[Vaclav Hanka]	Posthumous
	Variations A major: *Souvenir de Paganini*			Posthumous
	Two Songs to poems by Stefan Witwicki; *Gdzie Lubi* and *Zyczenie*	74/1, 5		Posthumous
	Waltz E flat major			Posthumous
1830	Four Mazurkas	6	Countess Paulina Plater	Schlesinger 1833
	Five Mazurkas	7	Paul Emile Johns	Schlesinger 1833
	Études C major, A minor, G flat major, E flat minor	10/1, 2, 5, 6	Franz Liszt	Schlesinger 1833
	Concerto for Piano and Orchestra, E minor	11	Friedrich Wilhelm Kalkbrenner	Schlesinger 1833
	Three Nocturnes	15	Ferdinand Hiller	Schlesinger 1834
	Waltz E flat major	18	Miss Laura Horsford	Schlesinger 1834
	Scherzo B minor	20	Thomas Albrecht	Schlesinger 1835
	Introduction to Polonaise for Cello and Piano	3	Joseph Merk	Mechetti 1831
	Grande Polonaise E flat major for Piano and Orchestra	22	Baronne d'Est	Schlesinger 1836
	Ballade G minor	23	Baron Stockhausen	Schlesinger 1836
	Mazurka F major	68/3		Posthumous

Date	Title	Opus No.	Dedicated to	First published
	Three Écossaises	72/3		Posthumous
	Four songs to poems by Stefan Witwicki: *Wojak, Hulanka, Posel* and Adam Mickiewicz:	74		Posthumous
	Precz z moich oczu			Posthumous
	Song to Witwicki's poem *Czary*			Posthumous
	Waltz E minor			Posthumous
	Nocturne C sharp minor *Lento con gran espressione*			Posthumous
1831	Étude C minor: 'Revolutionary'	10/12	Franz Liszt	Schlesinger 1833
	Waltz A minor	34/2	Baronne d'Ivry	Schlesinger 1838
	First of the 24 Preludes	28	Camille Pleyel	Pleyel 1840
	Allegro of proposed Concerto for Piano and Orchestra (rewritten as piano solo in 1841)	46	Miss Friederike Müller	Schlesinger 1841
	Two songs to poems by Stefan Witwicki: *Smutna Rzeka and Narzeczony*	74		Posthumous
	Song to poem by Ludwik Osinski: *Piosnka Litewska*		74	Posthumous
1832	Études E major, C sharp minor, C major	10/3, 4, 7	Franz Liszt	Schlesinger 1833
	Rondo E flat major	16	Caroline Hartmann	Schlesinger 1834
	Three Mazurkas	17/1, 2, 3	Madame Lina Freppa	Schlesinger 1834
	Grand Duo Concertante on themes from Meyerbeer's *Robert le Diable*, written in collaboration with Auguste Franchomme		Miss Adèle Forest	Schlesinger 1833
	Mazurka B flat major		[Miss Alexandra Wołowska]	Posthumous
	Mazurka D major			Posthumous
1833	Bolero	19	Comtesse Emilie de Flahaut	Prillip et Cie 1834
	Variations B major	12	Miss Laura Horsford	Paris 1833
	Études: A minor, E minor, G sharp minor, D flat major, G flat major, B minor	25/4, 5, 6, 8, 9, 10	Comtesse Marie d'Agoult	Schlesinger 1837
	Mazurka C major			Posthumous
1834	Mazurkas G minor, C major and B flat minor	24/1, 2, 4	Comte de Perthuis	Schlesinger 1836
	Étude A minor	25/11	Comtesse Marie d'Agoult	Schlesinger 1837
	Andante Spianato	22	Baronne d'Est	Schlesinger 1836
	Two Polonaises	26	Jozef Dessauer	Schlesinger 1836
	Mazurka A flat major		[Celina Szymanowska]	Posthumous
	Largo E flat major			Posthumous
	Cantabile B flat major			Posthumous
	Prelude A flat major		[Pierre Wolff]	Posthumous
	Fantaisie-Impromptu	66	[Baronne d'Est]	Posthumous
1835	Mazurka A flat major	24/3	Comte de Perthuis	Schlesinger 1836
	Two Nocturnes	27	Comtesse Apponyi	Schlesinger 1836

Date	Title	Opus No.	Dedicated to	First published
	Waltz A flat major	34/1	Countess Josephine Thun Hohenstein	Schlesinger 1838
	Mazurka G major	67/1	[Miss Anna Młokosiewicz]	Posthumous
	Mazurka C major	67/3	[Mrs Hoffmann]	Posthumous
	Waltz G flat major	70/1		Posthumous
	Waltz A flat major	69/1	[Miss Maria Wodzińska]	Posthumous
1836	Études A flat major, F minor, F major, C sharp minor, C minor	25/1, 2, 3, 7, 12	Comtesse Marie d'Agoult	Schlesinger 1837
	Four Mazurkas	30	Princess Maria Württemberg, née Czartoryska	Schlesinger 1838
	Two Nocturnes	32	Baronne de Billing, née de Courbonne	Schlesinger 1837
	Song to poem by Witwicki: Pierścien	74	[Miss Maria Wodzińska]	Posthumous
	Song to poem by Wincenty Pol: Lecą Liście z drzewa	74		Posthumous
1837	Impromptu A flat major	29	Comtesse Caroline de Lobau	Schlesinger 1837
	Scherzo B flat minor	31	Countess Furstenstein	Schlesinger 1837
	Funeral March	35		Troupenas 1840
	Four Mazurkas	33	Countess Roza Mostowska	Schlesinger 1838
	Variation in E major: 'Hexameron'			Paris 1837
	Song to poem by Adam Mickiewicz: Moja Pieszczotka	74		Posthumous
	Nocturne C minor			Posthumous
1838	Remainder of 24 Preludes	28	Camille Pleyel	Pleyel et Cie 1840
	Waltz F major	34/3	Baronne d'Eichthal	Schlesinger 1838
	Mazurka C sharp minor	41/4	Stefan Witwicki	Troupenas 1840
	Song to poem by Witwicki: Wiosna	74		Posthumous
1839	First Movement, Scherzo and Finale of B flat minor Sonata	35		Troupenas 1840
	F sharp major Impromptu	36		Troupenas 1840
	Two Nocturnes	37		Troupenas 1840
	Ballade F major	38	Robert Schumann	Troupenas 1840
	Scherzo C sharp minor	39	Adolf Gutmann	Troupenas 1840
	Two Polonaises	40	Julian Fontana	Troupenas 1840
	Three Mazurkas	41/1, 2, 3	Stefan Witwicki	Troupenas 1840
	Three Études			Paris 1840
	Canon in F minor			Posthumous
1840	Waltz A flat major	42		Pacini 1840
	Waltz F minor	70/2		Posthumous
	Waltz E flat major Sostenuto			Posthumous
	Song to poem by Józef Bohdan Zaleski: Dumka			Posthumous
1841	Polonaise F sharp minor	44	Princesse Ludmila de Beauvau, née Komar	Schlesinger
	Tarantella	43		Troupenas 1841
	Prelude C sharp minor	45	Princess Elisabeth Chernishev	Schlesinger 1841
	Ballade A flat major	47	Princesse Pauline de Noailles	Schlesinger 1841

Date	Title	Opus No.	Dedicated to	First published
	Two Nocturnes	48	Miss Laure Duperré	Schlesinger 1841
	Fantaisie F minor	49	Princess Catherine Soutzo	Schlesinger 1841
	Three Mazurkas	50	Leon Szmitkowski	Schlesinger 1842
	Mazurka A minor		Emile Gaillard	Chabal 1841
	Song to poem by J. Bohdan Zaleski: *Śliczny Chłopiec*	74		Posthumous
1842	Impromptu G flat major	51	Countess Jeanne Esterhazy, *née* Batthyany	Schlesinger 1843
	Ballade F minor	52	Madame Nathaniel de Rothschild	Schlesinger 1843
	Polonaise A flat major	53	Auguste Léo	Schlesinger 1843
	Scherzo E major	54	Countess Jeanne de Caraman	Schlesinger 1843
	Nocturne F minor	55/1	Miss Jane Wilhelmina Stirling	Schlesinger 1844
1843	Three Mazurkas	56	Miss Catherine Maberly	Schlesinger 1844
	Berceuse D flat major	57	Elise Gavard	Meissonier 1845
	Moderato E major		[Comtesse Sheremetieff]	Posthumous
	Nocturne E flat major	55/2	Miss Jane Wilhelmina Stirling	Schlesinger 1844
1844	Sonata B minor	58	Comtesse de Perthuis	Meissonier 1845
1845	Three Mazurkas	59		Brandus & Co 1845
	Barcarolle F sharp major	60	Baronne de Stockhausen	Brandus & Co 1846
	Songs to poems by J.B. Zaleski: *Dwojaki Koniec, Niema Czego Trzeba*	74		Posthumous
	Sonata for Piano and Cello begun	65	Auguste Franchomme	Brandus & Co 1847
1846	Polonaise-Fantaisie	61	Madame A. Veyret, *née* Kreisler	Brandus & Co 1846
1846	Two Nocturnes	62	Miss R. de Könneritz	Brandus & Co
	Three Mazurkas	63	Laura Czosnowska	Brandus & Co 1847
	Waltz D flat major	64/1	Countess Delfina Potocka	Brandus & Co 1847
	Waltz C sharp minor	64/2	Baronne de Rothschild	Brandus & Co 1847
	Waltz A flat major	64/3	Countess Katarzyna Branicka	Brandus & Co 1847
	Sonata for Piano and Cello finished	65	Auguste Franchomme	Brandus & Co 1847
	Mazurka A minor	67/4		Posthumous
	Veni Creator			Lost
1847	Song to poem by Zygmunt Krasiński: *Melodia*	74	[Countess Delfina Potocka]	Posthumous
1848	Waltz B major		[Mrs Erskine]	Lost
1849	Mazurka G minor	67/2		Posthumous
	Mazurka F minor	68/4		Posthumous

APPENDIX B

The Case of the 'Chopin–Potocka Letters'

Chopin's early biographers, some of whom, like Liszt, knew him personally, relied not on documents, but on their own reminiscences, those of others, and a certain amount of hearsay and gossip. The world of the 1840s was a small one, in which artists, aristocrats and professional people met each other across frontiers and knew a great deal about each other. It is therefore significant that not one of his early biographers dropped the slightest hint about the existence of any intimate link between Chopin and Delfina Potocka. Her other affairs were known throughout Europe, as was his with George Sand, but as far as his contemporaries were concerned, she was just another of the great ladies who, like Marcelina Czartoryska and Maria Kalergis, held a special position in his life because they were amongst the most gifted of his pupils, because they were *grandes dames* and because they were Polish. The published and unpublished correspondence of the period, including that of such renowned gossips as Balzac and Dumas, of the vindictive comtesse d'Agoult and of others who prided themselves on knowing everything that went on in Paris (and no regular affair could go on for long without everyone knowing about it), make no allusion, suppose nothing.

But in the last quarter of the nineteenth century a new kind of biography became popular: one which looked at artists in particular through the prism of their emotional lives. This worked well with a Liszt, but made Chopin's biography challenging, since there was so little to go on. It was at this moment that certain writers began to look for evidence to fill in the emotional lacunae in his life. An indeterminate affair was 'discovered' to fill his adolescence, a young Czech girl was dredged up to enliven the Bad Reinerz holiday, and then one of the most famous of all Polish historical gossips, Ferdynand Hoesick, hit on Delfina Potocka to add zest to the first few years in Paris. He hinted and suggested, found people who had been alive at the same time as Chopin, interviewed them and prompted them, and finally let fall that he knew of the existence of a batch of letters from the composer to the Countess allegedly kept under lock and key by puritanical 'descendants'. Others took this up, and soon a tradition had been created. The Countess herself began to come to life with the publication during the 1920s and '30s of much contemporary correspondence, particularly that of her celebrated lover, the poet Krasiński.

In 1939 a woman called Paulina Czernicka approached Radio Wilno, saying that she had several unpublished letters of Chopin's to Delfina Potocka, around which she could build a programme. With the outbreak of war, the plan came to nothing, and no more was heard until 1945, when the same lady, now resettled in western Poland, approached Radio Poznań, and broadcast extracts from letters allegedly written by Chopin. This naturally aroused enthusiastic interest, heightened by the fact that archives and collections throughout Poland had been methodically destroyed by the Germans during the war. But the enthusiasm waned as more extracts were published by Czernicka, with their overtly erotic content. A debate started up as to whether Chopin could or would have written such stuff, and whether he had or had not had a sexual relationship with Delfina Potocka.

The newly founded Chopin Society asked Czernicka to supply the originals so that they could verify them and publish this valuable find. She signed an agreement with them, promising to supply manuscripts and originals. A few months later, however, she stated that the originals were 'temporarily lost', but that she would produce photographs of them. She then explained that she had given some of the originals to a French officer in Wilno in 1939, and that these were now in France, but that others were hidden in Poland, and would be produced shortly. On the day she was supposed to bring them to Warsaw, the Chopin Society received a telegram from her saying that, as she was waiting for the train, the briefcase containing the originals had been grabbed by a thief employed by descendants of Delfina's family, who did not wish to see the compromising letters published. She fed the Society with various other stories, claiming on one occasion that the originals were in Australia, and on another that her aunt had them in America, and on a third that they were in France, but nobody has to this day seen any such originals. Paulina Czernicka committed suicide in 1949.

The provenance of the letters was no more probable than were their mystifying peregrinations. Czernicka claimed that she had obtained them from a relative who was a member of the Komar family, but although the name was the same, this particular Komar family had no traceable relationship in the last three hundred years with that into which Delfina was born, and lived in a completely different area of the country. Moreover, Delfina's Komars had died out, and her heirs were a Countess Tyszkiewicz and a Countess Raczyńska, neither of whom had the faintest recollection of any such correspondence existing. Furthermore, none of Czernicka's relatives had ever heard a word about any such letters.

Much has been written on Paulina Czernicka herself, and all the evidence from people who knew her points to her being a psychopath with a troubled emotional life. There was a strong vein of madness in the family (both her brothers and her mother also committed suicide), and she had from early life nurtured a cult of Chopin, avidly collecting every publication on the subject.

It was not until many years after her death that her papers were found and a full compilation made of the texts, which had hitherto been broadcast or printed only fragmentarily. It then became possible to look at the fundamental issue: whether or not these texts were genuine transcripts from letters written by Chopin.

A cursory reading of the texts, which include two full letters, one of them dated, and a hundred or so fragments, varying in length, will strike anyone who knows the authentic correspondence of Chopin in two ways. The first is that the style is indeed very 'Chopinesque', so much so in fact that one begins to wonder after a while at the abundance of turns of phrase, neologisms, puns and jokes which seem familiar. They are in fact familiar because they all occur in different forms or contexts in the authentic correspondence, though far less frequently. If this is indeed the real Chopin writing, he is trying to show off. The second thing that strikes one is the fact that this collection of texts provides, already made up into perfectly quotable passages, everything that the biographer and the historian vainly struggle to find in Chopin's real correspondence. This betrays little about Chopin's emotional life, let alone his sexual habits; here they are described in staggering detail. The authentic correspondence makes no judgements on other musicians or composers, and gives no clue as to how Chopin considered his music or how he felt about creating it. Czernicka's texts talk of nothing else: one is overwhelmed by the judgements on Liszt, Schumann, Berlioz, Mozart, Beethoven, Bach; by Chopin's statements about certain pieces of his own; by his observations on playing the piano, on the theory of music and just about anything related to it. The authentic correspondence also leaves one guessing at his relationship to the Polish Romantic movement in general and the poets, Słowacki, Mickiewicz and Norwid in particular. Czernicka's texts are full of vignettes and conversations which fill this gap too. Were these texts to be genuine, they would make the biographer's task much easier.

All the evidence points in the other direction. A historical examination of the texts reveals serious faults. The only dated letter is written from Chopin in Paris to the Countess in Paris, regarding a tryst for that evening. It is known that Delfina spent the whole of the year in question in Naples, having a torrid affair with Krasiński. Some have argued that Czernicka could have written down the wrong year when transcribing the original, but research has shown that in no year in which this letter could have been written were both Chopin and the Countess in Paris in the month given, which, written out in full, is unlikely to have been copied wrong. Several meetings are described which could never have taken place, and there are small mistakes, such as the fragments in which Chopin mentions sending Delfina books by Mickiewicz, Witwicki and Krasiński, in spite of the fact that when the letter purports to have been written Krasiński had only published one book, and that so anonymously that nobody in Paris knew who the author was.

In these texts Chopin talks much of the young poet Norwid, and refers to him in the same way as, and with greater respect than, he does to Mickiewicz. Mickiewicz was a national figure, generally regarded in Paris, by Frenchmen as well as Poles, as the spiritual cousin of Byron and Goethe. Norwid was a little-known young man in his twenties, who had published pieces here and there in periodicals and did not achieve full recognition in Poland until the beginning of the twentieth century, and did not become fashionable until the 1930s.

Another curious point is that the erotic passages reveal a distinctly post-Freudian association of sexual libido and artistic creativity which does not fit in with either the atmosphere or the psychological make-up of the society in which Chopin lived in the 1830s and '40s.

Finally, there is the evidence provided by a linguistic examination of the texts. Apart from the fact that the person writing one of the erotic passages gets his or her own gender mixed up at one stage, there are many examples of words which did not appear in Polish until the twentieth century, or else changed their meaning, and are used in the twentieth-century and not the nineteenth-century meaning. The texts are also full of word-endings and usages common to Galicia and Volhynia in eastern Poland, wholly different to those used in Warsaw and Mazovia, as in Chopin's authentic correspondence. Some of Chopin's own neologisms are here repeated with a different gender to the one they have in the authentic correspondence. There is also an avalanche of words such as 'art', 'artistic', 'creativity', 'work of art', 'inspiration', which are absent from the authentic correspondence and which, moreover, did not acquire their present meaning in the Polish language until after Chopin's death.

It is worth noting that amongst Paulina Czernicka's papers there are books on Chopin with underlined passages which can be recognised, only slightly amended, in her texts, and there are whole lines in her texts which are taken directly from statements by Chopin's pupils, published later, and from his own notes for a piano method. Her own manuscript texts are full of crossings out, of phrases added in different inks with a different pen, which suggests confection rather than copying.

There can be no doubt that these texts are forgeries, probably made during the 1930s, and that the forger was almost certainly Paulina Czernicka. One or two Chopin enthusiasts, however, have carried on championing the cause of their authenticity, and they had a field day in 1964 when a few photocopies, purporting to be of the originals, mysteriously appeared amongst the papers of the deceased composer Tadeusz Szeligowski. They came into the possession of his brother-in-law, living in England, Adam Harasowski, who for reasons which are not altogether clear did not publish them until 1973, in the periodical *Music and Musicians*, to support his view that some of the letters were genuine, while others were forgeries. The Warsaw Chopin Institute showed the photocopies to an expert graphologist, who declared them to be forgeries. A fierce champion of the authenticity of the letters, M. Gliński, showed them to another expert, who declared them to be copies of original letters written by Chopin. The Institute then handed them to the forensic department of the Polish Police, who carried out extensive and well-documented photographic tests which revealed that the photocopies were made by juxtaposing photographs of lines, words and expressions from facsimiles or photographs of authentic letters, and even traced from which publications certain words had been photographed. Who concocted these photocopies is not known, but they must be regarded as irrelevant to the issue. The entire body of 'letters' must be treated as forgeries, and the happy compromise that 'some of them are genuine' cannot be accepted. Nothing short of the discovery of original letters in Chopin's handwriting can alter the balance of the facts, which all testify to the whole story being an enormous and squalid hoax.

NOTES

Abbreviations

CFC – Chopin, Fryderyk, *Correspondance*, ed. B.E. Sydow, S. Chainaye & D. Chainaye

CJ – Czartkowski, Adam & Jeżewska, Zofia, *Fryderyk Chopin*

CLA – Liszt, Franz, *Correspondance de Liszt avec la comtesse d'Agoult*

Hoesick – Hoesick, Ferdynand, *Chopin*

KFC – Chopin, Fryderyk, *Korespondencja*, ed. B.E. Sydow

Lubin – Sand, George, *Correspondance*, ed. Georges Lubin

MH – Mirska, Maria & Hordyński, Władysław, *Chopin na Obczyźnie*

MS – Marix-Spire, Thérèse, *Les Romantiques et la Musique*

Niecks – Niecks, Frederick, *Chopin as Man and Musician*

SCFC – Chopin, Fryderyk, *Selected Correspondence*, ed. A. Hedley

Chapter 1: A Prodigy Restrained

1. *La Presse*, 5 November 1849.
2. On the funeral, see: *The Musical World*, 10 November 1849; Niecks, Vol. II, p.324; Théophile Gautier in *La Presse*, 5 November 1849; *Revue et Gazette Musicale de Paris*, 4 November 1849; Berlioz, *Selected Letters*, p.265, where he includes, probably erroneously, Paul de la Roche.

3. For documents relating to Nicolas Chopin's origins and move to Poland, see Introdution in Vol. I of CFC; also Gabriel Ladaique, *Les Ancêtres Paternels de Frédéric Chopin*; also Adam Massalski, *Niezbyt Ścisła Ankieta Personalna*.

4. Letter to Polish Literary Association, 16/I/1833, and to Fétis, 27/III/1836, in KFC, Vol. I, pp.224 & 227 respectively; also letter from Ludwika Jędrzejewicz to her brother, 21/III/1842, ibid., Vol. II, p.57; Article in *Gazeta Korespondenta Warszawskiego i Zagranicznego*, p.1733; see also Julian Fontana's introduction to Chopin's Complete Works, Paris 1853.

5. Eugeniusz Skrodzki (pseud. G. Wielisław) quoted in CJ, p.7.

6. Ibid., p.12; also K.W. Wójcicki, *Cmentarz Powązkowski*, Vol. I, p.202; and Eustachy Marylski on pp.55 & 56 of Ms. 7125 in Biblioteka Narodowa, Warsaw.

7. Eugeniusz Skrodzki, quoted CJ, p.12.

8. Nicolas Chopin to his son, 20/XI/1831, KFC Vol. I, p.188.

9. *Pamiętnik Warszawski*, 4th year, Vol. X, January 1818.

10. Aleksandra z Tańskich Tarezewska, *Historia Mego Zycia*, p.243.

11. A.E. Koźmian, *Wspomnienia*, Vol. I, pp.73 & 170.

12. J.U. Niemcewicz, *Nasze Przebiegi*, in *Przegląd Polski*, zeszyt 10, 1873, pp.72–81.

13. Wójcicki, op. cit., Vol. II, p.18; see also Hoesick, Vol. I, p.61.

14. KFC Vol. I, p.36.

Chapter 2: School Days

1. *Kurier dla Płci Pięknej*, Rok 1, Vol. 1, Warsaw 1823.

2. Letter to Wilhelm Kolberg, 19/VIII/1824, KFC Vol. I, p.40.

3. *Kurier Szafarski*, ibid., p.43.

4. Ibid., p.42.

5. Ibid., p.45.

6. Krystyna Kobylańska, *Nieznane Utwory Chopina w Zapomnianym Albumie*, pp.7–8.

7. Eugeniusz Szulc, *Nieznana Karta Warszawskiego Okresu Życia Chopina.*
8. Franciszek German, *Chopin i Literaci Warszawszcy*, p.228.
9. Quoted in Niecks, Vol. I, p.59.
10. Letter to Jan Białobłocki, 8/VII/1825, KFC Vol. I, p.48.
11. Letter to Jan Matuszyński, August 1825, ibid., p.52.
12. Letter to parents, 26/VIII/1825, ibid., p.53.
13. See Eugeniusz Szulc, op. cit.; A.E. Odyniec, *Wspomnienia*, pp.325–6 (although Odyniec places this evening in late 1826 or early 1827, he notes that Chopin was wearing the Lyceum uniform, which would seem to indicate a date prior to July 1826).
14. K.W. Wojcicki, op. cit., Vol. I, p.18. The evening probably took place in the house of Colonel Gutkowski, who died at the beginning of May 1826.
15. Letter to Elsner, 29/VIII/1826, KFC Vol. I, p.72.
16. Wanda Tomaszewska, *Chopin w Dusznikach*, p.88.

Chapter 3: Musical Genius

1. Letter to Elsner, 29/VIII/1826, KFC Vol. I, p.72.
2. Elsner to Chopin, 27/XI/1831, ibid., p.197.
3. Franciszek German, *Chopin i Literaci Warszawszcy*, pp.56ff.
4. Related to Friederike Müller, in Niecks, Vol. II, p.340.
5. Eugène Delacroix, *Journal*, Vol. I, p.270.
6. *Gazette Musicale de Paris*, 21 September 1834.
7. Letter to family, 12/VIII/1829, KFC Vol. I, p.93.
8. Letter to family, 20/IX/1828, ibid., p.83.
9. Mendelssohn to Fanny Hensel, ibid., p.263.
10. Letter to Tytus, 27/XII/1828, ibid., p.87.
11. *Gazette Musicale de Paris*, 15 May 1834.
12. Quoted KFC Vol. I, p.88.
13. See note ibid., p.487.
14. J. Reiss, *Ślązak Józef Elsner*, p.39.

15. Entry in register of the Warsaw Conservatoire, reproduced in Kobylańska, *Chopin w Kraju*, p.125.
16. Letter to parents, 8/VIII/1829, KFC Vol. I, p.90.
17. Ibid., p.91.
18. Ibid., p.92.
19. Letter to Tytus, 12/IX/1829, ibid., p.104.
20. Letter to parents, 12/VIII/1829, ibid., p.93.
21. Letter to family, 19/VIII/1829, ibid., p.96.
22. Letter to parents, 12/VIII/1829, ibid., p.93.
23. Letter to family, 19/VIII/1829, ibid., p.96.
24. Ibid.
25. Ibid.
26. Letter to parents, 12/VIII/1829, ibid., p.94.
27. Ibid.
28. Quoted in Niecks, Vol. II, pp.99–102.
29. Ibid.
30. Ibid.
31. Letter to family, 26/VIII/1829, KFC Vol. I, p.101.

Chapter 4: Adolescent Passions

1. *Kurier Warszawski*, No.230 (29/VIII/1829); *Gazeta Polska*, No.230 (30/VIII/1829) & 247 (16/IX/1829); *Dziennik Powszechny Krajowy*, 30/VIII/1829 & 15/IX/1829.
2. Oskar Kolberg's reminiscences in CJ, p.41.
3. Letter to Tytus, 20/X/1829, KFC Vol. I, p.109.
4. Letter to Tytus, 14/XI/1829, ibid., p.112.
5. Franz Liszt, *Chopin*, p.215.
6. Letter to Tytus, 14/XI/1829, KFC Vol. I, p.112.
7. *Kurier Warszawski*, 23/XII/1829.
8. *Kurier Warszawski*, 5/III/1829, p.309.
9. *Dziennik Powszechny Krajowy*, no. 62, 1830.
10. Karol Kurpiński's diary, in Hoesick, Vol. I, p.219.
11. Letter to Tytus, 27/III/1830, KFC Vol. I, p.115.

12. *Dziennik Powszechny Krajowy*, no. 77, 19/III/1830.

13. *Kurier Polski*, no. 107, 22/III/1830.

14. *Kurier Polski*, no 110, 26/III/1830.

15. *Kurier Polski*, no. 107, 22/III/1830.

16. Letter to Tytus, 27/III/1830, KFC Vol. I, p.116.

17. Letter to Tytus, 10/IV/1830, ibid., p.118.

18. Letter to Tytus, 17/IV/1830, ibid., p.121.

19. Letter to Tytus, 27/III/1830, ibid., p.116.

20. Letter to Tytus, 10/IV/1830, ibid., p.120.

21. Ibid.

22. Letter to Tytus, 3/X/1829, ibid., p.108.

23. Letter to Tytus, 15/V/1830, ibid., p.125.

24. Elsner to Chopin, 13/XI/1832, ibid., p.221.

25. Letter to Tytus, 5/VI/1830, ibid., pp.128–9.

26. Ibid., pp.126–7.

27. Letter to Tytus, 21/VIII/1830, ibid., p.130.

28. A. Rajchman, *Kolebka Chopina*.

29. Letter to Tytus, 31/VIII/1830, KFC Vol. I, p.132.

30. Letter to Tytus, 4/IX/1830, ibid., p.135.

31. Letter to Tytus, 18/IX/1830, ibid., p.138.

32. Letter to Tytus, 14/I/1830, ibid., p.113.

33. Letter to Tytus, 4/IX/1830, ibid., p.137.

34. Letter to Tytus, 5/X/1830, ibid., p.146.

35. K. Wójcicki, *Pamiętniki Dziecka Warszawy*, Vol. II, p.545.

36. Letter to Tytus, 5/X/1830, KFC Vol. I, p.145.

37. Letter to Tytus, 12/X/1830, ibid., p.147.

38. Chopin's Album Diary, p.12, in CFC Vol.II, p.210.

Chapter 5: Vienna

1. Letter to family, 14/XI/1830, KFC Vol. I, p.152.

2. Letter to Matuszyński, 22/XI/1830, ibid., p.153.

3. Letter to family, 1/XII/1830, ibid., p.158.

4. Ibid., p.155.

5. Letter to family, 22/XII/1830, ibid., p.160.
6. Letter to family, 1/XII/1830, ibid., p.157.
7. Ibid., p.156.
8. Ibid.
9. Ibid.
10. Letter to Tytus, 12/XII/1831, ibid., p.199.
11. Letter to Matuszyński, 26/XII/1830, ibid., p.162.
12. Ibid., p.156.
13. Letter to family, 22/XII/1830, ibid., p.161.
14. Romuald Hube's memoirs, Biblioteka Jagiellońska Ms. 6687/ II, p.63.
15. Letter to Matuszyński, 26/XII/1830, KFC Vol. I, p.166.
16. Ibid.
17. Ibid., p.163.
18. Ibid., p.162.
19. Ibid., p.163, and Letter to Matuszyński, 1/I/1831, ibid., p.170.
20. Fragment of Chopin's diary, ibid., p.167.
21. Letter to Elsner, 29/I/1831, ibid., p.171.
22. Letter to family, 22/XII/1830, ibid., p.161.
23. Letter to Matuszyński, 26/XII/1830, ibid., p.165.
24. Fragment of Chopin's diary, ibid., p.167.
25. *Allgemeine Musikalische Zeitung*, no. 30, 21 September 1831.
26. Letter to family, 22/XII/1830, KFC Vol. I, p.160.
27. Letter to Matuszyński, 26/XII/1830, ibid., p.164.
28. Ibid., p.161.
29. Letter to Matuszyński, 1/I/1831, ibid., p.168.
30. Ibid., p.162.
31. Stefan Witwicki to Chopin, 6/VII/1831, ibid., p.179.
32. Letter to parents, 16/VII/1831, ibid., p.182.
33. Fragment of Chopin's diary, ibid., p.167.
34. *Flora*, no.87, 30 August 1831.
35. Fragments of Chopin's diary, KFC Vol. I, pp.183–4.
36. See letter to Kumelski, 18/XI/1831, ibid., p.187.
37. Fragments of Chopin's diary, ibid., pp.185–6.

Chapter 6: Romantic Paris

1. Heinrich Heine, *Conditions in France*, quoted in Lloyd S. Kramer, *Threshold of a New World*, p.58.
2. Letter to Kumelski, 18/XI/1831, KFC Vol. I, p.187.
3. See Andrzej Jastrzębski, *Jański o Chopinie*.
4. Letter to Kumelski, 18/XI/1831, KFC Vol. I, p.186.
5. Letter to Tytus, 12/XII/1831, ibid., p.202.
6. Letter to Kumelski, 18/XI/1831, ibid., p.187.
7. Letter to Tytus, 12/XII/1831, ibid., p.201.
8. Ibid., pp.199–200.
9. Elsner to Chopin, 27/XI/1831, ibid., p.197.
10. Letter to Tytus, 12/XII/1831, ibid., p.203.
11. Letter to Tytus, 25/XII/1831, ibid., p.209.
12. Franz Liszt, *Chopin*, p.174.
13. Ibid., p.21.
14. Letter to Tytus, 12/XII/1831, KFC Vol.I, p.201.
15. Ferdinand Hiller, *Open Letter to Franz Liszt*, in MH, p.69; see also Niecks, Vol. II, p.8; Larry Todd, *Mendelssohn*, pp.253, 377
16. Letter to Tytus, 12/XII/1831, KFC Vol. I, p.201.
17. Quoted in Hoesick, Vol. II, p.91.
18. A. Orłowski to family, 9/III/1832, quoted in Hoesick, Vol. II, p.47.
19. G.A. Osborne, *Reminiscences of Frederick Chopin*, p.19. There are several errors of detail in his account, which was written fifty years after the event.
20. *Revue Musicale*, 3 March 1832.
21. Letter to Nowakowski, 15/IV/1832, KFC Vol. I, p.213.
22. Franz Liszt, op. cit., p.119.
23. Niecks, Vol. I, p.247: interviews with Liszt, Hiller and Franchomme.
24. Zofia Lissa, *Chopin w Świetle Korespondencji Wydawców*, pp.3ff.

25. Hector Berlioz, *Feuilleton* in *Journal des Débats*, 27 October 1849.
26. Juliusz Słowacki, *Dzieła*, Vol. II, pp.48 & 63.
27. Juliusz Słowacki to mother, 3/IX/1832, KFC Vol. I, p.216.
28. Ferdinand Hiller, *Open Letter to Franz Liszt*, in MH, p.69.
29. Franz Liszt, op. cit., p.146; also Hector Berlioz, *Les Années Romantiques*, p.399.
30. Liszt to Pictet, in MS, p.552.
31. Eugène Delacroix, *Journal*, Vol. I, p.365.
32. Quoted in Niecks, Vol. II, p.110.
33. Gutmann, quoted in Niecks, Vol. I, p.265.
34. Kornel Michałowski, *Nieznane Wspomnienie o Chopinie*, p.206.
35. Hiller, quoted in MH, p.69.
36. Letter to Tytus, 12/XII/1831, KFC Vol. I, p.199.

Chapter 7: Pianist *à la Mode*

1. Letter to Dominik Dziewanowski, Spring 1833, KFC Vol. I, pp.222–3.
2. Charles Hallé, *Life & Letters*, p.31.
3. Josef Filtsch to parents, in SCFC, p.216.
4. Ibid.; see also Niecks, Vol. II, p.101.
5. Quoted in MH, p.69.
6. H. de La Touche to George Sand, 31/VII/1844, Lubin Vol. VI, p.594.
7. Ibid.
8. Franz Liszt, *Chopin*, p.177.
9. Ernest Legouvé, *Soixante Ans de Souvenirs*, Vol. I, p.307.
10. Legouvé to Chopin, KFC Vol. I, p.421.
11. Custine to Chopin, n.d., ibid., p.207; see also MS, p.601, Appendix II.
12. Zofia Lissa, *Chopin w Świetle Korespondencji Wydawców*, p.10.

13. Ibid., p.8.
14. Ibid., p.10.
15. Inside cover of Chopin's 1834 diary, Chopin Society Ms. It is clear, from the presence of names such as that of Chopin's lodger Hoffmann, that this is a list of people who owed the composer money.
16. Antoni Orłowski to family, 29/XI/1832, in Hoesick, Vol. II, p.67.
17. J. Mycielski to wife, 26/IX/1852, in J.M. Smoter, *Spór o Listy Chopina do Delfiny Potockiej*, p.33.
18. Ibid., pp.31–2.
19. Letter to Tytus, 12/XII/1831, KFC Vol. I, p.204.
20. See George Sand to Grzymała, June 1838, ibid., p.438.
21. Franz Liszt, *Chopin*, p.210.
22. Letter to Franchomme, 18/IX/1833, KFC Vol. I. p.228.
23. Liszt, Chopin and Franchomme to Hiller, 20/VI/1833, ibid., pp.226–8.
24. Hector Berlioz, *Les Années Romantiques*, p.263; and *Selected Letters*, p.56.
25. Quoted in MH, p.69.
26. Ibid.
27. Matuszyński to family, SCFC, p.123.
28. MH, p.69. It is worth noting that Delfina Potocka's father, Stanisław Komar, died at Enghien in 1832, and that her brother later bought a villa there, so she may well have been renting a house in the vicinity in the mid-1830s (I was given this information by Dr H. Fornet, a local resident who made a search of the regional archives of Cergy-Pontoise).
29. *Revue Musicale*, 21 December 1833.
30. J.-J. Eigeldinger, *Koncerty Chopina w Paryżu*, p.161.
31. *Gazette Musicale*, 15 May 1834.
32. Rellstab, quoted in Hoesick, Vol. II, p.93.
33. Mendelssohn, quoted in Niecks, Vol. I, p.273.
34. MH, p.133.
35. Letter to Regina Hiller, May 1834, KFC Vol. I, p.303.

Chapter 8: Second Love

1. Liszt to Marie d'Agoult, 13/IX/1834, in CLA, p.113.
2. See Fanny Erskine's Paris Diary, in Jeremy Barlow, *Encounters with Chopin*, p.248.
3. Quoted in CJ, p.420.
4. Mikuli, quoted in J.-J. Eigeldinger, *Chopin vu par ses Élèves*, p.22.
5. Joseph Filtsch to parents, 19/VIII/1842, SCFC, p.221.
6. See J.-J. Eigeldinger, *Chopin vu par ses Élèves*, p.73.
7. On Chopin's teaching in general, see J.-J. Eigeldinger, *Chopin vu par ses Élèves*, pp.34–59; and Niecks, Vol. II, pp.174ff.
8. Rubio, quoted in Niecks, Vol. II, p.187.
9. Mikuli, quoted in J.-J. Eigeldinger, *Chopin vu par ses Élèves*, p.24.
10. Matthias, quoted in CJ, p.393.
11. Hector Berlioz, *Feuilleton* in *Journal des Débats*, 27 October 1849.
12. Legouvé, op. cit., Vol. I, p.307.
13. *Gazette Musicale de Paris*, 12 April 1835.
14. Minute-Books of the Association of Polish Ladies in Paris, Vol. III, pp.40–3, in Bibliothèque Polonaise, uncatalogued ms.
15. J.-J. Eigeldinger, *Koncerty Chopina w Paryżu*, p.166.
16. Letter to Kalasanty Jędrzejewicz, 16/VIII/1835, KFC Vol. I, p.260.
17. Franciszek German, *Fryderyk Chopin i Juliusz Słowacki*, p.159.
18. Ludwika Jędrzejewicz to Chopin, 15/XII/1835, KFC Vol. I, p.269.
19. Maria Wodzińska to Chopin, September 1835, ibid., p.261.
20. F. Wieck, quoted in MH, p.138.
21. Mendelssohn to Fanny Hensel, 6/X/1835, KFC Vol. I, pp.406–7.
22. Mendelssohn, *Letters to Charlotte and Ignaz Moscheles*, pp.125 & 138.

23. Maria Wodzińska to Chopin, September 1835, KFC Vol. I, p.262.

24. See A. Jełowicki, *Listy do Ksaweryny Chodkiewiczowej*, p.208; also Hoesick, Vol. II, p.124; and J.U. Niemcewicz's diary, Bibliothèque Polonaise, Ms. P.E. 501, p.70.

25. *Kronika Emigracji Polskiej*, Vol. IV, 22 February 1836, pp.109–10.

26. See Minute-Books of the Association of Polish Ladies in Paris, Vol. II, p.150 & Vol III, p.38, Bibliothèque Polonaise, uncatalogued ms.

27. *Kurier Warszawski*, 8 January 1836.

28. Józef Brzowski's diary, in CJ, p.225.

29. Mme Émile de Girardin, *Le Vicomte de Launay*, Vol. I, p.169.

30. Quoted by Marquis de Luppé, *Astolphe de Custine*, pp.200–1.

31. Ibid., p.248.

32. Custine to Chopin, 6/VI/1836, KFC Vol. I, p.419.

33. J.U. Niemcewicz's diary, Bibliothèque Polonaise, Ms P.E. 501, p.188.

34. Liszt to Marie d'Agoult, CLCA, p.170.

35. Marquis de Luppé, op. cit., p.186.

36. Teresa Wodzińska to Chopin, 14/IX/1836, KFC Vol. I, p.286.

37. Schumann to Heinrich Dorn, 14/X/1836, ibid., p.420.

38. Quoted in Niecks, Vol. I, p.310.

39. Ibid.

40. From Henriette Voigt's diary, quoted in Niecks, Vol. I, p.311.

41. Quoted in ibid., p.310.

Chapter 9: Art and Politics

1. Marie d'Agoult, *Mémoires*, p.208.

2. Alexandre Dumas, *Mémoires*, Vol. II, p.990.

3. Liszt to Marie d'Agoult, December 1839, CLCA, p.313.

4. Charles Augustin Sainte-Beuve, *Mes Poisons*, p.106.

5. Marie d'Agoult, *Mémoires*, p.210.

6. Quoted in James Billington, *Fire in the Minds of Men*, p.154.

7. Nourrit, quoted in Alexandre Dumas, *Mémoires*, Vol. II, p.613.

8. MS, p.530.

9. Berlioz to Liszt in *Gazette Musicale*, 11 August 1839.

10. Marie d'Agoult, *Mémoires*, p.210.

11. Ferdinand Denis, *Journal*, p.60.

12. CJ, p.212.

13. Ibid., p.213.

14. Ibid., p.214.

15. Ibid., p.215.

16. Ferdinand Hiller, *Open Letter to Franz Liszt*, in Niecks, Vol. II, p.8.

17. M. Karasowski, *Fryderyk Chopin*, Vol. II, p.75.

18. Heine, *Lutèce*, pp.48–9.

19. Marie d'Agoult, *Mémoires*, p.208.

20. See Z. Markiewicz, *Spotkania Polsko-Francuskie*, p.75.

21. Władysław Mickiewicz, *Żywot Adama Mickiewicza*, Vol. II, p.375.

22. Letter to Teresa Wodzińska, 1/XI/1836, KFC Vol. I, p.291.

23. Maria Wodzińska to Chopin, ibid., p.289.

24. Maria Wodzińska to Chopin, 25/I/1837, ibid., p.295; and Spring 1837, p.297.

25. A. Malvezzi, *La Principessa Cristina di Belgiojoso*, Vol. II, p.209.

26. CJ, p.219.

27. George Sand to Marie d'Agoult, 6/IV/1837, Lubin Vol. III, p.769.

28. Marie d'Agoult to George Sand, 8/IV/1837, ibid., p.807.

29. Custine to Chopin, Spring 1837, KFC Vol. I, pp.424–5.

30. CJ, pp.223–33.

31. Ibid., p.232.

32. Ibid., pp.234–5.

33. Chopin to Fontana, July 1837, KFC Vol. I, p.306.

34. Stanisław Egbert Kozmian to brother, July 1837, in Hoesick, Vol. II, p.145.

35. See Z. Jabłoński, *Chopin w Anglii*.

36. Letter to Teresa Wodzińska, 14/VIII/1837, KFC Vol. I, p.307.

37. See John Sellards, *Dans le Sillage du Romantisme*.

38. George Sand, *Journal Intime*, p.86.

39. Letter to Marie de Rozières, 2/XI/1848, KFC Vol. II, p.279.

40. See J. Słowacki to mother, February 1845, ibid., p.126; and Władysław Mickiewicz, op. cit., Vol. IV, p.255.

41. Quoted in Niecks, Vol. II, p.16.

42. Charles Hallé to parents, 30/XI/1836, in Jeffrey Kallberg, *Small Fairy Voices*, pp.51–2.

43. J.-J. Eigeldinger, *Koncerty Chopina w Paryżu*, p.148.

44. Heine, *Lettres Confidentielles*, in *Revue et Gazette Musicale de Paris*, 4 February 1838.

Chapter 10: Love Above All

1. MS, p.619.

2. Marquis de Luppé, op. cit., p.199.

3. George Sand to Grzymała, May 1838, Lubin Vol. IV, pp.428–39.

4. Balzac, *Lettres à Madame Hanska*, Vol. I, pp.584–5.

5. Letter to Grzymała, n.d., KFC Vol. I, p.325.

6. George Sand to Grzymała, May 1838, Lubin Vol. IV, pp.428–39.

7. Ibid., p.438.

8. George Sand to Grzymała, June 1838, ibid., p.445.

9. Letter to Grzymała, n.d., KFC Vol. I, p.325.

10. Félicien Mallefille to Chopin, ibid., p.441.

11. George Sand to Delacroix, 7/IX/1838, Lubin Vol. IV, pp.480ff.

12. Ibid.

13. See Curtis Cate, *George Sand*, p.457.

14. Custine to Sophie Gay, 22/X/1838, CFC Vol. II, p.279.

15. George Sand to Charlotte Marliani, Lubin Vol. IV, p.512.
16. Quoted in Marcel Godeau, *Le Voyage à Majorque de George Sand et Frédéric Chopin*, p.54.
17. Letter to Fontana, 15/XI/1838, KFC Vol. I, p.327.
18. George Sand, *Un Hiver à Majorque*, p.10; also George Sand to Christine Buloz, 14/XI/1838, Lubin Vol. IV, p.515.
19. Letter to Fontana, 3/XII/1838, KFC Vol. I, p.330.
20. George Sand to Grzymała, 3/XII/1838, Lubin Vol. IV, p.528.
21. Letter to Pleyel, 21/XI/1838, KFC Vol. I, p.443.
22. Letter to Fontana, 14/XII/1838, ibid., p.332.
23. George Sand to Gauthier d'Arc, 14/XI/1838, Lubin Vol. IV, p.521.
24. Letter to Fontana, 28/XII/1838, KFC Vol. I, p.333.
25. George Sand, *Un Hiver à Majorque*, p.107.
26. Letter to Fontana, 28/XII/1838, KFC Vol. I, p.332.
27. George Sand to Charlotte Marliani, 22/I/1839, Lubin Vol. IV, p.569.
28. Letter to Fontana, 14/XII/1838, KFC Vol. I, p.332.
29. Letter to Fontana, 28/XII/1838, ibid., p.333.
30. Letter to Grzymała, 12/III/1839, ibid., p.341.
31. George Sand, *Histoire de ma Vie*, Vol. XX, p.146.
32. George Sand to Charlotte Marliani, 22/I/1839, Lubin Vol. IV, p.569.
33. See George Sand, *Histoire de ma Vie*, Vol. XX, p.161, where she says that she would gladly have stayed on another two or three years, and George Sand to Charlotte Marliani, 22/I/1839, Lubin Vol. IV, p.560, where she has no intention of leaving.
34. For evidence discrediting an alleged excursion to Arenys de Mar by George Sand and Chopin, see *Por qui escribi Chopin in Arenys de Mar*; Curtis Cate, *George Sand*, p.476.
35. George Sand to Charlotte Marliani, 15/II/1839, Lubin Vol. IV, p.569.
36. George Sand to Charlotte Marliani, 26/II/1839, ibid., p.577.

37. *Un Hiver à Majorque*, written Autumn 1840, and *Histoire de ma Vie*, Vol. XX, started in 1848.

38. George Sand to Charlotte Marliani, 18/III/1839, Lubin Vol. IV, p.588.

39. Letter to Grzymała, 12/III/1839, KFC Vol. I, p.341.

40. Letter to Fontana, end of March 1839, ibid., p.342.

41. Letter to Fontana, 28/XII/1838, ibid., p.333.

42. Letter to Fontana, 12/III/1839, ibid., pp.339–40.

43. Ibid., p.340.

44. Letter to Fontana, n.d., ibid., p.338.

45. Letter to Grzymała, 12/IV/1839, ibid., p.345.

46. George Sand to Charlotte Marliani, 26/IV/1839, Lubin Vol. IV, p.646.

47. Letter to Fontana, 7/III/1839, KFC Vol. I, p.337.

48. George Sand to Charlotte Marliani, April 1839, Lubin Vol. IV, p.625.

49. George Sand to Charlotte Marliani, 26/IV/1839, ibid., p.645.

50. Letter to Grzymała, 2/6/1839, KFC Vol. I, p.349.

51. George Sand to Charlotte Marliani, 3/VI/1839, Lubin Vol. IV, p.663.

Chapter 11: Conjugal Life

1. George Sand to Charlotte Marliani, 15/VI/1839, Lubin Vol. IV, p.684.

2. George Sand to Charlotte Marliani, 20/VI/1839, ibid., p.688.

3. For this and other medical information, see: Czesław Sielużycki, *Chopin, Geniusz Cierpiący*; *O Zdrowiu Chopina*, and *Korekty do Ikonografii Chopinowskiej*; Sergiusz Gurewicz, *Miał Wyostrzoną Wrażliwość*; Sir James Clark, *A Treatise on Pulmonary Consumption*; John O'Shea, *Music and Medicine*; A. Laskiewicz, *Jak przebiegała Choroba Płucna Fryderyka Chopina*; Esmond R. Long, *A History of the Therapy of Tuberculosis and the Case of Frederick Chopin*.

4. The accounts of the Majorcan trip, and various anecdotes in Chopin's life as related in *Histoire de ma Vie*, are often either embellished or tendentious, or both, while the letter to Grzymała referred to (12/V/1847) contains one or two inaccuracies and one rather significant untruth: there is firm evidence of her having at least one affair while she was with Chopin.

5. George Sand to Charlotte Marliani, 20/VI/1839, Lubin Vol. IV, p.688.

6. Letter to Fontana, 8/VIII/1839, KFC Vol. I, p.353.

7. Ibid., pp.353–4.

8. George Sand to Grzymała, 8/VII/1839, Lubin Vol. IV, p.716.

9. George Sand to Charlotte Marliani, 24/VII/1839, ibid., p.726.

10. George Sand to Charlotte Marliani, 18/IX/1839, ibid., p.750.

11. Letter to Fontana, 25/IX/1839, KFC Vol. I, pp.357–8.

12. Letter to Grzymała, 29/IX/1839, ibid., p.358.

13. Letter to Fontana, 8/X/1839, ibid., p.366.

14. Berlioz to Liszt, 22/I/1839, *Les Années Romantiques*, p.399.

15. Letter to Fontana, 8/VIII/1839, KFC Vol. I, p.354.

16. Marie d'Agoult to Liszt, 19/I/1840, CLCA, p.360.

17. George Sand to Lamennais, 21/VII/1839, Lubin Vol. IV, pp.720–1.

18. Marie d'Agoult to George Sand, 20/VIII/1839, ibid., p.758.

19. George Sand to Charlotte Marliani, 28/IX/1839, ibid., p.757.

20. Marie d'Agoult to George Sand, ibid., p.798.

21. Marie d'Agoult to Liszt, 30/XI/1839, CLCA, p.321.

22. Liszt to Marie d'Agoult, ibid., p.346.

23. Marie d'Agoult to Liszt, March 1840, ibid., p.412.

24. S. Heller to Robert Schumann, 4/I/1840, quoted by L. Bronarski, *Stephen Heller a Chopin*, pp.1–3.

25. Friederike Müller's diary, in Niecks, Vol. II, p.340.

26. See catalogue of sale at Bonham's, London, 24 March 2009, lot 225; Hoesick, Vol. II, p.85.

27. Charlotte Moscheles, *The Life of Moscheles*, Vol. I, p.295.

28. Mendelssohn to Moscheles, in *Letters of Felix Mendelssohn to Charlotte and Ignaz Moscheles*, p.97.

29. See E. Perenyi, *Liszt*, pp.206–9.

30. Emil Smidak, *Moscheles*, p.121.

31. Quoted in Niecks, Vol. II, p.71.

32. Ibid., p.73.

33. Balzac to Eveline Hanska, 28/V/1843, in Balzac, *Lettres à Madame Hanska*, Vol. II, p.226.

34. Gaubert to George Sand, 1/IV/1840, in *Autour de Chopin et de George Sand*.

35. Friedericke Müller's diary, in Niecks, Vol. II, p.340.

36. George Sand to Hippolyte Châtiron, 2/II/1846, Lubin Vol. IV, p.861.

37. George Sand to Hippolyte Châtiron, 1/VII/1840, Lubin Vol. V, p.88.

38. Ibid., p.98.

39. Chopin to Grzymała, 13/VII/1842, quoted Aleksander Janta, *Losy i Ludzie*, pp.243–4.

40. George Sand to Maurice, 20/IX/1840, Lubin Vol. V, pp.132–3.

41. See MS, pp.579–80.

Chapter 12: The Church of Chopin

1. George Sand to Pauline Viardot, 18/IV/1841, Bibliothèque Nationale Ms, N.A.Fr. 16273, f. 36.

2. Marie d'Agoult to Lehmann, 21/IV/1841, quoted in SCFC, p.193.

3. George Sand to Pauline Viardot, 18/IV/1841, Bibliothèque Nationale Ms, N.A.Fr. 16273, f. 36.

4. Quoted in Niecks, Vol. II, p.78.

5. *Gazette Musicale de Paris*, 2 May 1841.

6. Quoted in Niecks, Vol. II, p.78.

7. *La France Musicale*, 2 May 1841.

8. *Gazette Musicale de Paris*, 2 May 1841.

9. Quoted in Niecks, Vol. II, p.279.

10. Quoted in Arthur Hedley, *Chopin*, p.131.

11. Schumann in *Neue Zeitschrift fur Musik*, no. 10 1841.

12. Schumann, *O Fryderyku Chopinie*, p.37.

13. Elsner to Chopin, 14/IX/1834, KFC Vol. I, p.246.

14. Franz Liszt, *Chopin*, p.10.

15. *Gazette Musicale de Paris*, 2 May 1841.

16. Schumann in *Neue Zeitschrift fur Musik*, no. 10 1841.

17. Quoted in Bronarski, *Chopin et l'Italie*, p.16.

18. Quoted in Arthur Hedley, *Chopin*, p.54.

19. Balzac, *Lettres à Madame Hanska*, 6/IV/1843, Vol. II, p.189.

20. Balzac, *Ursule Mirouet*, quoted in Balzac, *Correspondance*, Vol. IV, p.408.

21. Custine to Chopin, KFC Vol. I, p.422; and Delacroix, *Correspondance Générale*, Vol. II, p.286.

22. Anton Rubinstein, *La Musique et ses Représentants*, p.71.

23. Quoted in Niecks, Vol. II, p.100.

24. Letter to Fontana, 11/IX/1841, KFC Vol. II, p.34.

25. George Sand to Hippolyte Châtiron, 26/IV/1841, Lubin Vol. V, pp.29–30.

26. Witwicki to Zaleski, 2/V/1841, Stefan Witwicki, *Listy do J.B. Zaleskiego*, p.69.

27. Josef Filtsch to parents, 8/III/1842, SCFC, p.217.

28. Letter to Fontana, 20/VIII/1841, KFC Vol. II, p.31.

29. George Sand to Dr Gaubert, 1/VIII/1841, Lubin Vol. V, p.391.

30. Letter to Fontana, early June 1841, KFC Vol. II, p.20.

31. Letter to Fontana, 24/VIII/1841, ibid., p.33.

32. George Sand to Marie de Rozières, 11/VII/1841, Lubin Vol. V, p.361.

33. George Sand to Marie de Rozières, 29/VIII/1841, ibid., p.407.

34. George Sand to Marie de Rozières, ibid., pp.362–3; see also Teresa Czerwińska, *Dziennik Podróży Józefa Kalasantego Jędrzejewicza*.

35. Witwicki to Mickiewicz, 29/VII/1841, Bibliothèque Polonaise Ms., P.E. 696/13.
36. Wilhelm von Lenz, quoted in CJ, p.410.
37. Josef Filtsch to parents, 8/III/1842, SCFC, p.216.
38. *La France Musicale*, 27 February 1842.
39. George Sand to Hippolyte Châtiron, 4/III/1842, Lubin Vol. V, p.607.
40. Kornel Krzeczunowicz to Teofil Ostaszewski, 26/II/1842, Biblioteka Jagiellońska Ms, Przyb. 51/64.
41. Letter to Grzymała, n.d., KFC Vol. II, p.59.
42. George Sand to Pauline Viardot, 29/IV/1842, Lubin Vol. V, p.647.
43. George Sand to Delacroix, 28/V/1842, ibid., p.682.
44. Ibid.
45. Ibid.
46. Delacroix to Pierret, 7/VI/1842, Delacroix, *Correspondance Générale*, Vol. II, p.108.
47. Delacroix to Pierret, 22/VI/1842, ibid., p.114.
48. Ibid., p.111.
49 George Sand to Charlotte Marliani, 25/VII/1842, Lubin Vol. V, p.733.
50. Fontana to sister, early May 1842, Biblioteka Narodowa Ms, 7133, f.10.
51. See Kornel Michałowski, *Nieznane wspomnienie o Chopinie*, pp.204–5.
52. Marie de Rozières to A. Wodziński, erroneously dated in CFC, Vol. III, p.81.
53. Leonard Niedźwiedzki's diary, Polska Akademia Nauk, Kórnik, Ms, B.K. 2416, f. 133.
54. Ibid., f. 138.
55. George Sand to Pauline Viardot, 8/VI/1843, Lubin Vol. VI, p.163.
56. George Sand to Maurice, 6/VI/1843, ibid., p.156.

57. Delacroix to George Sand, 30/V/1842, Delacroix, *Correspondance Générale*, Vol. II, pp.104–5.

Chapter 13: The End of the Affair

1. George Sand to Charlotte Marliani, 28/X/1843, Lubin Vol. VI, p.253.
2. Maurice to George Sand, 18/XI/1843, ibid., p.287.
3. George Sand to Grzymała, 18/XI/1843, ibid., p.284.
4. George Sand to Ferdinand François, November 1843, ibid., p.915.
5. George Sand, *Histoire de ma Vie*, Vol. XX, p.160.
6. George Sand to Charlotte Marliani, June 1844, Lubin Vol. VI, p.565.
7. Zofia Rozengardt's diary, Biblioteka Jagiellońska Ms, 9261, f. 23, verso, entry for 2 January 1844.
8. Ibid., f. 24. The score in question has recently come to light in South Africa, still bearing the inscription in pencil.
9. Zofia Rozengardt to her brothers, 24/XII/1843, Biblioteka Jagiellońska Ms, 9292.
10. Charles Hallé, *Life & Letters*, p.34; and Wilhelm von Lenz, quoted in CJ, pp.416–17; Wilhelm von Lenz quoted in CJ, p.412. See A. Hedley, *Nieznana Uczennica Chopina*; also T. Niesmieyanova and S. Semienovsky, *Dnievnik Uchenitszy Shopena*.
11. George Sand to Ludwika Jędrzejewicz, July 1844, Lubin Vol. VI, p.574.
12. Letter to Marie de Rozières, 11/VIII/1844, KFC Vol. II, p.104.
13. George Sand to Charlotte Marliani, 18/IX/1844, Lubin Vol. VI, p.621.
14. George Sand to Pauline Viardot, 22/VIII/1844, ibid., p.605.
15. George Sand to Delacroix, 12/XI/1844, ibid., p.691.
16. Letter to George Sand, 5/XII/1844, KFC Vol. II, p.383.
17. Ibid.

18. Charles Hallé, *Life & Letters*, p.36.
19. Hector Berlioz, *Memoirs*, pp.465–6.
20. See Leonard Niedźwiedzki's diary, Polska Akademia Nauk, Kórnik, Ms, B.K. 2416, pp.221, 234, 131, etc.
21. Louis Blanc, *Histoire de la Révolution de 1848*, p.210.
22. Louis Moreau Gottschalk, *Notes of a Pianist*, p.33; also S. Frederick Starr, *Bamboula*, p, 60.
23. Solange to Marie de Rozières, 3/VII/1845, Lubin Vol. VII, p.9.
24. Letter to family, 13/VII/1845, KFC Vol. II, pp.136–7.
25. Ibid., pp.138–42.
26. George Sand to Marie de Rozières, 19/VII/1845, Lubin Vol. VII, p.63.
27. Quoted by Charlotte Marliani in letter to George Sand, 20/X/1849, Lubin Vol. IX, p.298.
28. George Sand to Marie de Rozières, 19/VIII/1845, Lubin Vol. VII, p.63.
29. Letter to family, 13/VII/1845, KFC Vol. II, p.141.
30. George Sand to Chopin, late September 1845, Lubin Vol. VII, p.97.
31. George Sand to Charlotte Marliani, 7/XI/1845, ibid., p.159.
32. Letter to family, August 1845, KFC Vol. II, p.146.
33. Letter to family, 12–26/XII/1845, ibid., p.155.
34. Ibid., p.157.
35. Turgenev to Pauline Viardot, November 1846, I.S. Turgeniev, *Lettres à Mme Viardot*, p.4.
36. George Sand, *Histoire de ma Vie*, Vol. I, p.267.
37. George Sand, *Lucrezia Floriani*, p.4.
38. Ibid. p.249.
39. Caroline Jaubert, *Souvenirs*, p.43.
40. Quoted in Z. Markiewicz, *Spotkania Polsko-Francuskie*, p.71.
41. George Sand to Marie de Rozières, 24/VII/1846, Lubin Vol. VII, p.430.
42. George Sand to Marie de Rozières, 18/VI/1846, ibid., p.378.
43. Delacroix to Villot, 16/VIII/1846, Delacroix, *Correspondance*

Générale, Vol. II, p.283; and Chopin to Franchomme, 30/VIII/1846, KFC Vol. II, p.165; Letter to Franchomme, 30/VIII/1846, ibid., p.398; J. Starzyński, *Delacroix et Chopin*, p.10.

44. Quoted in G. Lubin, *George Sand en Berry*, pp.28–9.
45. Quoted in S. Chainaye & D. Chainaye, *De quoi vivait Chopin?*, p.100.
46. Letter to Franchomme, 8/VII/1846, KFC Vol. II, p.396.
47. Letter to family, 11/X/1846, ibid., p.175.
48. Ibid., p.170.
49. Liszt to Marie d'Agoult, 10/II/1847, Liszt, *Correspondance avec la Comtesse d'Agoult*, Vol. II, p.374.

Chapter 14: An Ugly Fracas

1. Letter to family, 11/X/1846, KFC Vol. II, p.175.
2. Letter to family, 28/III/1847, ibid., p.193.
3. Ibid., p.191.
4. Delacroix, *Journal*, Vol. I, p.309.
5. Letter to family, 8/VI/1847, KFC Vol. II, p.204.
6. Letter to George Sand, 10/IV/1847, ibid., pp.190–1.
7. Letter to family, 28/III–19/IV/1847, ibid., p.194.
8. Letter to family, 8/VI/1847, ibid., p.204.
9. Ibid., p.203.
10. George Sand to Grzymała, 12/V/1847, Lubin Vol. VII, p.700.
11. Letter to family, 8/VI/1847, KFC Vol. II, pp.202 & 205.
12. George Sand to P.J. Hetzel, 12/V/1847, Lubin Vol. VII, p.703.
13. George Sand to Grzymała, 12/V/1847, ibid., pp.700–1.
14. Letter to George Sand, 15/V/1847, KFC Vol. II, p.200.
15. Letter to family, 8/VI/1847, ibid., p.204.
16. George Sand to Hortense Allart, 22/VI/1847, Lubin Vol. VII, p.756.
17. Solange to Chopin, 12/VI/1847, erroneously dated in KFC Vol. II, pp. 210 & 415.

18. George Sand to Marie de Rozières, 16?/VII/1847, Lubin Vol. VIII, p.12.

19. See Delacroix, *Journal*, Vol. I, p.322; also Chopin to George Sand, 24/VII/1847, KFC Vol. II, pp.417–18; Chopin to Ludwika Jędrzejewicz, 26/XII/1847, ibid., p.224 (*'w swoim sławnym liście mi pisała że zięć niezły'*); and Franchomme's account, in Niecks, Vol. II, p.200.

20. Delacroix, *Journal*, Vol. I, p.322.

21. Letter to George Sand, 24/VII/1847, KFC Vol. II, pp.417–18.

22. George Sand to Marie de Rozières, 25/VII/1847, in *Autour de Chopin et de George Sand*.

23. George Sand to Emmanuel Arago, 18–26/VII/1847, Lubin Vol. VIII, pp.18–49.

24. George Sand to Louis Viardot, 1/XII/1847, Bibliothèque Nationale Ms., N.A.Fr. 16273, ff. 69–72.

25. Quoted in Lubin Vol. VIII, p.49 note.

26. George Sand to Chopin, 28/VII/1847, ibid., pp.54–5.

27. Pauline Viardot to George Sand, 19/XI/1847, MS, pp.235–6; and Louis Viardot to George Sand, 19/XI/1847, postscript, quoted in SCLC, p.298.

28. George Sand to Pauline Viardot, 1/XII/1847, Bibliothèque Nationale Ms, N.A.Fr. 16273, f. 70.

29. See George Sand to Emmanuel Arago, 18–26/VII/1847, Lubin Vol. VIII, p.48.

30. George Sand to Marie de Rozières, 14/VIII/1847, ibid., p.72.

31. Franz Liszt, *Chopin*, p.247.

32. Letter to Ludwika Jędrzejewicz, 26/XII/1847, KFC Vol. II, p.225.

33. Quoted in S. Szenic, *Maria Kalergis*, p.183.

34. Quoted by Koźmian in *Przegląd Poznański*, Vol. IX, 1849, p.690.

35. Jeremy Barlow, *Encounters with Chopin*, p.246.

36. Letter to Ludwika Jędrzejewicz, 26/XII/1847, KFC Vol. II, p.225.

37. Jeremy Barlow, *Encounters with Chopin*, p.248.

38. Letter to Solange, 24/XI/1847, KFC Vol. II, p.424; and Princess Czartoryska to Chopin, end of December 1847, ibid., p.224.

Chapter 15: London and Scotland

1. Letter to family, 11/II/1848, KFC Vol. II, p.229.
2. Letter to Ludwika Jędrzejewicz, 10/II/1848, ibid., p.228.
3. G.A. Osborne, *Reminiscences of Frederick Chopin*, pp.102–3.
4. Josef Filtsch, quoted in SCFC, p.216.
5. G.A. Osborne, op. cit., p.102.
6. *Revue et Gazette Musicale*, 28 February 1848; also *Le Ménestrel*, 20 February 1848.
7. Custine to Chopin, erroneously dated in KFC, Vol. I, p.422.
8. Letter to Ludwika Jędrzejewicz, 26/XII/1847–6/I/1848, ibid., p.225.
9. Letter to Solange, 5/III/1848, ibid., p.431.
10. George Sand, *Histoire de ma Vie*, Vol. XX, p.254.
11. SCFC, p.309.
12. Letter to Fontana, 4/IV/1848, KFC Vol. II, p.239.
13. A.E. Koźmian in *Przegląd Poznański*, Vol. IX, 1849, p.687.
14. Letter to Marie de Rozières, private collection, Vienna.
15. Letter to Franchomme, 1/V/1848, KFC Vol. II, pp.434–5.
16. Letter to Gutmann, 6/V/1848, ibid., p.436.
17. See Ralph Waldo Emerson, *Journals & Miscellaneous Notebooks*, Vol. X, pp.285, 337, 442–3; and *Letters*, Vol. IV, p.84; also Letter to family, 19/VIII/1848, KFC Vol. II, p.266.
18. Letter to Grzymała, 4/V/1848, KFC Vol. II, p.244.
19. Letter to Grzymała, 13/V/1848, ibid., p.245.
20. Berlioz, *Memoirs*, pp.33–4.
21. Letter to Grzymała, 13/V/1848, KFC Vol. II, p.245.
22. Letter to Gutmann, 6/V/1848, ibid., p.436.
23. Letter to family, 19/VIII/1848, ibid., p.264.

24. Queen Victoria's diary, Windsor, entry for 15 May 1848.

25. Letter to unknown correspondent, 1/VI/1848, KFC Vol. II, p.246.

26. Letter to Grzymała, 2/VI/1848, ibid., p.249.

27. Quoted by Hoesick, Vol. III, p.183.

28. Letter to Gryzmała, 2/VI/1848, KFC Vol. II, p.249.

29. Letter to Grzymała, 21/X/1848, ibid., p.283.

30. William Thackeray, *Letters and Private Papers*, Vol. II, p.390.

31. Letter to family, 19/VIII/1848, KFC Vol. II, p.263.

32. Jane Welsh Carlyle, quoted in A. Bone, *Jane Wilhelmina Stirling*, p.66.

33. Thomas & Jane Welsh Carlyle, *Collected Letters*, Vol. XXIII, p.69.

34. *Daily News*, 10 July 1848.

35. Letter to family, 19/VIII/1848, KFC Vol. II, p.272.

36. Letter to Grzymała, 21/X/1848, ibid., p.283.

37. Kornel Michałowski, *Nieznane Wspomnienie o Chopinie*, p.211.

38. Letter to Grzymała, 2/VI/1848, KFC Vol. II, p.248.

39. Letter to family, 19/VIII/1848, ibid., p.272.

40. Mrs Grote to Alexandra Faucher (Wołowska), 3/VII/1848, Institut de France Ms, 6028, no. 72.

41. Letter to family, 19/VIII/1848, KFC Vol. II, p.269.

42. Letter to Grzymała, 2/VI/1848, ibid., p.249.

43. Letter to Grzymała, 18/VII/1848, ibid., p.253.

44. Kornel Michałowski, *Nieznane Wspomnienie o Chopinie*, p.211.

45. Letter to Franchomme, 11/VIII/1848, KFC Vol. II, p.257.

46. Letter to Thomas Albrecht, 1/IX/1848, Towarzystwo im. Fryderyka Chopina Ms.

47. G.A. Osborne, op. cit, p.101.

48. *Manchester Guardian*, 30 August 1848.

49. G.A. Osborne, op. cit., p.101.

50. Charles Hallé, *Life & Letters*, p.111; also S. Brookshaw, *Chopin in Manchester*, p.22.

51. Letter to Thomas Albrecht, 1/IX/1848, Chopin Society Ms.

52. Letter to Grzymała, 9/IX/1848, KFC Vol. II, p.274.
53. Ibid.
54. Letter to Franchomme, 11/VIII/1848, ibid., p.257.
55. Letter to Fontana, 18/VIII/1848, ibid., pp.259–60.
56. Letter to Grzymała, 1/X/1848, ibid., p.276.
57. Sir James Hedderwick, quoted in A. Bone, *Jane Wilhelmina Stirling*, pp.73–4.
58. Letter to Gutmann, 16/X/1848, KFC Vol. II, p.281.
59. Letter to Grzymała, 10/X/1848, ibid., p.278.
60. See Niecks, Vol. II, p.292.
61. Letter to Grzymała, 30/X/1848, KFC Vol. II, p.285.
62. Letters to Grzymała, 17–18/XI/1848, 30/X/1848, 17–18/XI/1848 respectively, ibid., pp.285 & 287.
63. Marcelina Czartoryska to Adam Czartoryski, 17/XI/1848, Biblioteka xx Czartoryskich Ms., Ew. XVII/841, kk.541–4.
64. Letter to Grzymała, 21/XI/1848, KFC Vol. II, p.289.
65. Leonard Niedźwiedzki private diary, Polska Akademia Nauk, Kórnik, Ms 2416, p.278.

Chapter 16: The Jealousy of Heaven

1. Letter to Solange, 30/I/1849, KFC Vol. II, p.292.
2. Letter to Solange, 13/IV/1849, ibid., p.294.
3. See Delacroix, *Journal*, Vol. I, p.364.
4. Pauline Viardot to George Sand, KFC Vol. II, p.450.
5. Letter to Grzymała, 18/VI/1849, ibid., p.299.
6. Letter to Ludwika Jędrzejewicz, 25/VI/1849, ibid., p.301.
7. Marcelina Czartoryska to Władysław Czartoryski, 16/V/1849, Biblioteka xx Czartoryskich Ms, Ew. XVII/951, k.107.
8. Letters to Grzymała, 28/VII/1849 & 3/VIII/1849, KFC Vol. II, pp.309–11 & 312.
9. Ibid., p.312.
10. Ludwika Jędrzejewicz to Kalasanty Jędrzejewicz, Towarzystwo im. Fryderyka Chopina Ms.

11. George Sand to Ludwika Jędrzejewicz, 1/IX/1849, KFC Vol. II, p.458.

12. Cyprian Norwid, *Czarne Kwiaty*, in *Pisma Wybrane*, Vol. V, pp.37–9.

13. For details of Chopin's last apartment and its furnishings, see Henri Musielak, *Dokumenty dotyczące Spadku po Chopinie*.

14. See Zaleski to Koźmian, J.B. Zaleski, *Korespondencja*, Vol. II, p.128.

15. George Sand to Étienne Arago, 11/XI/1849, *Autour de Chopin et de George Sand*, no. 28.

16. Aleksander Jełowicki to Ksawera Grocholska, 21/X/1849, KFC Vol. II, pp.318–21.

17. Jules Janin, *Lettres a sa Femme*, Vol. I, p.476.

18. Pauline Viardot to George Sand, KFC Vol. II, p.464.

19. George Sand to Étienne Arago, 11/XI/1849, in *Autour de Chopin et de George Sand*; see also Z. Krasiński, *Listy do Jerzego Lubomirskiego*, p.525; Grzymała to Auguste Léo, KFC Vol. II, p.462; Sand to Étienne Arago, 11/XI/1849, in *Autour de Chopin et de George Sand*.

20. Solange Clésinger, *Frédéric Chopin, Souvenirs Inédits*, p.229.

21. Quoted in Niecks, Vol. II, p.321.

22. Ludwika Ciechomska's account (in CJ, p.321, originally printed in *Kurier Warszawski*, 7 August 1882), which claims, among other things, that Gutmann was not in Paris at the time, must be treated with caution. Gutmann's presence is attested in Grzymała's, Solange's and Niedźwiedzki's accounts.

23. George Sand, *Visages du Romantisme*, p.83.

24. See Ludwika Jędrzejewicz to Kalasanty Jędrzejewicz, Towarzystwo im. Fryderyka Chopina Ms; and Henri Musielak, *Dokumenty dotyczące Spadku po Chopinie*.

25. Cyprian Norwid, in *Dziennik Polski*, Poznań, 25 October 1849, no. 117.

26. Anton Rubinstein, *Autobiography*, p.119.
27. Saint-Saëns, *Portraits et Souvenirs*, pp.102, 106.
28. Elias Canetti, *Party in the Blitz*, London 2005, p.3.
29. Delacroix to Grzymała, 7/I/1861, KFC Vol. II, p.467.
30. Solange Clésinger, *Frédéric Chopin, Souvenirs Inédits*, p.226.

SOURCES

A. Manuscript

Biblioteka xx Czartoryskich, Kraków:
Letters from Chopin to Grzymała (Ew. XVII/1173, 651–3), from
Princess Marcelina Czartoryska to Prince Adam Czartoryski
(Ew. XVII/841) and to Prince Władysław Czartoryski (Ew.
XVII/951). File on Charity Concert, 4/IV/1835 (IV/5664)

Biblioteka Jagiellońska, Kraków:
Romuald Hube's Memoirs (Ms.6687, II), letter from Kornel
Krzeczunowicz to Teofil Ostaszewski (Przyb. 51/64), diary,
papers and correspondence of Zofia Rozengardt-Zaleska
(9261), diaries of Józef Bohdan Zaleski (9158, I)

Biblioteka Narodowa, Warsaw:
Eustachy Marylski's memoirs (copy) (7125), Julian Fontana's
letters to sister (7133), Chopin's letters to Fontana (copy)
(7125)

Bibliothèque Nationale, Paris:
Correspondence of Pauline Garcia-Viardot (N.A.Fr. 16272 and
16273), Correspondence of Comtesse Marie d'Agoult
(N.A.Fr. 25175 and 25187)

Bibliothèque Polonaise, Paris:
Zofia Rozengardt-Zaleska's diary (fragment, copy) (P.E.543/30),
Julian Urzyn Niemcewicz's diary (P.E. 500–4), letters from
Marie d'Agoult to Adam Mickiewicz (M.A.M. 480), Albert

Grzymała's personal notebooks (uncatalogued at time of study), minute-books of the Benevolent Association of Polish Ladies in Paris (vols. 1–3), Letters of Stefan Witwicki to Adam Mickiewicz (M.A.M. 696), letter from Albert Grzymała to A. Kożuchowski (P.E. 466/II), letter from Princess Marcelina Czartoryska to Dr Seweryn Gałęzowski (P.E.)

Institut de France, Paris:
Correspondence of Alexandra Wołowska-Faucher (6028), letter from Chopin to Alkan (1988)

Polska Akademia Nauk, Kórnik:
Leonard Niedźwiedzki's diary (2416)

Bibiliothèque Historique de la Ville de Paris:
Fonds Sand, M.237, G.3880, G.5532, Letters from the Marquis de Custine, Henri Hyacinthe de la Touche and Stefan Witwicki

Royal Library, Windsor Castle:
Queen Victoria's personal diary (by kind permission of Her Majesty the Queen)

Towarzystwo im. Fryderyka Chopina, Warsaw:
Letters from Chopin to Albrecht, Grzymała, George Sand and others, Chopin's private diaries for 1834, 1848, 1849

B: Printed

Agoult, Marie de Flavigny, comtesse d', *Mémoires*, Paris 1927

Apponyi, Rodolphe, comte, *Vingt-cinq ans à Paris*, Vol. II, Paris 1913

Attwood, William G., *The Lioness and the Little One: The Liaison of George Sand and Frederic Chopin*, Columbia 1980

— *Fryderyk Chopin: Pianist from Warsaw*, New York 1987

Autour de Chopin et de George Sand: Manuscrits, lettres autographes, livres, documents et souvenirs, Issoudun 1988

Balzac, Honoré de, *Lettres à Madame Hanska*, Vols I & II, Paris 1968

— *Correspondance*, Vol. IV, Paris 1966

Barlow, Jeremy, *Encounters with Chopin: Fanny Erskine's Paris Diary 1847–8*, in John Rink & Jim Samson (eds), *Chopin Studies*, No. 2, Cambridge 1994

Beaumont-Vassy, vicomte de, *Les Salons de Paris et la Société Parisienne sous Louis Philippe Ier*, Paris 1866

Berlioz, Hector, *Correspondance Inédite*, Paris 1879

— *Les Années Romantiques. Correspondance 1819–42*, Paris n.d.

— *Memoirs*, trs. David Cairns, London 1974

— *Selected Letters*, London 1966

— *Selected Letters*, ed. Hugh Macdonald, London 1995

Billington, James H., *Fire in the Minds of Men: Origins of the Revolutionary Faith*, London 1980

Blanc, Louis, *Histoire de la Révolution de 1848*, Paris 1880

Bone, Audrey, *Jane Wilhelmina Stirling*, n.p. 1960

Brault, *Une Contemporaine*, Paris 1848

Brion, Marcel, *La Vie quotidienne à Vienne à l'époque de Mozart et de Schubert*, Paris 1959

Bronarski, Ludwik, *Stephen Heller a Chopin*, in *Ruch Muzyczny*, No. 20, Warsaw 1960

Brookshaw, Susanna, *Concerning Chopin in Manchester*, n.p. 1951

Cate, Curtis, *George Sand*, London 1975

Chainaye, S. & Chainaye, D., *De Quoi vivait Chopin*, Paris 1951

Chopin, Fryderyk, *Correspondance*, ed. B.E. Sydow, S. Chainaye & D. Chainaye, 3 vols, Paris 1953

— *Korespondencja Fryderyka Chopina*, ed. B.E. Sydow, 2 vols, Warsaw 1955

— *Korespondencja z Rodziną*, ed. Krystyna Kobylańska, Warsaw 1972

— *Korespondencja z George Sand i jej Dziećmi*, ed. Krystyna Kobylańska, 2 vols, Warsaw 1981

— *Selected Correspondence*, trs. Arthur Hedley, London 1963

Clark, Sir James, *A Treatise on Pulmonary Consumption*, London 1837

Clésinger, Solange, *Frédéric Chopin, Souvenirs inédits*, in *Revue Musicale de la Suisse Romande*, No.5, Hiver 1978

Comettant, O., *Histoire de cent mille pianos et d'une salle de concert*, Paris 1890

Czartkowski, Adam & Jeżewska, Zofia, *Fryderyk Chopin*, Warsaw 1970

Czeczot, Zbigniew & Zacharias, Andrej, *Comparative Graphic Expert Examination of Four Specimens of Letters Allegedly Written by Frederick Chopin*, in *Chopin Studies 1*, Warsaw 1985

Czerwińska, Teresa, *Dziennik Podróży Józefa Kalasantego Jędrze-jewicza*, in *Rocznik Chopinowski 21*, Warsaw 1995

Delacroix, Eugène, *Journal*, Paris 1893, Vol. I

— *Correspondance Générale*, ed. Joubin, Paris 1936, Vols I & II

— *Further Correspondence*, ed. Lee Johnson, Oxford 1991

Denis, Ferdinand, *Journal*, ed. P. Moreau, Fribourg 1932

Eigeldinger, Jean-Jacques, *Chopin vu par ses élèves*, Neufchâtel 1970

— *Koncerty Chopina w Paryżu w latach 1832–1838*, in *Rocznik Chopinowski 17*, Warsaw 1985

Elsner, Józef, *Sumariusz moich utworów muzycznych z objaśnieniami o czynnościach i działaniach moich jako artysty muzycznego*, Kraków 1957

Emerson, Ralph Waldo, *Journals & Miscellaneous Notebooks*, ed. Merton M. Sealts Jr, Harvard 1973

— *Letters*, ed. Ralph A. Rusk, Columbia 1939

Fajer, Lucjan, *Chopin's Letters Allegedly Written to Potocka: Statement by Expert*, in *Chopin Studies 1*, Warsaw 1985

Ferra i Perello, *Chopin and George Sand in the Cartuja de Valldemosa*, Palma 1932

German, Franciszek, *Chopin i Literaci Warszawscy*, Warsaw 1960

— *Chopin i Mickiewicz*, in *Rocznik Chopinowski 1*, Warsaw 1955

— *Chopin i Witwicki*, in *Annales Chopin*, No. 5, Warsaw 1960

— *Fryderyk Chopin i Juliusz Słowacki. Dzieje nieprzyjaźni dwóch na słońcach swych przeciwnych bogów*, in *Rocznik Chopinowski 18*, Warsaw 1989

— *Karol Lipiński i Fryderyk Chopin*, in *Zeszyt Naukowy Akademii Muzycznej we Wrocławiu*, No. 51

Girardin, Madame Émile de, *Le Vicomte de Launay*, 4 vols, Paris 1857

Gliński, M., *Chopin: Listy do Delfiny*, New York 1970

Godeau, Marcel, *Le Voyage à Majorque de George Sand et Frédéric Chopin*, Paris 1959

Gottschalk, Louis Moreau, *Notes of a Pianist*, London 1881

Grabowski, Ambroży, *Wspomnienia*, Vol. II, Kraków 1909

Gurewicz, Sergiusz, *'Miał wyostrzoną wrażliwość': o niektórych właściwościach choroby Fryderyka Chopina*, in *Ruch Muzyczny*, No. 21, 1979

Hallé, Sir Charles, *Life & Letters*, London 1896

Hanson, Alice M., *Musical Life in Biedermeier Vienna*, Cambridge 1985

Hedley, Arthur, *Chopin*, London 1947

Heine, Heinrich, *Lutèce*, Paris 1855

Heller, Stephen, *Lettres d'un musicien romantique à Paris*, ed. Jean-Jacques Eigeldinger, Paris 1981

Hoesick, Ferdynand, *Chopiniana*, Warsaw 1912

— *Chopin*, 3 vols, Kraków 1967

Hoffmanowa, Klementyna z Tańskich, *Pamiętniki*, Berlin 1849

Jabloński, Z., *Chopin w Anglii*, in *Ruch Muzyczny*, No. 7, 1960

Jack, Belinda, *George Sand*, London 1999

Janin, Jules, *Lettres à sa femme*, ed. Mergier, Vol. I, Paris 1973

Janta, A., *Losy i Ludzie*, London 1961

Jastrzębski, Andrzej, *Jański o Chopinie*, in *Ruch Muzyczny*, No. 11, 1977

Jaubert, Caroline, *Souvenirs*, Paris 1881

Jełowicki, Aleksander, *Listy do Ksaweryny Chodkiewiczowej*, ed. Franciszek German, Warsaw 1964

Kallberg, Jeffrey, *Chopin at the Boundaries: Sex, History and Musical Genre*, Harvard 1996

— *Small Fairy Voices: Sex, History and Meaning in Chopin*, in John Rink & Jim Samson, *Chopin Studies*, No. 2, Cambridge 1994

Kański, J., *Niedokończony Festiwal i Czeskie Chopiniana*, in *Ruch Muzyczny*, No. 20, 1968

Karasowski, M., *Fryderyk Chopin*, 3 vols, Warsaw 1882

Karłowicz, Mieczysław, *Niewydane dotychczas pamiątki po Chopinie*, Warsaw 1904

Kobylańska, Krystyna, *Korespondencja Fryderyka Chopina z Rodziną*, Warsaw 1972

— *Rękopisy utworów Chopina – Katalog*, 2 vols, Kraków 1977

— *Nieznane utwory Chopina w zapomnianym albumie*, in *Ruch Muzyczny*, No. 20, 1972

— *Chopin w Kraju*, Kraków 1955

— *Korespondencja Fryderyka Chopina z George Sand i jej Dziećmi*, 2 vols, Warsaw 1981

— *Odnaleziony list Chopina*, in *Ruch Muzyczny*, No. 26, 1990

Koźmian, A.E., *Listy*, Lwów 1894

— *Wspomnienia*, 3 vols, Poznań 1867

Kramer, Lloyd S., *Threshold of a New World: Intellectuals and the Exile Experience in Paris 1830–1848*, Ithaca 1988

Krasiński, Zygmunt, *Listy do Delfiny Potockiej*, ed. Z. Sudolski, 3 vols, Warsaw 1975–76

— *Listy do Jerzego Lubomirskiego*, ed. Z. Sudolski, Warsaw 1965

Krzywon, Ernst, *Heinrich Heine und Polen*, Vienna 1972

Ladaique, Gabriel, *Les Ancêtres paternels de Frédéric Chopin*, in Daniele Pistone, *Sur les Traces de Frédéric Chopin*, Paris 1984

Laskiewicz, A., *Jak przebiegała choroba płucna Fryderyka Chopina*, in *Rocznik Polskiego Towarzystwa Naukowego na Obczyźnie*, No. 18, London 1968

Legouvé, E., *Soixante ans de souvenirs*, Vol. I, Paris 1886

Łętowski, Ludwik, *Wieczór u Pana Chopina w Paryżu*, in *Miscellanea*, Vol. I, Kraków 1860

Lissa, Zofia (ed.), *The Book of the First International Musicological Congress Devoted to the Works of F. Chopin*, Warsaw 1963

— *Chopin w Świetle Korespondencji Wydawców*, in *Muzyka*, No. 1, 1960

Liszt, Franz, *Chopin*, Leipzig 1879

— *Correspondance de Liszt avec la comtesse d'Agoult*, Vols I & II, Paris 1933

Long, Esmond R., *A History of the Therapy of Tuberculosis and the Case of Frederick Chopin*, n.p. 1956

Lubin, Georges, *George Sand en Berry*, Paris 1967

Luppé, marquis de, *Astolphe de Custine*, Monaco 1957

Malvezzi, A., *La Principessa Cristina di Belgiojoso*, Vol. II, Milan 1936

Marix-Spire, Thérèse, *Les Romantiques et la Musique: Le Cas George Sand*, Paris 1954

Markiewicz, Z., *Śpotkania Polsko-Francuskie*, Kraków 1975

Massalski, Adam, *Niezbyt Ścisła ankieta personalna. Przyczynek do biografii Mikołaja Chopina*, in *Ruch Muzyczny*, Rok XXXV, No. 24, 1 December 1991

Mendelssohn, Felix, *Letters to Charlotte and Ignaz Moscheles*, London 1888

Merlin, comtesse, *Souvenirs et Mémoires*, Paris 1836

Michałowski, Kornel, *Nieznane wspomnienie o Chopinie – Ignacego Krzyżanowskiego*, in *Rocznik Chopinowski 17*, Warsaw 1985

Mickiewicz, Władysław, *Żywot Adama Mickiewicza*, 3 vols, Poznań 1892

Mirska, Maria, *Szlakiem Chopina*, Warsaw 1949

Mirska, Maria & Hordyński, Władysław, *Chopin na Obczyźnie*, Kraków 1965

Moscheles, Charlotte, *The Life of Moscheles, with Selections from his Diaries and Correspondence*, 2 vols, London 1873

Musielak, Henri, *Dokumenty dotyczące spadku po Chopinie*, in *Ruch Muzyczny*, Nos 14, 15, 16, 1978

Niecks, Frederick, *Frederick Chopin as Man and Musician*, 2 vols, London 1890

Niemcewicz, J.U., *Nasze Przebiegi*, in *Przegląd Polski*, zeszyt 10, 1873

Niesmieyanova, T. & Semienovsky, S., *Dnievnik Uchenitsy Shopena*, in *Muzikalnaya Zhizn*, No. 4, Moscow 1960

Norwid, Cyprian Kamil, *Pisma Wybrane*, ed. J.W. Gomulicki, Vol. V, Warsaw 1968

— *Listy*, Warsaw 1937

Odyniec, A.E., *Wspomnienia z Przeszłości opowiadane Deotymie*, Warsaw 1884

Osborne, G.A., *Reminiscences of Frederick Chopin*, in *Proceedings of the Musical Association*, Sixth Session, London, 5 April 1880

O'Shea, John, *Music and Medicine: Medical Profiles of Great Composers*, London 1990

Perenyi, E., *Liszt*, London 1975

Pezda, Janusz, *Ludzie i Pieniądze: Finanse w Działalności Adama Jerzego Czartoryskiego i jego Obozu na Emigracji w latach 1831–1848*, Kraków 2003

Prochazka, J., *Chopin und Bohmen*, Prague 1968

Przybylski, T., *Fragmenty Dziennika Karola Kurpińskiego*, in *Muzyka*, No. 4, 1975

Radcliffe, Philip, *Mendelssohn*, London 1967

Rajchman, A., *Kolebka Chopina*, in *Echo Muzyczne, Teatralne i Artystyczne*, No. 424, Warsaw, 2 November 1891

Reiss, Józef, *Ślązak Józef Elsner*, Katowice 1936

Rubinstein, Anton, *Autobiography*, Boston 1890

— *La Musique et ses représentants*, Paris 1892

Rudzki, Edward, *Delfina Potocka*, Warsaw 1990

Ruhlmann, Sophie, *Chopin-Franchomme*, in *Chopin w Kręgu Przyjaciół*, Warsaw 1996

Rzewuska, Countess Rozalia, *Mémoires*, Rome 1939

Sainte-Beuve, Charles Augustin, *Mes Poisons*, Paris 1926

Saint-Saëns, Camille, *Portraits et souvenirs*, Paris n.d.

— *Correspondance Générale*, ed. Bonnerot, Paris 1958

Samson, Jim (ed.), *The Cambridge Companion to Chopin*, Cambridge 1992

Sand, George, *Lettres Inédites de George Sand et de Pauline Viardot*, ed. Thérèse Marix-Spire, Paris 1959

— *Correspondance*, ed. Georges Lubin, Vols III–IX, Paris 1967–72

— *Histoire de ma Vie*, Vols I–XX, Paris 1854–56

— *Lucrezia Floriani*, Paris 1853

— *Un Hiver à Majorque*, Paris 1869

— *Journal Intime*, Paris 1926

— *George Sand, Visages du Romantisme*, Bibliothèque Nationale, Paris 1977

Schumann, Robert, *O Fryderyku Chopinie*, Katowice 1963

Sellards, John, *Dans le Sillage du Romantisme: Charles Didier 1805–64*, Paris 1933

Servadio, Gaia, *The Real Traviata: The Biography of Giuseppina Strepponi*, London 1994

Sielużycki, Czesław, *Chopin, Geniusz Cierpiący*, Warsaw 1999

— *O zdrowiu Chopina: Prawdy, Domniemania, Legendy*, in *Rocznik Chopinowski 15*, Warsaw 1983

Sikorski, Andrzej & Mysłakowski, Piotr, *Rodzina Matki Chopina: Mity i Rzeczywistość*, Warsaw 2000

Sikorski, Józef, *Wspomnienia Szopena*, in *Biblioteka Warszawska*, December 1849

Skarbek, Fryderyk, Count, *Pamiętniki*, Poznań 1878

Słowacki, Juliusz, *Dzieła*, Vol. II, Wrocław 1949

Smoter, J.M., *Spór o Listy Chopina do Delfiny Potockiej*, Kraków 1976

Soszalski, Ryszard & Wójcik, Władysław, *Examination No.ZKE-*

P–2871/74 of Frederick Chopin's Letters to Delfina Potocka, in *Chopin Studies 1*, Warsaw 1985

Starr, S. Frederick, *Bamboula: The Life and Times of Louis Moreau Gottschalk*, New York 1995

Starzyński, J., *Delacroix et Chopin*, Paris 1962

Stock-Morton, Phyllis, *The Life of Marie d'Agoult, alias Daniel Stern*, Johns Hopkins UP, 2000

Szenic, S., *Maria Kalergis*, Warsaw 1963

Szulc, Eugeniusz, *Nieznana Karta Warszawskiego okresu życia Chopina*, in *Rocznik Chopinowski 18*, Warsaw 1989

Tarczewska, Aleksandra z Tańskich, *Historia Mego Zycia*, Warsaw 1967

Thackeray, William Makepeace, *Letters and Private Papers*, ed. G.N. Ray, Vol. II, Cambridge 1945

Todd, R. Larry, *Mendelssohn: A Life in Music*, Oxford 2003

Tomaszewska, Wanda, *Chopin w Dusznikach*, in *Muzyka*, No. 4, 1961

Turgenev, I.S., *Lettres à Madame Viardot*, Paris 1907

Witwicki, Stefan, *Listy do Józefa Bohdana Zaleskiego*, Lwów 1901

Wodziński, A., *Les Trois Romans de Frédéric Chopin*, Paris 1886

Wójcicki, K.W., *Cmentarz Powązkowski*, 3 vols, Warsaw 1855–58

— *Pamiętniki Dziecka Warszawy*, 2 vols, Warsaw 1974

Wróblewska-Straus, Hanna & Markiewicz, Katarzyna, *Fryderyk Chopin i Bracia Kolbergowie na tle epoki*, Warsaw 2005

Zaleski, Józef Bohdan, *Korespondencja*, 2 vols, Lwów 1901

Zieliński, Tadeusz A., *Ilu nauczycieli miał Chopin?* In *Ruch Muzyczny*, Year XXXVI, No. 6, 22 March 1992

C: Contemporary Newspapers and Periodicals

Gazeta Korespondenta Warszawskiego i Zagranicznego, Warsaw 1818

Pamiętnik Warszawski, Warsaw 1818

Kurier dla Płci Pięknej, Warsaw 1823

Kurier Warszawski, Warsaw 1820–30

Gazeta Polska, Warsaw 1829

Dziennik Powszechny Krajowy, Warsaw 1829–30

Kurier Polski, Warsaw 1829–30

Gazeta Warszawska, Warsaw 1818, 1849

Dziennik Polski, Poznań 1849

Tygodnik Literacki, Poznań 1840

Tygodnik Emigracji Polskiej, Paris 1835

Kronika Emigracji Polskiej, Paris 1836

Trzeci Maj, Paris 1842

Dziennik Narodowy, Paris 1841

La France Musicale, Paris 1841

Revue Musicale, Paris 1832, 1833

Gazette Musicale de Paris, Paris 1834, 1835, 1839, 1841

Journal des Débats, Paris 1835, 1849

Revue et Gazette Musicale de Paris, 1838, 1848, 1849

La Presse, Paris 1849

Le Ménestrel, Paris 1841

Daily News, London 1848

Musical World, London 1849

Manchester Guardian, Manchester 1848

Allgemeine Musikalische Zeitung, Leipzig 1831

Flora, 30 August 1831

Neue Zeitschrift fur Musik, Leipzig 1834–41

INDEX

FC indicates Fryderyk Chopin

Index